Politics,
Writing,
Mutilation

Politics, Writing, Mutilation

The Cases of Bataille, Blanchot, Roussel, Leiris, and Ponge

Allan Stoekl

UNIVERSITY OF MINNESOTA PRESS, MINNEAPOLIS

The University of Minnesota Press
gratefully acknowledges assistance provided by
the Andrew W. Mellon Foundation for publication
of this book.

Published by the University of Minnesota Press,
2037 University Avenue Southeast, Minneapolis, MN 55414
Printed in the United States of America

Library of Congress Cataloging in Publication Data

Stoekl, Allan.
  Politics, writing, mutilation.

  Bibliography: p.
  Includes index.
  1. French literature—20th century—History and criticism.
2. Politics in literature. 3. Utopias in literature. 4. Modernism
(Literature). I. Title.
PQ307.P64S76 1985   840'.9'00912   85-8594
ISBN 0-8166-1299-4
ISBN 0-8166-1300-1 (pbk.)

Chapter 1, "Politics, Mutilation, Writing," copyright © 1984
by Allan Stoekl, is reprinted from *Raritan* 3, no. 3 (winter
1984) with permission of the author. Chapter 5, "Ponge's
Photographic Rhetoric," copyright © 1984 by the University of
Wisconsin Press, is reprinted from *Sub-Stance* 41 (winter 1984)
with the permission of the publisher.

The University of Minnesota is
an equal-opportunity educator and employer.

D'autres sont rebelles à l'angoisse. Ils
rient et chantent. Ils sont *innocents* et je
suis *coupable*. Mais que suis-je à leurs
yeux? un *intellectuel* cynique, tortueux,
malaisé. Comment supporter d'être lourd
à ce point, odieux, méconnu? J'accepte,
étonné de l'excès.

Bataille, *Le Coupable*

Contents

Acknowledgments

Paul de Man's interest and encouragement enabled me to write this book. It is dedicated to his memory. I also want to thank my editors Wlad Godzich and Lindsay Waters for their support of this project, and Virginia Hans for her excellent copyediting.

A. S.

Introduction
Utopias of Conflict,
Urtexts of Deconstruction

It has become a commonplace of criticism to argue that modernist literature is about language itself. Avant-garde textual practice in some way fundamentally disrupts the quotidian usefulness and precision of language; behind the facade of utility we find another language, which is the real realm of modernity. Language becomes a universe unto itself, an absolute realm that refers to the senselessness of its own origins.

This article of modernist faith is accurate, up to a point. Each of the authors dealt with in this book—Georges Bataille (1897–1962), Maurice Blanchot (b. 1907), Raymond Roussel (1877–1933), Michel Leiris (b. 1901), and Francis Ponge (b. 1899)—posits a realm of language that not only calls attention to its own workings, but shows that what is often considered most peripheral is really the central phenomenon of language. Thus both Roussel and Leiris, for example, attempt to see the fundamental statements of language as functions of puns: their writing is, at least to a certain extent, generated out of phonic similarities between words, similarities that might then uncover rather bizarre links between the meanings of words. Others, like Blanchot and Ponge, see a profound silence or death at the heart of writing, and write what amounts to a silencing of language as we know it. These projects tend to cross over: thus Roussel and Leiris are concerned, in one way or another, with the silence of their language, just as Blanchot and Ponge are occupied with the phonic or written configurations of the words they use, and with the multiple meanings—and problems—that lie behind each word.

It is not hard to see these avant-garde realms of language as utopias: they are realms where language as it should be—not as it is—is displayed. Marxist critics, among them Lukács, were quick to point out that the apparent disruptions of modernism were in fact an admission of sterility, the carrying out of a revolution on an abstract ideal plane, where risks— and benefits—amounted to zero. In this view, avant-garde practice is restricted to an elite social sphere, since it can have little to say to people confronted with the problems of everyday life; it finally becomes a reactionary tool—its formal disruptions are merely reflections of bourgeois decay and are eminently appropriable by certain forces of order.[1] Other critics, such as Julia Kristeva, argued that avant-garde formal subversion was inherently revolutionary, not reactionary: they held that the disruptions of language were the product of a predenotative "semiological flux"—that is, of a state of language outside the repressive strictures of logic and signification—and that the avant-garde text returned to liberate these forces in language and society. In this view, the most important avant-garde texts brought off a dialectical union between logic/denotation and the liberated flux of a subversive force of signification. But on the other hand, Kristeva maintained, certain writers, such as Louis-Ferdinand Céline, fundamentally misunderstood the revolutionary implications of their language practice and mistakenly associated it with fascism.[2]

There may, in fact, be a third possibility. As we read these five authors, we will attempt to see not only the utopian denial or denegation of various political problems, but their *return* as well. Modernist texts may be the locus of an irresolvable struggle between different ideological forces, rather than the repository of a single one: we will attempt to read the space where that struggle occurs, where it is denied, and, conversely, where it can be read, perhaps through its very denial. To read a space between political positions and political rewritings, one need not be "neutral" oneself. Yet, as we shall see, the violence of inward conflict in the texts we propose to read cannot simply be exiled from critical consideration. These five authors, in different ways, focus on the problem of automutilation and sacrifice. This phenomenon of inner sacrifice is by no means a dead letter for criticism itself today: in fact it may be the most important one that we as readers of "literature" face.

The inner violence of major characters (on a thematic level) mirrors the self-directed violence of language (in silence, in wordplay, in *writing*) in the modernist novels, autobiography, and poetry we propose to examine. Thus the models of a utopian future depicted in these writings double the utopias of language worked out by the writings on a formal level. The utopian future that is most explicitly prefigured by Bataille—

but that also lurks under the surface, so to speak, in the other writers—is one which would attempt to imagine, somehow implemented in society, the radical negativity and unrecoverable (but crucial) violence that occurs between sacrificer and victim, or ultimately, as we shall see in our reading of Bataille, between two opposing ideological forces that collide head on. But the question always returns: what will be the political manifestation of the squandered energy of sacrifice in society? Can fiction or poetry, as utopian texts, somehow foresee it?

The irony here is that the critic who would read these writings closely and perhaps dismiss their utopian desire for strategic destruction is inescapably formed by a method of interpretation that was itself the result of the intervention (proposed by our authors) of sacrifice/doubling/auto-mutilation. This method is, of course, deconstruction.

By calling these writings "urtexts of deconstruction" we do not wish to imply that there are not other "urtexts" as well: Kant, Hegel, Nietzsche, Kierkegaard, and Heidegger are a few names that come to mind as authors of such "urtexts." But these authors are (in a different way) authors of "urtexts" of existentialism as well, whereas the authors treated in this book were totally unacceptable to larger literary and philosophical movements (such as existentialism),[3] and they constitute a specific and crucial moment in contempory French literature and philosophys out of which appeared the writings of critics who, in the United States at least, have come to be called "poststructuralists" (Michel Foucault, Jacques Derrida, Gilles Deleuze, to cite three names).

It at first seems strange to attempt to place in literary history (or in the history of philosophy) critics who are engaged in the *critique* of a history (or histories) based on metaphysical or dialectical models of causation, production, or presence. As is by now well known, the very model of literary *influence* has been put into question by these influential writers. But this (non)influence extends back in time as well: the interest in the model of sacrifice that is exhibited in the "urtexts of deconstruction" is much more than a quirk of 1930s or 1940s intellectual life; instead it is an affirmation of a dualist view of historical progress, in which productive history is itself opened out at key junctures by a negativity that escapes appropriation. We face the somewhat paradoxical situation, then, of considering a group of authors whose "influence" has been to point toward the impossibility of a coherent theory of influence. There are other "influences" as well: the privileging, in one way or another, of *writing* or inscription over speech, of force over dialectical articulation, of writing referring to its own status as anterior heterogeneous force.

Perhaps the very critique of history that comes out of a reading of these "urtexts" has condemned them to exile from established histories of twentieth-century French literature. Of course (as we all know), symbolism came first, then surrealism, then existentialism, then the New Novel. Necessarily falling between the cracks of this history are the authors we shall read in this book. There is a certain logic to this: one simply cannot teach Bataille's obscenity or Blanchot's opacity in a high school. These then, as well as others (Céline, Artaud, Klossowski) are necessarily *minor* authors, not because they lack "importance" but because of a subversiveness that can never be erected and displayed as a law of the land. Yet, ironically, each of these authors would *join* his subversion to a view of a transformed society: this utopian vision is one of the impossible establishment of a subversive principle (Bataille's expenditure, Blanchot's silence, Roussel's textual machine, etc.) in conjunction with a society or social experience that somehow embodies this subversion. It is that utopian instant of conjunction, the violent meeting of irreconcilable forces, that is the moment of sacrificial death (the conjunction of sacrificer and sacrificed), as are also those doubles of sacrificial doubling, the "difference and repetition" of Deleuze, the "differance" or "dissemination" of Derrida. Thus the *minor* subversion of the "urtexts" that we mentioned a moment ago is soon transformed into the *inescapable* subversion of our contemporaries. (They in turn reflect back on their urtexts and reveal them to be inescapable as well.)

To what extent is our reading of these "urtexts" inevitably formed by the methods of "deconstructive" interpretation? To the extent that philosophical texts are deconstructed, the necessity of deconstruction is derived from the necessity of the text itself. Yet it is the very notion of necessity that is necessarily deconstructed. Consider Hegel: once we have deconstructed a dialectical text that lays claim to absolute knowledge—a knowledge that, on its own terms, we must recognize as absolute—[4]our own text takes on the inescapability of the text it deconstructs, because the irreducibility of the deconstructive reading is the irreducibility of the negativity it reads positioned in the dialectic. Thus the reading and rewriting of the dialectic will never be the "same" again: they will be irreducibly different.

Does this mean that deconstructive texts—say, for example, Derrida's readings of Husserl or Plato—[5]have *supplanted* those philosophers, have gone beyond them in precision of argument and subtlety of analysis? It certainly is true that neither Bataille nor Blanchot practices the kind of close reading that Derrida especially is known for; whereas Bataille or Blanchot posit the necessity of a nonknowledge at the heart of absolute knowledge, of death or madness at the end of history, they, nevertheless, do not arrive at it through a rigorous reading of a philosopher, a reading that shows how certain forms of negativity (called nonknowledge, "differance," the "pharmakon," or whatever) are necessary to a given system and are at the same time necessarily excluded from it. Some might argue that Derrida's analysis clearly has a power that the analyses of his forerunners lack because, rather than positing a need for a certain kind of experience or negativity, he simply draws that negativity out of the points of radical incoherency in the text he is reading. Bataille and Blanchot might condemn the very "idea" of a positive, constructive philosophy, but their method is a continuation of such a project, because they continue to put forward "notions" (as in Bataille's "notion of expenditure"). Derrida, on the other hand (like Deleuze and Foucault), merely *reads*. The strength of his reading, the fact that it is so compelling, may lie in its following through an argument and pointing out how a heterogeneous element is both necessary to that argument and necessarily exiled from it. This strength is also a weakness, however, in that Derrida's insistence on *writing* is done at the cost of excluding the more "positive" realms of politics and problems of ideology.

A fundamental concern of the "urtexts" has thus been lost in the later deconstructive writers. As we shall see in our readings of these authors, the experience of mutilation—the (self)inscription or (re)writing of sacrifice (or the sacrifice of [re]writing)—is never simply separable from a political dualism. Indeed the violence of this rending dualism may be a function of the conflict between writing and politics. Bataille wrote, just before World War II, "I myself am WAR";[6] by this he meant that the conflict of political forces and armies was somehow "inside" himself: the self-differentiating victim/sacrificer was a war of conflicting ideological tendencies.

Bataille had to suture this mutilation, this war, as did all the other authors we shall read here. This suturing in any author is inevitable, because the space of conflict and mutilation is unknowable, and unusable. Bataille's and the others' unknowable space of conflict is the juncture between the desire for a just, rationalized society and the desire for a society that recognizes the human tendency to expend rather than conserve. What form would such a dual society take? Or a question of equal interest: how would the individuals experience the conflict of such a society "inside" themselves?

In the contemporary deconstructive critics, mutilating dualism has been depoliticized. The "pharmakon" (in Derrida's "La Pharmacie de Platon") may very well be both poison and cure, but both of those options are presented outside of a political context. Deconstruction, then, is not apolitical because its radical negativity cannot be put to work in a dialectic (nor, conversely, is it political because it *can* be used),[7] but instead because in it the sides in conflict are rigorously depoliticized. We might, therefore, argue that although the "urtext" of deconstruction attempts to silence, cover, or misread a space of conflict between inevitably politicized forces (such as the conflict between Marxist revolutionaries and fascist traitors in Bataille's *Le Bleu du ciel* [*Blue of Noon*]), a contemporary version of deconstructive criticism refuses to acknowledge that those conflicting forces might already *be* politicized.

We have reached a point at which we recognize how contemporary deconstructive critics, in their method of reading, seem to have gone beyond the "urtexts"—but at the same time, the "urtexts" always return, providing a dualistic model from which one cannot simply escape (one can escape neither its politics nor its dualism). Our critical text will then be a reading double of the written "urtext." The utopian juncture of the "urtext," the mythical space of solution and hypostasis where the two conflicting sides are reconciled—or where their conflict is made comprehensible, is somehow shoehorned into language—is inevitably doubled in our own deconstructive critical text by the very act of rationally analyzing (and hence attempting to master) the utopia. (The critique of utopia is incessantly at war with itself because in its mastery of, or effort to completely understand, utopia, it itself is utopian.)

But just as the ideology of utopia obscures, so utopia critically turns on its own obscurity: in the end—and at the end of this book, the last chapter—we shall attempt to locate the irreducible point of conflict where the double bind or duality of our own text is read in conjunction with the (self) critical utopia—of language, or politics—of these (and our) "urtexts."

There are, then, three major problems with which we are concerned in this book: first of all, a critical reading of these five authors of the 1930s, 40s, and 50s; second, the problem of the rereading and repetition of these authors performed by Derrida and Foucault; and third, the attempt to elaborate a theory of reading that accounts for—but does not necessarily "synthesize"—both the deconstructive reading that revolves around the irruption of a radical negativity in language and writing, and another reading, a (hostile) repetition of the deconstructive reading, which concerns itself with the consequences of a nonrecuperable negativity in the social/political sphere, as represented, foretold, and mediated in our avant-garde (modern utopian) authors.

The chapters dealing with Blanchot, Roussel, Leiris, and Ponge contain this procedure in microcosm. The first part of each chapter presents the fundamental outline of a deconstructive reading of the author in question; the second shows how this approach, while indispensable, excludes another fundamental set of problems, that of politics and the incessant attempt to resolve an irresolvable political conflict. In each chapter we shall show how these two problems (conflict in language, conflict in politics) are repetitions of each other, and are heterogeneous to each other. No simple dialectical procedure can guarantee the erasure of negativity in writing or in the automutilating politics presented by these authors, and no dialectical procedure can guarantee the simple coordination of these two radically *different* fields.

The last two chapters of this book repeat on a large scale what takes place in the chapters devoted to individual authors. Chapter 7 is concerned with the deconstructive readings of Bataille and Blanchot done by Derrida and Foucault; in this it repeats the fist movement of each chapter. We examine the ways in which both Derrida and Foucault retain a fundamental set of problems found in Bataille and Blanchot (most notably the Nietzsche/Hegel conflict), while at the same time stripping the political conflict, and hence the political specificity, of the texts they read. Conversely, a return to Bataille and Blanchot—but especially Bataille—will necessarily imply a *return* to those political problems and binds. Thus in chapter 8 we return to, and repeat, the political and social conflict that was stripped by Derrida and Foucault. (This corresponds to the problem that appears in the second part of the chapters we have devoted to individual authors—the problem of reading a text politically.) To effect this return, we must not simply posit a self-satisfied political position of our own that gives the final word on our authors, but instead we must "recognize" that our own position, which cannot simply escape the problems of deconstruction, necessarily repeats the automutilating social and political binds we read in others. If our authors face and conceal the problem of a painfully double position that embraces both constructive political action and the radically unregenerate violence of doubled sacrifice, inscription, and death, we as readers face the same double bind, this time between the ultimately coherent approach of a constructive political reading and the apolitical loss figured in the methods of deconstruction. Louis Marin's *Utopiques: jeux d'espaces* [*Utopias: Play of Spaces*] embodies for us such a bind in a critical text; our own text is one dialectical stage beyond his, however, to the extent that we "recognize" the bind that is implied in his, and our own, position. But how can we "recognize" a bind that by its very nature is unusable and unrecognizable?

A critical method inevitably returns to *read*, and, because our approach is political even in its recognition of the automutilation of political positions and readings, we must work out a theory of ideology. This is what we try to do in chapter 8: ideology for us, however, is less the error or mendacity of a given theory or picture of the world (as it is in any Marxism, no matter how liberal or accommodating that Marxism may be), than it is the refusal to read in one's own text the various painful political binds and betrayals that are generated by the avant-garde "necessity" of both coherence and incoherence. (But this refusal, when read through the gaps that make it possible, reveals the very violent conflict it seeks to do away with. In this way ideologies or utopias become radical textual and sociopolitical critiques in spite of themselves.) This is the notion of ideology that grounds our readings of the authors presented in chapters 1 to 6; of all the authors, Bataille is the least ideological in that he is the most capable of facing the metamorphoses of his predicament, of trying to see what social or historical forms the violence of sacrificial negativity has taken and will take. On the other hand, to believe that one has simply escaped ideology or utopia is a fully ideological gesture, an attempt to put critical violence to work. To face the conflict between the necessity and impossibility of our notion of ideology or utopia is to face the final—and first—automutilation of our approach.

Our readings of these authors are selective, focusing on one or several of the author's works to the exclusion of others. Yet the works examined are in each case central to an understanding of other works by the same author. The two novels by Bataille that we examine—*Le Bleu du ciel* [*Blue of Noon*] and *L'Abbé C.*—are the most thorough attempts in his oeuvre to foresee, in fiction, the effects of the implementation of sacrificial negativity in society.

Blanchot's *Le Très-Haut* [*The Most High*] is exemplary among his novels because in it we can see the generation (in Blanchot's prose) of the withering away of both the sociopolitical sphere and the sphere of concrete descriptive detail. This double elision is one of the most notable features of Blanchot's prose style, as seen in novels such as *Thomas l'obscur* [*Thomas the Obscure*] and *L'Arrêt de mort* [*Death Sentence*]. By reading *Le Très Haut*, then, we can see the logic behind—and the irresolvable conflict in—Blanchot's larger novelistic practice.

Roussel's *Locus Solus* is, along with *Impressions d'Afrique*, [*Impressions of Africa*] the most important example of his celebrated writing method. That method is most often seen as an aleatory-mechanical production of stories, in which the actual significance of the recounted events is greatly eclipsed by the cleverness (or profundity) of the writing procedure. Thus the examination of an episode of *Locus Solus* is decisive for the understanding of Roussel's work when it indicates a subject matter, a thematics, that leads out of the question of the impersonal generation of texts and into the social and historical problems of conflict and repressive violence that virtually all readers of Roussel have neglected. (That violence itself, however, is inseparable from mechanized motivation and revivification.)

Leiris's five-volume autobiography (counting *L'Age d'homme* [*Manhood*], is generally seen as his most important project. Within that project, the most incisive readers of Leiris— such as Jeffrey Mehlman and Philippe Lejeune—have recognized the importance of Leiris's attempt to write an autobiography that recounts not so much events in his life as his experience of the mutations of language itself. But when we examine a section of volume II of *La Règle du jeu* [*Rules of the Game*], we find that its importance lies in the fact that it demonstrates how Leiris's language games are linked to a larger problem of political commitment and betrayal, which doubles the problems of language, and which throws the autonomy of language into doubt.

Finally, in Ponge's case we examine several pivotal texts ("Texte sur l'électricité," ["Text on Electricity"] "Scvlptvre") that enable us to understand the basis of his writing method, which focuses on minute descriptions of physical objects—and which transforms writing itself into a totally dead yet superalive object. We then read several equally important pieces that demonstrate the impossibility Ponge faces in linking his seemingly apolitical object-texts to social concerns—a project of no little importance to Ponge, since he was (and is) a committed communist.

Politics, Writing, Mutilation

Chapter One
Politics, Mutilation, Writing

In the 1930s, in essays such as "La Notion de dépense" ["The Notion of Expenditure"], "La Structure psychologique du fascisme" ["The Psychological Structure of Fascism"], and "La Critique des fondements de la dialectique hégélienne" ["The Critique of the Foundations of the Hegelian Dialectic"],[1] Georges Bataille audaciously joined such basic tenets of Marxism as class struggle and the dialectical movement of history to a notion of "production" that deviated from the traditional positions. of Marxism. This "production" stresses not utility, conservation, and labor, but orgiastic sexuality and the ritual destruction of goods. However, Bataille came up against the fact that there may be a fundamental incompatibility between progressive political revolution on the one hand and, on the other, the affirmation of sexual effervescence and delirious expenditure: such an incompatibility is never recognized in his essays, but it lies just under the surface of much of Bataille's fiction. The tensions and conflicts that result from an attempt to live within an incompatibility of this type are what obsess Bataille in *Le Bleu du ciel*, [*Blue of Noon*] a novel written in 1935 but first published only in 1957. The confidence exuded by the essays—which hold that Marxism must be identified with explosive sexuality and expenditure—is replaced, in *Le Bleu du ciel*, by exhaustion and despair. Like many on the left, Bataille recognized an affinity between the tendency to "expend" and fascism, and he also recognized that delirious crowds, ecstatic destructive drives, and the glamour of excess may be compatibile less with the ''Front populaire'' than with the Führer. The menace of fascism is the given of every important work by Bataille. Thus what is crucial to Bataille—and to us—is the troubled nature of his opposition to fascism. Of particular concern to him was the degree to which the writer's own valorization of ''excess,'' ''expenditure,'' and ''effervescence'' potentially puts him in complicity with fascism in the very act of opposing it. *Le Bleu du ciel*, written barely a year after ''La Notion de dépense,'' implicitly recognizes this problem by attempting to envision a hero who embodies both the sexul subversiveness of Don Juan and the desire to bring off a constructive social revolution. Through his defiance of the Commander, Don Juan had symbolized for Bataille a defiantly destructive energy, an emblem of ''expenditure,'' who had the advantage of being a popular figure in the West—and specifically so in the France of 1935, thanks in part to the resurgence of interest in Kierkegaard and in his reading of the Don Juan myth.[2]

In *Le Bleu du ciel*, we will argue that Troppmann (Bataille's Don Juanesque hero) is lost in a labyrinth of impotence and self-betrayal. Important figures in *Le Bleu du ciel* are women whom the narrator finds emblematic of certain modes of being. These women are Lazare, Xénie, and Dorothea (''Dirty''). Lazare in the novel is associated with a Marxism with fundamental affinities to Christianity. The equation here is a Nietzschean one, with a link established between a politics (Marxism) and a religion (Christianity) of *ressentiment*; Lazare the revolutionary cannot conceive of a politics that does not involve the martyrdom of the revolutionary leader, or the ''salvation'' of the ''souls'' of the workers. The ''real-life'' model for Lazare was Simone Weil, who eventually converted to Christianity, as Bataille had predicted she would. Xénie, on the other hand, is a very rich dilettante who is interested in Marxism only because it is stylish, while Dorothea, although devoted to an orgiastic expenditure of force, seems to be more or less apolitical. Her only political affiliation is an assigned one, when Troppmann imagines her ''blood-red'' dress as a Nazi flag. Fleeing the political stalemate represented by Lazare in the grim year 1934, Troppmann quits Paris and arrives in Barcelona, in the midst of a conflict between Catalan separatists and Spanish Federalists. He is followed there by all three women—by Xénie, whom he tries to lose, by Lazare, of whom he is terrified, and by Dorothea, to whom he is attracted and whom he follows from Spain to Nazi Germany. Torn between these women, and the unacceptable alternatives they seem to represent, Troppmann sinks into a profound sexual and political impotence. While in Barcelona, for example, he wants to aid the separatists, but finds himself thwarted by the choices he sets for himself. He can (along with a group of revolutionaries) either storm an arsenal or storm a prison, and he prefers the prison even though the arsenal is a much more practical target. The dilemma represents the difference between a useful revolutionary action and a purely violent, destructive one. To storm a prison, as Troppmann wishes, is symbolic of "spending without reserve," as against any more practical but less ecstatically liberating strategy. In the end he accomplishes nothing in Barcelona. Caught between a pragmatic revolt and a pure revolt that cannot be harnessed to any ideology (except perhaps to that of Sade), Troppmann simply leaves.

Torn between the Christian Marxism of Lazare, to which he (perversely) feels more and more akin, and the sinister but absolute defiance of Dorothea, Troppmann begins to sense that he may be in the position of betraying both himself and Marxism, thereby arriving at an unwitting complicity with the fascists. From the perspective of a thoroughly reasonable doctrine like Marxism, he must see even himself as a potential enemy. He faces the fact that even a liberal Marxism may have an inherently absolute status, which becomes manifest whenever it is confronted with a radical deviation. In this chapter I will consider the various strategies posited in *Le Bleu du ciel* for liberating Troppmann's and Dorothea's "tendency to expend" from the guilty complicity with fascism that seems always to characterize it. These strategies are extraordinarily painful and self-lacerating. Troppmann's guilt is a kind of automutilation, in which the leftist turns against himself and betrays his own inevitably rational political doctrine.

The most salient characteristic of "expenditure," as presented in the writings of Bataille, however, is its status as a *duality*, as embodied in both the automutilating madman (who in himself is double, both sacrificer and sacrificed), and the sacrificial couple. Indeed, it may be that guilt and self-betrayal are not peripheral to "spending without return," but are in some ways actually central to it. Never directly confronted in any of Bataille's essays, this is a problem that nevertheless haunts them all and therefore necessarily haunts any reading of Bataille. (The classic text on affirmed automutilation in Bataille is the essay "La Mutilation sacrificielle et l'oreille coupée de Vincent Van Gogh" (I, 258) ["Sacrificial Mutilation and the Severed Ear of Vincent Van Gogh"].

Finally—and this may be the most important part of the argument presented in the pages that follow—this dualistic political bind, perhaps inevitably conjoined to any phenomenon of expenditure, is also inextricably bound to the problem of *writing*.

I

Bataille's *Le Bleu du ciel* presents its hero, Henri Troppmann, as a modern-day Don Juan, yet at first we would hesitate to think of Mozart's *Don Juan* in the context of Bataille's novel. As Kierkegaard points out in his interpretation of Mozart's opera, the character Don Juan (in the opera) is musical; in Bataille's novel, however, Troppmann is a singularly unmusical character. To understand what in fact has happened to Don Juan's music in Bataille, and what has come to replace it (and what the significance of that replacement is), we must first look at Kierkegaard's presentation of Don Juan in *Either/Or* (vol. I).

Don Juan for Kierkegaard is, like music, without preparation and formation, continuation and permanence.

Speech and dialogue are not for him, for then he would be at once a reflective individual. Thus he does not have a stable existence at all, but he hurries in a perpetual vanishing, precisely like music, about which it is true that it is over as soon as it has ceased to sound, and only comes into being again, when it again sounds. (101)[3]

Thus Don Juan, like music, is at the antipodes of the written and reflective experience. His nature is a "perpetual vanishing," but it is also a perpetual present to the extent that the temporal deferrals and reversals of writing are excluded from it.

In Kierkegaard's view, there is a very real interrelation between a written Don Juan on the one hand, and comedy—and irony—on the other. Kierkegaard contrasts Mozart's Don Juan with comic Don Juans, like that of Molière. In Molière's Don Juan, the reversal of the humorous situation—the pratfall—takes place in lieu of the irresistible force of Mozart's Don Juan. And ratiocination occurs instead of musical effervescence; the scheming, planning and deferring talking and writing of Molière's Don Juan contrasts sharply with the "immediate concrete" of Mozart's Don Juan.

If I allow Don Juan to be in financial straits, harassed by creditors, he at once loses the ideality he has in the opera, and becomes comic. (108)
It would be quite consistent with the spirit of modern comedy for Don Juan to know the tedious barriers of actuality. (111)

Thus (Mozart's) Don Juan's endless seductions are not calculated or planned; they occur immediately. Opposed to this immediacy are not only the literary devices and tropes of comedy ("burlesque" and "parody"; see p. 130) but the retribution of codified law and temporalized procedure—symbolized by the Commander, or Stone Guest. This stony Commander is clearly not only the outraged parent of one of Don Juan's victims, but the embodiment of the military and legal state apparatus. The Commander is the embodiment of the same principle of reversal (the same trope) that one finds in comedy:

It is quite proper that irony should so dominate this piece [Mozart's *Don Juan*]; for irony is and remains the chastener of the immediate life. Thus, to cite only one example, the Commandant's return is prodigious irony; for Don Juan can overcome every obstacle, but a ghost, you know, cannot be killed. (120)

Law, retribution, and the reversal of irony frame Mozart's opera, for the opera begins with the Commander's death, and ends with his return. Just as Kierkegaard shows that the musical "centrality" of Don Juan suffuses all the other characters (except the Commander), so too he shows that the periphery of the opera—its beginning and end—opposes that solar centrality. Time, reversal, and language can be seen to frame, oppose, and ironize the effervescence of the immediate.

We should note, though, that there appears, in the term "irony," a certain doubleness. The same term used by Kierkegaard to describe the closure of the opera by the Commander is also used to describe the way in which Don Juan suffuses Elvira in the opera.

Don Juan's incomparable irony ought not to be something external, but should be concealed in Elvira's essential passion. They must be heard simultaneously. (121)

"Irony" is thus used by Kierkegaard in a double sense; it is both the up-setting of Don Juan by the Commander *and* the possession of at least one of the central characters (Elvira) by Don Juan. Don Juan, at his most musical (the moment he "possesses" Elvira), is in some way ironic—a term that we previously saw as the element, in the Commander, that spelled defeat for Don Juan. The fact that Don Juan's "echoing" of Elvira is an internal irony, as opposed to the Commander's external irony, does not seem to solve the problem; it only indicates that what is radically external to Don Juan may also be the internal element that goes to make his musicality—his immediate possession of the other characters (except the Commander)—possible.

There is a chance, then, that Don Juan's centrality and immediacy (Kierkegaard compares his position in the opera to the position of the sun in the solar system) may in fact be constituted through its opposite; the light of the sun may be crossed with darkness—and that opposite, that darkness, is precisely a temporal movement that is both retributive (the law of the Commander) as well as, in some way, inherently reversing and thus ironic. Perhaps the Commander must finally be seen as textual: he is both a legal code, and a reversible (and reversing) literary trope. It is a strange union: the stone sober retribution linked to the pratfalls and reversals of comedy. Yet if irony is double, its very "nature" is one of reversibility—and thus it seems likely that it will be tied to its reverse. If everything irony touches reverses itself and is doubled, it also seems possible that Don Juan's effervescence, when coming into contact with it, will be doubled and reversed. Don Juan's double, of course, is the retribution, irony, and death of the Commander. . . .

We use the word "possible" here advisedly—for what can *possible* mean in the context of a law that is somehow doubled by irony and comedy? But if we can *join* comedy and the retributive yet coherent legal text together in the dead figure of the Commander, to what extent can we speak of a possible recognition of the peripheral death and textuality at the center of the effervescence of Don Juan? Can we posit a text that recognizes the problem of irony we have seen in Don Juan, and that attempts to rewrite the stone-dead Commander at the center of Don Juan's immediacy?

Such a rewriting of Kierkegaard (one that would be as much about writing and textuality as about Don Juan) would be forced to recognize a Don Juan who is written at the moment of his greatest effervescence. The reversal of irony and the coherent analysis/retribution of the legal code would always double, as well as constitute, in this Don Juan, an effervescence that would be contaminated by that irony and coherency, an effervescence that, for that reason, would always again confront its other, death. Each side of this dyad would transgress the other, thus creating in Don Juan a self that "is" (as well as engages in) automutilation. It is possible that such a rewriting is the novel *Le Bleu du ciel* whose hero, Troppmann, is, as we will see, the written and writing victim of pratfalls (and repressive militarism) and who is also the perpetrator of sexually explosive, yet analyzed and analyzable, acts. This oxymoronic written effervescence will always manifest itself as double, and hence a host of symptoms—the doubling of automutilation, the simultaneity of sex and death, the identity of immediacy and time resulting in a circular or repetitious time—will always again constitute a text that would be an opera at the moment in which it is a novel (and, in the process, rewrites a philosophical text). If the Commander represents the reflective instance (for Kierkegaard), does it not make sense that another text, reflecting on Kierkegaard's, and reflexively "aware" of the writing (both ironic and coherent) that Kierkegaard tries to exile to the periphery, would be the Commander to Kierkegaard's Don Juan? Yet "Bataille" is the battle between the two, rather than the final (impossible) triumph of one over the other—for, as we know, the Commander is already double, since he is the internal element that makes Don Juan "possible."

II

Le Bleu du ciel is clearly about a "modern" Don Juan; the hero, Tropp-mann, defies the Commander, and, in his effervescence, attempts to be the kind of seducer that Mozart and Kierkegaard envisioned. Tropp-mann's very name, however, indicates that there are problems in reen-acting (or rewriting) Don Juan: he is excess-man ("trop"), a parody of the Nietzschean "superman"—and indeed, his name even indicates the trope, be it irony or parody. Thus he embodies the excess of not only the lover but that reversal of the lover, the murderer (the historical Tropp-mann was, in fact, a nineteenth-century murderer who bit off the finger of his executioner), as well as the writing of the literary figure (the trope and the man). Troppmann's excesses and his writing are intimately con-nected. Unlike Mozart's Don Juan, Troppmann is as impotent as he is (or would be) effervescent; his writing—for Troppmann is an intellec-tual, writing in 1934—underscores both his sexual and his political im-potence. It is his writing, in fact, that is central not only to Troppmann's impotence, but (as we will see) to his "release" from his impotence, and to the final critique of that release.

Both Troppmann's impotence and his monstrous excess (the two things that distinguish him from Kierkegaard's Don Juan) are functions of writing. Troppmann is a writer, rather than a singer; his ecstasy can only be banged out on a typewriter in the early morning, "toutes portes ouvertes" (414; 48) ["leaving all the doors open"].[4] From the very first his relation to writing is one of automutilation: his writing is double, involving the mutilation of the writing subject who is both sacrificer and and sacrificed, victim and torturer. Troppmann describes his childhood:

Je passais les heures d'études à m'ennuyer, je restais là, presque immobile, souvent la bouche ouverte. Un soir, à la lumiere de gaz . . . j'avais saisi mon porte-plume, [et] le tenant, dans le poing droit fermé, comme un couteau, je me donnai de grands coups de plume d'acier sur le dos de la main gauche et sur l'avant-bras. . . . Je m'étais fait un certain nombre de blessures sales, moins rouges que noirâtres (à cause de l'encre). Ces petites blessures avaient la forme d'un croissant, qui avait en coupe la forme de la plume. (454; 106)

I used to while away my study hours, just sitting there, scarcely moving, often with my mouth hanging open. One evening, under the gaslight . . . I had grasped my pen and, holding it in my clenched fist like a knife, I repeatedly buried the steel nib in the back of my left arm and forearm. . . . I inflicted a number of dirty cuts, more blackish than red because of the ink. The small cuts were crescent-shaped, like the nib seen in cross-section.

Pen piercing flesh, black ink and red blood on white skin: the auto-biographical account recounts its origins (the child's earliest writing) as openmouthed incomprehension and sexually impotent violence. This apparently mindless violence soon takes on a larger significance, how-ever, when it is repeated in the account of Troppmann's encounter with the Commander.

We have already seen, in our brief discussion of Kierkegaard's version of Don Juan, that the Commander may in fact be an internal constituent of Don Juan. The written Commander—both comic and legal—at the heart of the effervescent must be seen as a double of the self-mutilating writing at the beginning of Troppmann's autobiography. Just as the author is initiated into his writing and written self through a violence to the integrity of his "self," so too he constitutes himself as Don Juan only through the recurrent violation of his Don Juan by the Commander. The sacrificer and sacrificed in "primitive cultures," the automutilating mad-man—figures evoked by Bataille in his essays of the 1930s—all appear here in the dyad Troppmann/Commander.

It should first be noted that there is little defiance in Troppmann's embrace of the Commander. Despite the fact that this defiance was the element in Don Juan's comportment toward the Commander that Bataille in other writings valued the most (see V, 92), in *Le Bleu du ciel* Tropp-mann is sick and feverish, and seems to be calling the Commander and asking him to deliver him from his impotence and suffering. Troppmann associates the Commander with a black apparition: the tablecloth at the final meal of Don Juan and, more importantly, the "banderole noir" ["black streamer"] that hangs outside Troppmann's hotel in Vienna (409; 41). Later, Troppmann is terrified by a black shadow outside his window that "tomba du ciel ensoleillé" (439; 84) ["fell out of the sunny sky"], which he identifies with the Commander. This darkness, seen out-side the window, is clearly associated with the entry of death: Tropp-mann looks at the "black streamer" just before he attempts to hang him-self. The "streamer," finally, is compared with a stream of ink that opens in Troppmann's head. Troppmann's call to the Commander, his attempted suicide, his experience of ink in the head, his willing assump-tion of the role of victim, are less the defiance of Don Juan than they are the calculated self-destruction of a doomed man. Because of that calcula-tion, moral terms such as "guilt" and "innocence" inevitably confront Troppmann; unlike Don Juan, in his very weakness Troppmann cannot be above such considerations.

For that reason, Troppmann's calling of the Commander, and the Commander's militarism, inevitably take on a political significance. The Commander himself must be seen as double, but double in a sinister way, since his entry is marked by the "black streamer" hung to commemorate Dollfuss, a fascist slain by fascists (409; 42). The Commander, the black stain on the white sky, the black banner of death poised at the window, all these not only double the inscription of violence of writing (black ink and blood on white skin) but signal a kind of double—and violently self-mutilating—fascism as well. The Commander is here the instance of the deleterious retributive code in the form of fascist law.

The death and mutilation facing Troppmann (which he inflicts or calls down upon himself) are fascist. It is clear that his implicit guilt, his calling in the Commander, must be seen in a larger context. Troppmann is a Marxist intellectual with a "mauvaise conscience à l'égard des ouvriers" (448; 98) ["an inner feeling of guilt toward the workers"]. This guilt comes from the fact that he himself is double. The Commander in Troppmann is a function of Troppmann's complicity with the fascists, and yet Troppmann himself is an avowed Marxist. On the one hand Troppmann the Marxist believes in the possibility of a rationalized, coherent society in which wealth is evenly distributed; on the other he is a (would-be) Don Juan who would embrace an experience that departs from the coherent and rational. But is it possible for the Marxist intellectual, like Troppmann, *not* to betray Marxism (and thus not ally himself with the fascists and call in a fascistic Commander) while devoting himself to a practice that goes beyond production and utility?

Marxism, observing Troppmann, must conclude that he has embraced fascism. Any interest that radically goes beyond the rational and codified (and perhaps even liberalized) "closed economy" of production and consumption can only be seen by a Marxist as a betrayal. But there is more to Troppmann than simply a capitulation to and complicity with the fascists. To be sure, a Marxist Don Juan automutilates when he embraces a rational Marxist code at the moment he attempts to experience sheer effervescence. For the time being, at this point in the novel, Troppmann is the typical impotent intellectual, torn by his "guilt": he can neither forsake the Marxist revolutionaries he goes to aid in Barcelona, nor can he wholeheartedly aid them. But as Don Juan, Troppmann always implies a rewriting or repetition of defiance before the Commander. To that extent, he embodies a defiance of rationalized yet repressive law—not in the name of another law, but out of simple effervescence. If indeed Troppmann could break this always threatened complicity with the fascists, and really defy them, he might be able to experience an unadulterated effervescent sexuality; he might be able to become the musical

Don Juan. That, however, would appear to involve both the definitive supersession of his guilt (and complicity with fascism) and the embrace of a wholehearted and coherent revolutionary activity (because only this type of activity can hope to defeat fascism). How can this take place if his defiance is directed not only against a repressive and illegitimate code (fascism), but against, inevitably, a legitimate but rationalized one (Marxism) as well? Once again we confront Troppmann's "guilt": how can Troppmann engage in an effervescent activity, and avoid the guilt and impotence that necessarily goes along with that effervescence? How can the guilty conscience (and its self-mutilation) be done away with, and the two seemingly opposite (but equally necessary) alternative modes of action—the coherent and the effervescent—be engaged in? Can some form of political action be worked out that implements both coherency and effervescence? Can this be done *outside of* automutilating writing?

We will argue, in the pages that follow, that the very movement of *Le Bleu du ciel* as a novel is made possible not only by writing, but by the doublings and repetitions—the metamorphoses—of writing itself. Just as the black-banner Commander on the blank sky was a double of Troppmann's childhood wounds, so too other episodes of the novel will repeat this configuration, this bind, this guilt—the doubled automutilation of black and white—while impossibly trying to find a way out of it. Yet the ultimate question of the guilt of writing will prove to be very much an open question.

One possible route open to Troppmann is that demonstrated by M. Melou, the stepfather of Troppmann's revolutionary friend, Lazare. It is, in fact, in Melou's discourse—as written and reported by the autobiographical Troppmann—that a way out of guilt and automutilation might be seen. Melou is first presented by Troppmann as a comic figure (423; 62), but Troppmann starts to respect him when they talk of the future of the revolutionary masses of Europe.

Melou, as a communist, recognizes the possibility that the working classes of Europe will "perish" in the rise of fascism. It is clear that he is thinking of a disaster more radical than a simple political or even military defeat. Troppmann then questions him: "Si la classe ouvrière est foutue, pourquoi êtes-vous communistes—ou socialistes?—comme vous voudrez—" (424; 63) ["If the working classes are done for, why are you both communists—or socialists—or whatever?"] Melou recognizes Troppmann's perplexity and the real problem in his question. He answers:

"En effet . . . pourquoi sommes-nous encores socialistes—ou communistes? Oui, pourquoi?" Il parut s'abîmer dans une méditation imprévue. Il laissa peu à peu tomber, du haut de son immense buste, une petite tête longuement barbue. Je vis ses genous anguleux. Après un silence gênant, il ouvrit d'interminables bras, et, tristement, il les éleva:

"Les choses en arrivent là, nous ressemblons au paysan qui travaillerait sa terre pour l'orage. Il passerait devant ses champs, la tête basse—il saurait la grêle inévitable—

. . . .
. . . .
. . . .

"Alors—le moment approchant—il se tient devant sa recolte et, comme je le fais maintenant moi-même" (sans transition, l'absurde, le risible personnage devint sublime, tout à coup sa voix suave avait pris quelque chose de glaçant) "il élevera ses bras vers le ciel—en attendant que la foudre le frappe—lui et ses bras—"

Il laissa, sur ces mots, tomber ses propres bras. (425; 63–64)

"In fact . . . why are we socialists—or communists? Why, indeed?" He seemed to sink into unforeseen meditation. Little by little from the summit of his immense trunk, the tiny head and its long beard began to droop. I noticed his bony knees. At the end of an uncomfortable silence he stretched out two interminable arms and sadly lifted them up, "Things have come to this. We're like a farmer working his land for the storm, walking down his fields with lowered head—knowing that the hail is bound to fall—

. . . .
. . . .
. . . .

"And then—as the moment approaches—standing in front of his harvest, he draws himself erect and, as I now am doing" (with no transition, this ludicrous, laughable character became noble: that frail voice, that slick voice of his was imbued with ice) "he pointlessly raises his arms to heaven, waiting for the lightning to strike him—him, and his arms—"

On these words, his own arms fell.

Melou's remarks have a precision that Troppmann's often lack. While the self-mutilation of a vacant child is the model for Troppmann's writing, Melou's statement at least allows him provisionally to escape one of Troppmann's binds. How can the intellectual devoted to "expenditure" still manifest solidarity with the working classes and not betray them? Melou presents the growth of the working class as organic growth, the effervescence of plant life. The intellectual watches over this growth and aids it. This metaphor of organic growth allows Melou (and Troppmann, who is citing him) neatly to fuse the notion of production with the idea of the explosive sexuality of Don Juan. (Bataille used the same image of organic growth some fifteen years later, in *La part maudite* [*The Cursed Share*] to illustrate the "excessive" tendencies of both nature and man as a self-reflexive phenomenon of nature.) As opposed to the closed circle of mechanical production and use, organic growth is immediate and open-ended, exploding and proliferating without end or goal. But we must assume that the metaphor of organic growth includes the workers of the industrial and mechanical world.

Destruction has been divorced from the proliferation of growth. The farmer or the leftist intellectual is no longer culpable; while his gesture of raising his hands is "useless," and while he is passive, he has still found a way out of the "guilt" of Troppmann and the risk that Troppmann faces of being assimilated by the fascists. Death and the negativity of annihilation cannot be definitively escaped, just as Don Juan was inevitably retaken by the Commander; guilt, however, can be exiled to the extent that the intellectual goes down with the troops that he has (like crops) somehow raised. He does not give up his solidarity with them. Nor is he preparing the workers for some "higher" meaning or value, beyond the instant of their growth: he only "worked the land for the storm." The affirmation of growth is now (for the intellectual) beyond both reappropriation through utility and betrayal through fascism and death; the intellectual can therefore be an instantaneous Don Juan, without the risk of collusion with the right. When death comes, it comes from outside the dyad workers/intellectuals.

The doubled sacrificial relation, however, is still to be found in this text; it is, in fact, the text itself. While the intellectual is not actively guilty of sacrificing the workers, of mutilating himself and his doubles, he *is* guilty of sacrificing his own language: "Il laissa, sur ces mots, tomber ses propres bras" ["On these words, his own arms fell"]. The arm of the sacrificer falls, but in this case on language itself. Troppmann doubles Melou, by citing his text. (Melou's text is one that could only be cited, for Melou himself would never publish words that his friends would regard as scandalous.) Troppmann mimics his discouragement ("par contagion, j'eus un geste découragé" ["I too, as if it were contagious, made a gesture of discouragement"]) and repeats (by rewriting) his words. In doing so, however, he mutilates them: large sections of what Melou said are missing, replaced by neat rows of dots, black puncturing white. It is impossible to know what inevitably unacceptable formulations have been lost or repressed in the interstices of this text. This censorship involves an active destruction of meaning, which is quite different from the passive resistance offered by the "farmer" in Melou's little speech. The guilty automutilation of writing—the doubling of victim and sacrificer, the cutting of pen in flesh, the penetration of black in the empty whiteness of consciousness—is now transposed to the unwritten text itself; pen in flesh becomes pen in text, expurgating through the process of replacing words (and sense) with a grid pattern of dots. The Commander is metamorphosed as rewriting through expurgation and suppression.

The rows of dots that represent a textual violence double an action described by the passage. Men spring from plowed rows, like crops, and the storm cuts them down. Words spring from rows of type and are cut down in the process of citation. Citation doubles the action of the storm—a storm from which it was necessary, as we saw, for Melou and Troppmann to dissociate themselves. If Melou/Troppmann doubles the storm by bringing his hand down violently on his words, then his recurrent guilt in the destruction of his men (and himself) must be considered. His complicity may not be expunged, but only transferred to an action that he actively directs against the text.

Finally, we recognize in this passage a return of the impotence of Troppmann as a literary "revolutionary." Once again, his solution—which in itself is only a displacement of culpability, rather than an effacement of it—is accomplished only in writing. Troppmann is still the parodic Don Juan, impotent, haunted by his mother-in-law who resents his abandonment of her daughter (414; 48), incapable of either aiding the revolutionaries in Barcelona or experiencing the sexual excess to which—perhaps for lack of anything else—he seems to want to devote his life. He can only write.

There is, in fact, one final scene—a "climatic" one—in which it seems that Troppmann's sexual and political impotence is resolved. It appears that for once his automutilation and guilt have been overcome. Having left Spain, Troppmann and Dorothea change trains in Trier, Germany. With its newly consolidated Nazi regime, Germany is a strange backdrop for what takes place. The lovers take a walk and, tempted by a secluded site, suddenly couple, balanced on the edge of an abyss. In the abyss is a cemetery, each grave marked with a candle.

A un tournant du chemin un vide s'ouvrait au-dessous de nous. Etrangement, ce vide n'était pas moins illimité, à nos pieds, qu'un ciel étoilé sur nos têtes. Une multitude de petites lumières, agitées par le vent, menaient dans la nuit une fête silencieuse, inintelligible. Ces étoiles, ces bougies étaient par centaines en flammes sur le sol: le sol où s'alignait la foule des tombes illuminées. Je pris Dorothea par le bras. Nous étions fascinés par cet abîme d'étoiles funèbres. Dorothea se rapprocha de moi. Longuement elle m'embrassa dans la bouche. Elle m'enlaca, me serrant violemment: c'était, depuis longtemps, la première fois qu'elle se déchainait. Hâtivement, nous fimes, hors du chemin, dans la terre labourée, les dix pas que font les amants. Nous étions toujours au-dessus des tombes. Dorothea s'ouvrit, je la dénudai jusqu'au sexe. Elle-même, elle me dénuda. Nous sommes tombés sur le sol meuble et je m'enfoncai dans son corps humide comme une charrue bien manoeuvrée s'enfonce dans la terre. La terre, sous ce corps, était ouverte comme une tombe, son ventre nu s'ouvrit à moi comme une tombe fraiche. Nous étions frappés de stupeur faisant l'amour au-dessus d'un cimetière étoilé. Chacune des lumières annonçait un squelette dans une tombe, elles formaient ainsi un ciel vacillant, aussi trouble que les mouvements de nos corps mêlés. Il faisait froid, mes mains s'enfonçaient dans la terre: je dégrafai Dorothea, je souillai son linge et sa poitrine de la terre fraîche qui s'était collée à mes doigts. Ses seins, sortis de ses vêtements, étaient d'une blancheur lunaire. Nous nous abandonnions de temps à autre, nous laissant aller à trembler de froid; nos corps tremblaient comme deux rangées de dents claquent l'une dans l'autre.

Le vent fit dans les arbres un bruit sauvage. Je dis en bégayant à Dorothea, je bégayais, je parlais sauvagement:

"—mon squelette—tu trembles de froid—tu claques des dents—"

Je m'étais arrêté, je passais sur elle sans bouger, je soufflais comme un chien. Soudain j'enlaçai ses reins nus. Je me laissai tomber de tout mon poids. Elle poussa un terrible cri. Je serrai les dents de toutes mes forces. A ce moment, nous avons glissé sur un sol en pente.

Il y avait plus bas une partie de rocher en surplomb. Si je n'avais, d'un coup de pied, arrêté ce glissement, nous serions tombés dans la nuit, et j'aurais pu croire, émerveillé, que nous tombions dans le vide du ciel. (481–82; 143–45)

At one turning in the path, an empty space opened beneath us. Curiously, this empty space, at our feet, was no less infinite than a starry sky over our heads. Flickering in the wind, a multitude of little lights was filling the night with silent, indecipherable celebration. Those stars—those candles—were flaming by the hundred on the ground: ground where ranks of lighted graves were massed. We were fascinated by this chasm of funereal stars. Dorothea drew closer to me. She kissed me at length on the mouth. She embraced me, holding me violently tight; it was the first time in a long while that she had let herself go. Leaving the path across plowed earth, we took the lover's dozen steps. We still had the graves below us. Dorothea opened wide, and I bared her to the loins. She in turn bared me. We fell onto the shifting ground, and I sank into her moist body the way a well-guided plow sinks into earth. The earth beneath that body lay open like a grave; her naked cleft lay open to me like a freshly dug grave. We were stunned making love over a starry graveyard. Each of the lights proclaimed a skeleton in its grave, and they thus formed a wavering sky, as unsteady as the motions of our mingled bodies. It was cold. My hands sank into the earth. I unbuttoned Dorothea, smirching her underclothes and breast with the cold earth that stuck to my fingers. Emerging from her clothes, her breasts were of a lunar whiteness. We let go of one another from time to time, simply letting ourselves quiver with cold: our bodies were quivering like two rows of teeth chattering together.

The wind made a wild sound in the trees. I said to Dorothea in a stammer (I was stammering and talking wildly), ''—My skeleton—You're shivering. Your teeth are chattering—''

I stopped and lay on top of her, heavy and still, panting like a dog. Abruptly I clasped her naked buttocks. I fell on her with my full weight. She uttered a terrific scream. I clenched my teeth as hard as I could. At that moment we began sliding down the sloping ground.

Farther down, the rock formed an overhang. If I hadn't stopped our slide with my foot, we would have fallen into the night, and I might have wondered with amazement if we weren't falling into the void of the sky.

In this expressionistic landscape, the solid limits of previous sexual dilemmas have disappeared; Dorothea and Troppmann fall into the ''void.'' The passage must be seen in a political context as well as in the more obvious sexual light: we see here the elimination of the writer's guilty conscience and individuality, as well as the supersession of his sexual impotence. The instantaneous yet seemingly eternal moment of sexual union—the moment in which the woman, like the soil, is sown with seed—takes place in a limitless expanse where sky and earth are identical. For a moment, it seems the couple will hover ''in the void of the sky,'' neither in the tombs below, nor in the sky above, caught in neither of the binds that these alternatives represent.[5] This effervescence has a political significance as well because the erotic couple is here presented as the true revolutionary unit, defiantly coupling in Nazi Germany. (Bataille later wrote—in 1951—of the erotic couple as the political basis for a utopian future, in the last chapter of his *Histoire de l'érotisme* [VIII, 135].) In one moment, then, which could just as easily be an eternity, death and writing have been forsaken, to be replaced by a unification that is both sexually and politically potent.

Yet this potency comes at the end of, and is made possible by, a narrative chain of metamorphoses and doublings. It cannot be read outside of that context. Just as for a moment (in our process of reading) we experience an unlimited unification, so now the point of view of our position is immediately doubled, and reverses itself (in the same way that the lovers were reversed and would have fallen into the tombs below, had not Troppmann stuck out his foot to stop them). We now recognize that this episode not only serves as a climax for a series of written events (which constitute the novel), but that the very elements of the scene—the tombs (and Dorothea's womb as tomb), the fires and stars in the night, the skeleton, the cutting into the earth, the spilling of excess seed as well as its recuperation, the tropic reversal and fall—all indicate a continuation of the same series of metaphors that constituted the earlier metastatements on writing and death in this novel (and whose repetitions and doublings constitute its narrative movement): the boy stabbing his skin; the oblivion and retribution of the Commander; the mutilation of writing itself in the process of citation. Rather than escaping these problems, the lovers only hover over them momentarily; they eventually fall back to isolation, impotence, and duality: "nous étions peu de chose l'un pour l'autre, tout au moins dès l'instant où nous n'étions plus dans l'angoisse" (481; 143) ["We mattered little to one another, not, at least, after anxiety abandoned us"].

Thus the explosion of sexuality outside of the limits of the two individuals (and their automutilations) cannot be sustained; as explosion, it is always again textual. The "return to earth" at first, however, would seem to be a disastrous fall to fascism, impotence, and death. After the incident in Trier, Troppmann's and Dorothea's relationship once more decomposes. After the moment of liberation, Troppmann discovers Dorothea's nude body beneath "une robe de soie d'un rouge vif, du rouge des drapeaux à croix gammée" (484; 148) ["a bright red silk dress—the red of swastikaed flags"]. Not only Dorothea, but the experience in Trier itself must now be recognized as a kind of fascist ceremony, a parody of the ideology of farmer, blood, and soil ("Nous n'étions pas moins excités par la terre que par la nudité de la chair" [482; 145] ["We were as excited by earth as by naked flesh"]). Finally, in the last scene of the novel, the too-human Troppmann sees in the obscene baton manipulations of a Hitler Youth leader the sadistic agression that will soon be loosed on Europe—and that will certainly be unconcerned with the "supplications" of nervous intellectuals who oppose it (487; 151). It seems that we have come full circle, and have returned to the impotence and guilt of the writer, that well-meaning man who cannot cast his lot without reserve with the Marxists and who therefore finds himself in (unwilling) complicity with the fascists.

There may be more to the sundered consciousness of the writer than this, however. Troppmann at the end of his story points out that Trier is fertile to the point that it has produced that authority on production, Karl Marx himself (483; 146). Marx, as Troppmann informs us, is now buried near London. Now it was in London that the first scene of *Le Bleu du ciel* took place: in it, the drunken Dorothea (or, as Troppmann calls her, "Dirty") recalls her childhood and the drunken collapse of her mother (388; 12). Thus the novel ends with the birth and childhood of Marx, and ends with his death and the childhood of Dorothea. The novel describes a circle: in its repetitious or circular time, the problem of writing occurs in the space between the incessant death and rebirth of Marx. As the locus of socialization for Marx—Troppmann mentions Marx's middle-class childhood as well as his birth—Trier represents Marx's initiation into language. Troppmann in mentioning this detail perhaps intends to point out the irony of the triumph of Nazism in Marx's birthplace, but another reading is just as possible. A boy seen on the street, who reminds Troppmann of Marx as a child, may serve as a reminder as well of the genesis or production of Marxian language. The view of Dorothea in her blood-red dress may consequently be a *critical* view both of her and of the ''escape'' (from political and sexual impotence) that she and Troppmann experience at the moment of orgasm. At the same time, however, the redness of Dorothea's dress may be double, signaling both a complicity with Nazism and the intervention of a communist (red) critique. (If Dorothea had chosen the official Nazi color, she would have worn a brown dress.) Thus Dorothea, too, in her revolt, may be as torn as Troppmann.

If indeed writing is double, and always turned against itself, then the writing at the end of the novel must be seen as not only in complicity with death, impotence, and guilt (the things to which one falls back) but as an analytic (and rational) tool that criticizes fascism. Thus the momentary ''climax'' and solution of the novel may be opened out not only by a writing of impotence, reversal, and defeat, but by its double, a powerful, analytical writing. This writing finds that the ''moment'' of resolution or escape was in fact already in complicity with fascism and its ideals of apolitical and atextual utopian solutions.

Writing must be seen as double, and caught in a bind that mirrors Troppmann's. It supports and makes possible the momentary experience of effervescent sexuality, and then (or at the same instant) criticizes and betrays that effervescence and its pretentions. Not only is it double, but it is both integral to and radically opposed to Don Juan's (or his double Troppmann's) moment of effervescent sexuality. Into immediacy there is always introduced the temporality of writing. We must recognize the complicity of that writing with self-rending death; indeed it becomes clear that, as presented in *Le Bleu du ciel*, explosive sexual expenditure cannot be definitively separated from what is radically opposed to it: analysis, and the silence and absence of death. In this light, Troppmann's bizarre tendencies, which seem like indications not only of impotence but even of sickness, come to be seen as integral parts of the momentary sexual experience. Incestuous necrophilia and the vision of Dorothea as womb and tomb are both indications of Troppmann's weakness, but are also integral to the divided force of sexuality. Hence Bataille's rewriting of Kierkegaard—the metamorphosis of sexuality into death—is a function of the inevitable writing of sexuality. Bataille was never, in any of his works, capable of simply separating sexuality from death, immediacy from the self-mutilation of inscription. Nor was he capable of ignoring the importance of the analysis of experiences of sexuality and death, for analysis is, through writing, the double of death.

What then of fascism and Marxism? If the novel is circular, its ending leading back to its beginning, it seems likely that any political "solution" is not fully separable from an open-ended process of rereading and rewriting. Troppmann is certainly politically impotent, but at the same time, by the end of the novel, we see a powerful critique of any "solution" to that impotence. Indeed it seems impossible to fully disengage effective action from betrayal, sincerity from guilt; the only disengagement from guilt the novel can offer is itself guilty. Just as Troppmann is caught between coherent doctrines and explosive sexuality, so, in the same way, language itself is torn between complicity with a totalizing law and complicity with a death that escapes that law. In this context, fascism is positional: at one moment surfacing in the sheer death associated with the Commander, at another as his retributive formalized law; at one point as the inevitable guilt of the leader of the defeated workers, at another as the escape from that guilt in a moment of sexual "communication." It seems clear that for Bataille fascism was (like the black streamer marking the death of Dollfuss) itself double, and was an inherent function of language. To attempt to escape it would paradoxically result in an inevitable return to it. *Le Coupable* [*The Guilty One*] (1944) was neither the first nor the last work of Bataille to deal with betrayal and guilt. The only option was to continue the written critique—impotent and powerful—of the experience both of total loss and total coherence. It is only through that critique that the ideals of Marxism are to be approached, if indeed we continue to recognize the possibility of a coherent doctrine (like Marxism) that is itself constituted through the intervention of the momentary (in the same way that the momentary is constituted through the intervention of the coherent and the deferred). (If we do not see Marxism constituted through the momentary or effervescent, Marxism becomes a mere balancing of the books, a settling of accounts that is a double of the totalization [or "homogeneity"] of fascism.)

If, for a moment, we recall our initial rereading of Kierkegaard, we might postulate that Bataille, in *Le Bleu du ciel*, is merely recognizing what is repressed in Kierkegaard's text: that writing, manifesting itself as both analysis and death, constitutes what is radically different from itself, namely, the immediacy of sexuality. The Commander, as repressive or rational law and simple death, is always already at the heart of effervescence. And just as the Commander frames Mozart's *Don Juan*, while at the same time (as periphery) penetrating to the heart of the opera, so too Marx frames (with his birth and death) *Le Bleu du ciel*, while penetrating to the heart of the novel (its climax) with the force of a critique of sexuality. It may be, then, that *Le Bleu du ciel* must be seen as a metastatement on writing in excess—as death and analysis—as well as a commentary on the dilemmas of the writer.

Chapter Two
Blanchot and the
Silence of Specificity

The problem of Maurice Blanchot as right-wing propagandist[1] is a most perplexing one: rightist articles in the 1930s, hermetic works of fiction and Heideggerian criticism in the 1940s. Blanchot's early political polemics would seem not only to be written by a different man from the critic and novelist, but on a different planet as well. Where is the law—"où est la loi"—of Blanchot's fiction? To attempt to answer this question, and to see how Blanchot's post-1930s writing involves not a simple ideology but an impossible attempt to strip and finally silence all ideologies (and to broach, finally, the problem of the status of that impossible silencing), we will examine first Blanchot's reading of his contemporaries in his collection of essays *Faux pas* [*False Step*] (1943), and then Blanchot's treatment of the modern absolute State in his 1948 novel, *Le Très-Haut* [*The Most High*].

I

In light of Blanchot's political writings of the 1930s, it is tempting to see in Blanchot's interest in Henry de Montherlant's *Solstice de juin* [*June Solstice*] (in *Faux pas*, 360–63)[2] an affirmation on Blanchot's part of the celebration by Montherlant of the French surrender of June 1940. An examination of Blanchot's text reveals something quite different— namely, that Blanchot advocates a kind of stripping of Montherlant's text, and it is precisely the political moment of Montherlant that he would

22

discard. While Blanchot affirms the "insolence" of Montherlant's elitism ("une oscillation entre le juste et le faux: . . . exaltation spectaculaire de l'instant et effort violent pour dominer celui qui domine" [363] ["an oscillation between the true and the false: . . . a spectacular exaltation of the moment and a violent effort to dominate the one who dominates"]), this Nietzschean attitude is stopped short of politics. Blanchot condemns in Montherlant "une idéologie qui semble à peine supérieure aux meditations habituelles des écrivains perdus dans la politique" ["an ideology that seems hardly superior to the habitual meditations of writers lost in politics"]—a fascist ideology that in the future, according to Blanchot, will not be actively suppressed, but will simply disappear in silence, or in the supersilence of the imagined sound of the sea or the rolling of the waves. To drive home the point, Blanchot quotes Montherlant against himself: "Les journaux, les revues d'aujourd'hui, quand je les ouvre, j'entends rouler sur eux l'indifférence de l'avenir, comme on entend le bruit de la mer quand on porte à l'oreille certains coquillages" (363) ["When I open the newspapers and reviews of today, I hear rolling over them the indifference of the future, as one hears the sound of the sea by putting certain shells up to the ear"]. (These indeed are the last words of *Faux pas*; after them, in large letters, at the bottom of the page, is "FIN.")

The same process, the stripping away of specificity and the repetition of silence, can be seen to take place throughout this first volume of Blanchot's critical writings. The opening essay in *Faux pas*, "De l'angoisse au langage" ["From Dread to Language"], significantly rewrites the title of one of Georges Bataille's favorite books, Pierre Janet's *De l'angoisse à l' extase* [*From Dread to Ecstasy*]. In Blanchot it is no longer a positive term toward which one moves, be it simple ecstasy or simple death, but it is a movement through which language itself, the language of the text, becomes the embodiment of an initially posited "dread." The writer has nothing to say; his "dread" is this nothing, and his task is to say and write this nothing: "le rien est sa matière" (*Faux pas*, 11; 5) ["nothing is his material"]. But, paradoxically, simply giving up or allowing mere chance to do the work is not enough. As soon as one allows chance to do one's work (as in the case of "automatic writing"), one is no longer disinterested: one is no longer writing nothing. Because of this, the most rigorous writing about nothing—and the most intimately tied to "dread"—is the most carefully worked out, the *least* left to chance. It is finally the reflection on the status of writing, the necessity of an order that escapes order, that is the final stage of any experience of "dread": "Tout ce qui est écrit a pour celui qui l'écrit le plus grand sens possible, mais aussi ce sens que c'est un sens lié au hasard, que c'est le nonsens. . . . Il [le texte] garde un peu de sens du fait qu'il ne reçoit jamais tout son sens, et il est angoissé parce qu'il ne peut être pure angoisse'' (26; 19–20) ["Everything that is written has, for the one who writes it, the greatest meaning possible, but also has this meaning that it is a meaning bound to chance, that it is a non-sense. . . . It (the text) retains a little meaning from the fact that it never receives all its meaning, and it is filled with dread because it cannot be pure dread'']. The final stage of this "development" of "dread" is the stripping away of all other concerns, and the focus of writing on the radical dilemma—the "dread" —of a writing that rigorously is nothing.

Many of the other essays in *Faux pas*, focusing on writers such as Camus, Sartre, and Jünger bear out this approach. In each essay the political moment in, or orientation of, the work discussed is dismissed. Sartre's Orestes in *Les Mouches* [*The Flies*] is dismissed by Blanchot as a mere rationalist, opposing a hypocritical and brutal order—rather than the sacrilegious hero of Greek myth (see pp. 82–92; we will return to this essay later). Clearly, the target here is Sartre's political notion of "engagement," muted but already clearly presented under the Occupation. Similarly, the reading of Ernst Jünger's *On the Marble Cliffs* as a political novel is dismissed as a "too simple allegorical interpretation," despite the fact that the "Chief Ranger" in that novel is clearly identifiable with Hitler (see p. 298).

With these critical positions in mind (which devalue the problem of politics and conflate it with the problem of language), it is not difficult to see how a commentator as perceptive as Michel Foucault essentially can identify the problems of law with those of language in a novel by Blanchot, *Le Très-Haut*.[3] In an article devoted to Blanchot, "La Pensée du dehors" ["The Thought of the Outside"],[4] Foucault comes to associate the self-transgressions (or "dread") of the law (Foucault, 533–37) with language (540–43). The hero of *Le Très-Haut*, Henri Sorge, embodies the law of a phantasmic totalitarian State. The law of this State seems literally untransgressible because all transgressions, no matter how brutal, can be recuperated or put to use by the law. It is only when Sorge, as representative of the law, finally transgresses it (at the very end of the novel), that the self-transgression of language replaces depicted and recuperable violence. Sorge's transgression of the law is brought about through his death as sacrificial victim, as god. This death, in Foucault's view, is tied to the movement and liberation of language: "Mais peut-être cette mort de Dieu est-elle le contraire de la mort (l'ignominie d'une chose flasque et visqueuse qui éternellement palpite), et le geste qui se détend pour la tuer libère enfin son langage" (537) ["But perhaps this death of God is itself the opposite of death (the ignominy of a flaccid and viscous thing that eternally throbs), and the gesture that relaxes in order to kill it finally liberates its language"]. Finally, it is language itself rather than any relation to the law that comes to characterize the subject: "[Un] Langage qui n'est parlé par personne: tout sujet n'y dessine qu'un pli grammatical. [Le langage] ouvre un espace neutre où nulle existence ne peut s'enraciner" (543) ["(A) language which is spoken by no one: any subject sketches out there only a grammatical fold. (Language) opens a neutral space where no existence can take root"]. Somewhere in all of this, however, the register of discourse has changed, and the disfigured corpses and plague victims that litter *Le Très-Haut* have been replaced by the problematics of language. There is of course nothing morally or intrinsically "wrong" with that replacement, but it does pose a problem: if, in *Le Très-Haut*, as in his essays, Blanchot is concerned primarily with a model of "dread" and transgressive death of and in language, why do we see depicted in the novel a city that (at least in the opening chapters) resembles Paris under the Occupation, and why is there a regime or State that mirrors the absolutely totalitarian Stalinist State?

In other words, it would seem that, unlike Blanchot's criticism, *Le Très-Haut* poses problems that depart from the realm of language and that are explicitly concerned with legal and finally political questions (after all, the hero of the novel, its main character, is as much the State as it is Henri Sorge). (In this context it goes without saying that the move from politics and the State to language may be as much a political move as a gesture of language.) We might turn the tables on Foucault and ask (if the novel on a major level is concerned with the problem of politics): what, if any, political or legal significance is there to the shift from law and politics to language in the novel? This returns us to our initial question concerning the political position of Blanchot's writings, for a novel that in the immediate postwar period deals with the State and law will very likely touch on the phenomenon of right-wing totalitarianism, either explicitly or, as is more likely, as a space or hollow where that totalitarianism has been eradicated or erased.

II

To put the novel *Le Très-Haut* in perspective, we must recall that the postwar period was one in which the questioning of the State had attained a crucial importance. The "end of history," affirmed by Kojève after Hegel and Marx, was seen both in the Stalinist state but also, in a sinister parody, in the recently destroyed fascist states. Julien Benda, Arthur Koestler, George Orwell, Georges Bataille, and Czeslaw Milosz among others in the late 1940s questioned the claim made by the State at the "end of history" for the total allegiance of the intellectual. Both Stalinism and fascism proclaimed that, as the culminating point of history, they made further revolution unnecessary. These two views of the "end of history," so different in other ways, were in agreement on this point: negativity that could not be put to use by the State had literally no status whatsoever, and the intellectual who could not affirm in the totality of his being the absolute State was self-condemned to utter marginality. Thus Bataille chose eroticism, Milosz chose exile—but for the all-powerful and all-correct State such revolt was utterly insignificant.

Facing this problem, Blanchot in *Le Très-Haut* presents an exaggerated or parodied Hegelian State for which unrecuperable negativity simply does not exist. The State and its representatives, like the narrator, Henri Sorge, exist in a kind of closed circularity to which negativity is invisible. All negativity, no matter how destructive and pointless on the surface, inevitably goes toward consolidating the final and absolute State. Thus the ever-spreading violence of this State—which must always justify means by ends—is seen, when pushed to its logical conclusion in *Le Très-Haut*, to be an affirmation of an apocalyptic and nihilistic destruction of the earth.[5]

There are of course characters in the novel who rebel against this omnipresent State. Bouxx wants to lead an uprising that would topple the tyranny of the State; Sorge, the functionary, writes him a letter that tries to set him straight: "Vous faites fausse route en attaquant les bureaux, l'administration, tout l'appareil de l'Etat. Ils ne comptent pas. Si vous les supprimez, vous ne supprimerez rien. Si vous les remplacez par d'autres, vous les remplacerez par les mêmes." (*Le Très-Haut*, 171) ["You are on the wrong track when you attack the offices, the administration, and all the apparatus of the State. They don't count. If you suppress them, you suppress nothing. If you replace them with others, you replace them with the same."] No matter how violent or definitively destructive Bouxx's rebellion might be, in the end it must always dialectically reverse itself and affirm the State. The State absorbs all.

A letter from Sorge to Bouxx, written prior to the one cited above, affirms Bouxx's impotence when he writes. If Bouxx's revolution is a sham, anything he writes or says about it will be a sham as well: "Vous avez la superstition de ce qui est écrit. Vous vous préoccupez excessivement des commentaires, des consignes, des rapports. Ce sont des copies ignorantes." (149–50) ["You are superstitious about the written. You are excessively preoccupied with commentaries, written orders, reports. These are ignorant copies."] The same thing, however, applies to Sorge. If Bouxx is impotent so is Sorge, but on another level. Sorge in the same letter writes: "Je pénètre tout, rappelez-vous bien cela; c'est pourquoi je ne pourrai plus tenir longtemps. J'ai honte." (150) ["I penetrate into everything, bear that in mind; that is why I will not be able to hold on much longer. I am ashamed."] Sorge's shame, his humiliation as the perfect State functionary, is due to the fact that, at the "end of history," there can be nothing more to say, just as there can be no more revolutionary events. The writer, like Sorge, is caught in a double bind: as writer he must write, but as functionary he cannot. As functionary he can only repeat what the State decrees; he is impotent. "La lumière était si faible que je pouvais à peine écrire: pendant tout ce temps, je ressentis combien le caractère humiliant de mon existence ici dépassait l'humiliation de toutes les autres, parce que moi, je devais lire, écrire, réfléchir" (149) ["The light was so weak that I could hardly write: during all this time, I felt to what an extent the humiliating character of my existence here went beyond the humiliation of everyone else, because in my case I had to read, write, and reflect"]. Sorge is no more a writer than Bouxx is a revolutionary: to really write or reflect would be somehow to distance oneself from others, or from the State. That distance is impossible; all writing is of the State. Yet Sorge is nevertheless a writer; even though he shows, a number of times, that he is incapable of writing or speaking, he still must differ from (and with) the State. The necessity/impossibility of this difference is at the basis of Sorge's shame and guilt. This dilemma is resolved at the very end of the novel when, at the moment of his death, Sorge is at least capable for the first time of speaking, if not writing. In that way, his humiliation, his shame, is overcome. To that single moment of communication we must now turn.

That Sorge becomes a sacrificial victim at the end of the novel has been noted by several critics.[6] His transformation seems most unexpected; to go from being a perfect representative of the State to being the only individual capable of a radical enough revolt to defy the appropriating powers of the State is quite a leap. As do the writings of Bataille and Leiris, for example, Le Très-Haut puts forward a sacrificial experience—the transgressive death of Sorge at the very end of the novel—that defies the all-encompassing State. What is most interesting is that here the radical negativity of death is explicitly connected with the possibility of the use of language.

The most salient event that we associate with Sorge's death is the final phrase of the novel: "Maintenant, c'est maintenant que je parle" (243) ["Now, it is now that I speak"]. Jeanne Galgat, Sorge's murderess and nurse, has finally, by the last chapters of the novel, recognized Sorge for what he is: the "Très-Haut," the "high" victim/god who embodies the law and the definitive defiance of the law at the moment of his death. Yet by Sorge's own reckoning the most salient aspect of his death is his speaking at the moment of death ("maintenant"). His last words are a reflexive awareness that *now*, at the very end, his first words, and the first words of his self-narration, can appear. The impotence that we saw in Sorge's communication as an embodiment of the State is here replaced by a language that is "tied to a non-sense" (to use Blachot's formulation in "From Dread to Language"), a language that confronts and is finally "about" the point at which the most rigorous formulation of language impossibly embodies or knows the experience that most radically escapes it.

Language refers now not to the workings of an absolute knowledge, but to its own workings, which definitively defy absolute knowledge. But language itself is rigorous, it is not simple death: thus its own reflexivity as to its status is an absolute knowledge that goes one step further than the knowledge embodied in the State, and at the same time language's self-knowledge is a radical defiance of any definitive closure of a system. If there is any system that embraces or is unified with that which transgresses it, it is transgressive language itself, rather than any model of a State, or political position of a State. The reflexive language of "non-sense" is the only movement that can defy the appropriation by the State: any political point, no matter how transgressive, will always be useful to the State (*Le Très-Haut* demonstrates this over and over)—and simple death outside of language is eminently appropriable in any Hegelian system. *Le Très-Haut* is a circular novel: the last words point to a blank—silence, death—that in turn leads to a resumption of the telling of the story (since the last words are "it is now that I speak"). Only at the end of the novel can the story be told—once again—about language. Now finally Sorge can speak his story—and he must always return to speak what will be more than his letters that argue in favor of absolute recuperation by the State—the story of his movement on the way to a language that defies the State and State-sense by being about its own impossible embrace of itself as the disruption of itself. Thus *Le Très-Haut* all along has been narrated by a language of "non-sense," and by a "dead" man. Only a "dead" narrator re-speaking himself as a living narrator could work to a climax in which language itself in its embrace of death defies the State. If he were not dead, not the speaking sacrificial victim, Sorge would only speak the infinite and eventless nonhistory of the State as absolute knowledge.

We can see a certain justice in Foucault's remarks that Sorge is a kind of modern Orestes, defying the State powers. Indeed Blanchot, in *Faux pas* (in his essay on Sartre's *Les Mouches*) had called for a more radical Orestes than Sartre's—an Orestes who really could defy the State. Sorge the dead narrator must be seen here in the light of Blanchot the critic.

Blanchot's critical texts feature the stripping of the specificities of the politics of the works on which they comment. At this point we can see why *Le Très-Haut*, which at first seems to be a sort of political novel, refuses to identify the "State" it depicts as either a fascist or Stalinist one. A "minor" language—which would parallel the impotent writing of Sorge the functionary—can give details about a political process. But in *Le Très-Haut*, the only function of the "minor" language is to lead to the "major" language with which the narrative ends, and begins again. The "minor" language shows the ahistorical breakdown of the State and leads the way to the "major" language. The "minor" is thus written from the "point of view" of the "major" (if we can write of such a thing); "minor" language *as* "minor" language is what the victim/god/criminal Sorge will touch on as he accounts for the repetitious final appearance of a "major" language. Thus the "author" of this "major" writing—Blanchot—will be unwilling to write of extraneous "minor" details, and Sorge the god will be incapable of it. In fact, Sorge will write of those who attempt to identify themselves with the specificity of a historical position as those who bury themselves in a kind of pit of history—and who thus imprison themselves, thereby inadvertently aiding the all-appropriating State: "l'inculpé . . . se voyait enfermé dans cette histoire comme dans une prison" (218) ["the accused . . . saw himself locked in this history as in a prison"]. See also pp. 191–92: "des êtres . . . s'étant rendus aveugles à l'universelle bienveillance de l'Etat, se jettent effrontément dans la profondeur de l'histoire" ["beings . . . having made themselves blind to the universal benevolence of the State, throw themselves impudently into the depths of history"]. Finally, this self-condemnation to history must be seen as a dyadic phenomenon, in which two opposing absolute knowledges struggle against each other and reappropriate each other's negativity: "on pouvait bien dire que les illégalités les plus violentes faisaient secrètement office du droit . . . mais l'horreur vague qu'elles inspiraient prouvait aussi que le crime avait changé du camp" (218) ["one could well say that the most violent illegalities secretly acted as the law . . . but the vague horror that they inspired proved also that crime had changed sides"]. This interchangeability of States and crimes underlines their identity from the point of view of the narrator as victim/god at the moment of death, and from the point of view of the author as the one who affirms definitive defiance by that victim. Any attempt at establishing a new history as anything other than the defiance by Orestes/Sorge must result in a death or violence that rebounds on the misreader of history. The violence depicted in the novel is for that reason the very opposite of a violence associable with an attempt on the author's part to promote either fascism

or Stalinism; it is, in fact, a function of the demonstration of the consequences of locking oneself in history. The only way out of this violence
is the stripping of history of its detail; this is accomplished by the repetitious death and speech of the victim. The new parodic absolute knowledge introduced at the end of the novel is a forgetting of the deleterious
and exchangeable details of States and histories.

At this point we have little interest in pointing out the ideology of
Blanchot's position. Of course we could argue that Blanchot's position,
far from being an echo of a right-wing ideology, is in fact much closer
to a simple bourgeois liberalism that sees fascism and Stalinism as identical totalitarian evils. We cannot however bring up this political question
at this point because to do so would result in the bulldozing of the argument and position that Blanchot has gone to great lengths to establish. If
Blanchot has demonstrated the necessity of the problem of language and
the demise of the problem of political and historical specificity, it is
clearly regressive to accuse him of making a given political move (to the
extent that, in doing so, we ignore the complexities of his dialectic).

If, however, we respect Blanchot's argument and follow it through,
there are still problems in his position. How, in the fiction of *Le Très-
Haut*, does the transition from Sorge as representative of the State to
Sorge as victim/god/Orestes take place? If there is a radical discontinuity
between realms, how is a point of "communication" established between
them? That point of communication, we would be justified in inferring,
must somehow move from a political sphere—even if only a stripped
one—to a sacrificial sphere. There must be, then, a common "ground"
between the spheres, and if there is, perhaps Blanchot himself has not
exiled the problems of politics and history as definitively as it might at
first seem. It is to this problem that we now turn.

III

Le Très-Haut is a novel that is constructed out of silences, out of "neutral
spaces"—spaces of irreconcilability, of incongruence or impossibility
between entities. On a "minor" level, such spaces exist between the
impotent citizens of the State who cannot communicate with each other
(153), or between that which characterizes "legitimate" State functions
and that which characterizes "illegitimate" State crimes. But these silences or gaps, like the pit of history, can be all too easily filled at the
next stage of the infinite or timeless elaboration of absolute knowledge.
The only "silence" or "space" that does not simply serve this knowledge—the only major one—would seem to be found at the point where

Sorge speaks and dies, where language meets its other, death—and where the novel ends and recommences.

Yet how does Sorge's status change—from embodiment of law to transgressive god—and how does language concomitantly change, from tool to impossible knowledge? Evidence begins to appear, in the next-to-last chapter of the novel, that indicates that Jeanne Galgat regards Sorge as more than a simple patient; at the end of the chapter, speaking to Sorge, she states: "*Je sais que tu es l'Unique, le Suprême. Qui pourrait rester debout devant toi?*" (224; italics in the original) ["*I know that you are the Unique, the Supreme. Who could remain standing before you?*"] But the crucial turning point—and necessarily a neutral space, a silence of juncture—can be found in the last chapter. Sorge writes:

tout contre moi, un bruit intermittant, de sable coulant et s'écoulant, un halète-ment ralenti à l'extrème, comme si quelqu'un avait été là, respirant, s'empê-chant de respirer, caché juste contre moi. Je voulais ouvrir les yeux, me déga-ger, mais alors, avec horreur, je compris que mes yeux étaient déjà ouverts et déjà regardaient et touchaient et voyait ce que nul regard n'aurait dû atteindre, ne pouvait supporter. (233)

right against me, an intermittent noise, of sand flowing back and forth, an ex-tremely slowed-up panting, as if someone had been there, breathing, keeping himself from breathing, hidden just next to me. I wanted to open my eyes, get myself loose, but then, with horror, I understood that my eyes were already open and already looked at and touched and saw what no look should have attained, or could tolerate.

In the very next paragraph, Jeanne pulls "Une grosse montre, un re-volver, une boîte de cigarettes bourrée de papiers" ["A thick watch, a revolver, a cigarette box stuffed with papers"] out of a basket. The re-volver, of course, will be used shortly to "kill" Sorge, and the "thick watch" may very well indicate that time and its revolutions or cycles ("a revolver") are at stake here. The noises described earlier—the intermit-tent sound of flowing sand, the stifled breathing of someone next to Sorge—are the noises of silence or are the hallucinated noises in a silent room. They closely parallel the ultimate silence at the end of the novel: the sacrificial pair united yet radically split; the silence that is also a repe-titious sound; the experience by the victim of that which is radically other ("my eyes . . . already looked at . . . what no look should have attained").

The silence, the neutral space of the end/beginning of the novel is therefore made possible by another silence that prefigures it and doubles it—a silence within (or "hidden just next to") the text, a space of articulation that makes the "final" silence possible by joining Sorge the functionary to Sorge the victim, Jeanne the nurse to Jeanne the sacrificer, the State to the definitive defiance of the State. From this point on Sorge's "death," and all it indicates is a necessity. Watch and revolver in this context are only the indicators within the "fiction" of the novel that repetition, identity, and violence *between* neutral spaces has taken place—for if the novel is "about" anything, it is about the progression in radicality from one neutral space to the next.

The silence of flowing sand is more than just a space of intersection within the novel, however. It is a neutral space—of silence and violation—between *Le Très-Haut* and Blanchot's critical texts. It is on the same note of silence, or on the more complex waves of silence, that *Faux pas* ends. Blanchot quotes Montherlant against himself, and the suppression of a part of Montherlant's text—its oblivion—is compared to the emptiness of the sound of the sea. Water and sand, two elemental forces that spread throughout *Le Très-Haut*, can be seen to be associable, then, with silence and revelation, repression and awareness, death and language. The neutral space of transition of *Le Très-Haut* both covers over or represses in silence a transition—from State to transgression of the State—and reveals behind itself, so to speak, another, larger problem. The neutral space *in Le Très-Haut* refers us to a political problem, and the ensuing oblivion of that problem—namely, the question of the politics of Montherlant's *Solstice de juin*.

Of course the wave/silence does not refer simply to a political moment in another text, but instead to the incessant or repetitive *absence* of such a moment in that text. Montherlant reads Montherlant, and cancels out his own and others' politics with a few lines referring to the empty sound of the sea in a shell just next to the ear. Blanchot performs the same operation on Montherlant (by quoting him against himself)—but more explicitly, and at a higher level of "reflexivity." Blanchot holds Montherlant to a more rigorous silencing than the one Montherlant would perform on himself in his politically naive and garrulous self-portrait. Finally Blanchot makes internal Montherlant's silencing sound of the sea at a point in his own text (his novel) where Sorge "hears" the sound of flowing sand, where the functionary is joined to the god, where the State as knowledge is joined to the State as knowledge of its own impending but impossible demise. (That "death" of the State at the end of the novel—and the concomitant death of Sorge—is what decrees the always-already-stripped political status of the State throughout the novel.)

But this movement from one silencing to another, from one text to another, is not simply a dialectical one: it is a movement of repetition and return. Just as *Le Très-Haut* is circular, this intertextual movement is repetitious; what is repeated from text to text is the identical stripping procedure, and the identical conflict between political, historical, or textual sense, and that which is death or silence to that sense.

The neutral space of flowing sand in *Le Très-Haut* thus silences and conveys more than simply the metamorphosis of Sorge. In its repetitive silence—in wave after wave—it conveys the violent repetition or doubling of texts. And since it is a movement of difference and repetition (each text, repeating the preceding, violently differs from it), it calls into question what is different in each text. What is different, of course, is the political moment that is defied.

At a crucial neutral space and point of transition in the novel a functionary is metamorphosed into a defiant god, and a series of political and textual differences is recalled. The re-speaking by the god (by a "major" speech) is a silencing or stripping of political specificity; the series of violent rewritings inevitably recalls those stripped specificities. (It is not only a question of Montherlant's positions, of course; Sartre's Camus's, and Jünger's also come into play.)

The question inevitably appears at this point: which is the most radical silence in *Le Très-Haut*? Even if the silence of the silencing sounds of sand or breathing (233) might defy the political reticence of the novel and invoke the ghosts of political positions, we must as least at first agree that *the* transgressive point in the novel is that at which Sorge dies and speaks (243). There are perhaps a series of silences or spaces within the novel, but they lead up to, and culminate in, that last moment.

We might have to revise this position, however, if we consider what is at stake in the silence of flowing sand. The waves of noise/silence indicate in the negative the very repetitions and reversals of political positions that that white noise/silence would do away with. In order for the novel to present a circular progression—the incessant movement from functionary to god—one neutral space has to eclipse another. The neutral space at the end of the novel—the juncture of speech and death—has to cover over the neutral space where the text of the novel joins with the neutral spaces of a series of political readings. The repetition of the final/initial "silence"—the end of the novel—both silences and reveals the silence of flowing sand. The primacy of the last/first space is based on the fact that it is a kind of final refinement of a series, in that all the irrelevancies of particular positions have been purged from it, and all that remains is the reflexive question of language itself. But is it this simple? The silence of the last words of the novel, which call attention only to themselves in the presence of death ("it is now that I speak") are an impossible articulation with simple death. The silence/noise of flowing sand, on the other hand, is a point of articulation with other texts, with other waves of repetition—either those that appear as shadow images of ideologies *in* the novel, or those that appear through a repressed movement of critical readings of other texts. Thus a movement of textual articulation (of intertextuality), as well as the point of articulation from man to god, is lost when only the juncture of speech and death "stands" as the culmination—the end—of the novel. One could argue of course that the silence/noise of sand is always returned to (because the novel is circular), but the fact remains that on a certain level of reflexive awareness the moment of the meeting of speech and simple death is the beginning and end of the novel, the apparently major point at which the god dies and is reborn through his speech.

Ironically, then, the point at the end of the novel at which it would be the most aware of the primacy of language is also a point at which that primacy is done away with. It is the other point of silence, a juncture of political and depoliticized text, of functionary and god, that is the most textually "aware," because it is a point of intertextuality, a point at which the closed circularity of the book is opened out to a larger disseminating movement. This juncture is not necessarily a point of political awareness, but instead is a point at which the stripping of political positions and differences is negatively indicated.

The consequences of this are far-reaching. The simple attempt at a loss or forgetting of the intertextual nexus is in effect the repression of a series of political silencings. Conversely, the reading of the neutral space of flowing sand is not only the reading of a chain of political maneuvers and political silences, but is the realization that the "outside" of the novel is not simple death, but *another text*. Rather than a repetition of the same, we see the repetition of the same with a difference—the difference between political defiances, hence between political positions that are defied, and between the ways the critic/writer defies those positions.

The return to the space of flowing sand, therefore, is the return to the primacy of the revelation/repression of repetitious textuality (the "box stuffed with papers"), the specificity of defied political positions, and the shuddering guilt of the writing, hence intellectual, functionary/god. This last point—the humiliation and culpability of the intellectual—becomes apparent when we recall that it was as a writer and a functionary that Sorge experienced his shame, degradation, and impotence: thus a return to a point prior to Sorge's sacrificial death, to a point between his status as functionary and as god, will be a return to Sorge's humiliation, to his self-destructive double bind. Indeed the guilty bind of Sorge the writer—the position *between* intellectual fidelity and independence—perfectly repeats the transition point, the silence/noise of sand in which employee met god. Conversely, Sorge's death at the end of the novel represents a kind of clear conscience in which the abasement and guilt of the writer has been left behind, and has been replaced with the potency of the spoken "now." It should be clear, however, that the impossibility of going beyond the specificities of political defiances and dilemmas also entails the impossibility of the loss of the guilty conscience of the writer. Since the position of functionary held by the writer cannot simply be left behind (it is always joined to the position of god), the guilt associated with the opening-out, hence betrayal, of the functionary's status cannot simply be transcended: it is always a point of return. Finally, the specificities of the writer's guilt are indissociable from the *impossible* self-awareness of a textuality that sees its "end" as an opening-out *not* onto a simple "death" or "nothing" through which it incessantly loses itself, but onto an incessantly repeating and differing movement of political (and politically stripped) texts.

Our earlier position, that Blanchot's novel represents a form of bourgeois ideology, may be accurate. (We are justified in returning to this question to the extent that we have seen the incessant importance of different political positions as elements to be defied—hence to be confronted and questioned—in Blanchot's writings.) The point at which intertextuality is raised and effaced is the point from which the identification fascism = Stalinism becomes possible. This identification is then simply another political position—undefined and undefied, to be sure. The *joining* of *Le Très-Haut* with a specific series of writings, on the other hand, raises the question: which political positions are to be defied? It is interesting to note in this context that *Faux pas* ends not with a defiance of Sartre's "engagement," but with the defiance of Montherlant's already defied crypto-fascism. (The silence of the ending of *Faux pas* is then reinscribed at a fundamental turning point of *Le Très-Haut*.) The important question that comes out of this may revolve not around Blanchot's putative right-wing or bourgeois ideology, but instead around the question of which ideology is to be situated in the most pivotal space of defiance. This in itself is a kind of political question.

What justifies us in asking *which* political questions are to be defied? Another question might be: how can we avoid interrogating the politics of the defiance of political positions, when certain positions, such as Montherlant's, are given privileged locations (i.e., at the end of *Faux pas*)? What is the status of the refusal to consider directly the space *between* the defied political position and the position that defies it? What is the political significance—if any—of the specific position defied, and the way in which it is defied? The very placement of the Montherlant essay and the silence with which it—and *Faux pas*—ends indicates a surreptitious priority of defiance: a defiance that is finally obscured by the sacrificial end of Sorge at the final moment of *Le Très-Haut*. Yet the move to forget political positions—itself a political position—inevitably puts these questions beyond the reach of Blanchot's novelistic or critical practice. That if anything is the political dilemma of Blanchot.

We can contrast this refusal of certain questions by Blanchot with the positions taken by Georges Bataille in certain of his essays and novels. In writings like *La Part maudite* and *Le Bleu du ciel*, Bataille explicitly asks *which* political positions are to be defied, and what the written neutral spaces (between defier and defied) will be, in inevitably utopian texts.

We must therefore pose the problem of the differences between Bataille's and Blanchot's utopias.[7] Bataille's and Blanchot's novels and critical writings *are* utopias, in that they attempt to envisage the impossible spaces in and between sacrificial textual and political experiences, and in that they were written in a (bourgeois) civilization founded upon the refusal to envisage sacrifice.

Chapter Three
Roussel's Revivifications
of History

I

Michel Foucault's 1963 essay, *Raymond Roussel*, is still probably the most thorough commentary on this writer's work. Foucault's analysis starts, and always returns to, the short work by Roussel that makes his fantastic inventions and machinery much more fantastic than they would at first seem: *Comment j'ai écrit certains de mes livres* [*How I Wrote Several of My Books*]. Significantly, Roussel's procedure of writing was unknown in his lifetime, and his writing was dismissed as that of a madman (except, of course, by the surrealists; they vainly looked for some secret, occult meaning in Roussel's novels). *Comment j'ai écrit . . . ,* prepared for publication just before Roussel's suicide in 1933, informs us that a number of his works—among them *Impressions d'Afrique* and *Locus Solus*—were in fact written through the use of a kind of mechanical procedure. The method consisted of taking apparently random phrases or expressions—children's nursery rhymes, the name and address of Roussel's bootmaker, and so on—and breaking them up to create different phrases that sounded nearly the same when read aloud, but that had quite different meanings(55)[1]. The various phrases, with their different meanings, were then reconstructed in a paragraph or story that had somehow to account for all of them and that would lead from one to the other. The most famous example of this procedure is a paragraph in *Impressions d'Afrique* that describes the statue of a helot made out of corset stays, rolling on rails of gelatine.

Of course knowing that this method is "behind" the novels explains both everything and nothing. It certainly does not explain why certain phrases were disarticulated and others were not. Nor does it explain why certain "sound alike" expressions were formulated, while other, equally likely, were excluded.[2] Beyond this, *Comment j'ai écrit . . .* contains only a few examples of this method; most of the phrases used to generate the novels in question have presumably been lost, so that the bases for the generation of the various stories will always remain something of an enigma.

Foucault's project, vast in scope, attempts to see forms of this phenomenon—the rhetorical breakdown and reconstruction of language (which Foucault explicitly links to the problem of tropes and figural language)—reflected on a thematic level in Roussel's writing. If Roussel's novels are about anything, they are about the repetitions and mutations of the language that generates them. Time is circular, with the endpoint identical to the point of origin; the repetitions of language within nonidentity are in fact series of figural reversals. Foucault cites Du Marsais on tropes:

Les mots sont parfois détournés de leur sens primitif, pour en prendre un nouveau qui s'en éloigne plus ou moins, mais que cependant y a plus ou moins de rapport. (24)

Words are sometimes turned away from their original meaning, to take on a new one that more or less is at a distance from it, but which nevertheless more or less relates to it.

This circular time and repetitious nonidentity is represented most typically in Roussel by the machine, like the "hie à dents" ["paving beetle"] in *Locus Solus* or the "métier à aubes" ["paddle loom"] in *Impressions d'Afrique*. The latter is a giant loom mounted over a river; Foucault informs us that much of its description comes from the Larousse Encyclopedia's description of the Jacquard loom. The loom in Roussel, however, differs in one important way; its inventor, Bedu, has designed it so that, instead of being operated by a person consciously choosing thread and working out the design, the *chance* movements of the river drive it and cause a preprogrammed image to be woven. The loom is somehow able to take the random currents and coordinate them so that they result in a coherent design. Apparently this near-miraculous feat is made possible by a mysterious black box that contains various mechanisms that not only do not appear in the Larousse, but that also are exiled from Roussel's text.

Without describing his writing practice (that could only be done, according to Foucault, posthumously) Roussel, through a machine, presents a figure of that method. Just as chance and design combine to produce stories (stories of machines), so the things described embody the same impossible union of the lack of presiding consciousness (randomness) and purposeful plan. A "mise-en-abîme" situation: the machine itself, the loom, presents another inverted and occulted double, by weaving as it does an image of Noah's ark, the *opposite* of the weaving machine suspended over but reaching into the waters of the river. In Roussel's writing method, language is doubled, inverted, and repeated—and the procedure behind that method is hidden and at the same time manifested in a figure: the figure of the machine. The machine (the loom) in turn repeats the random/determined movements (of the writing procedure), but occults them in the unfathomable workings of the black box. The image of the ark is a figure of both the weaving machine and Roussel's writing machine: it represents the chance meeting of opposites within a confined or demarcated space—opposites that will go on to reproduce and that will repopulate the earth.

La machine (reproduction sourde du procédé) reproduit une image dont le symbole surchargé la designe elle-meme dans sa ressemblance avec le procédé; et ce qu'elle montre au spectateur en une image muette mais distincte, c'est ce qu'elle est au fond d'elle-même: arche sur l'eau. Le cercle est parfait, comme est parfait le grand cycle des aubes, des matins et des mots, qui, chacun à leur tour, plongent dans le courant du langage et y puisent sans bruit l'enchantement des récits. (84)

The machine (a hidden reproduction of the procedure) reproduces an image whose overburdened symbol designates itself in its resemblance to the procedure; and what it shows the spectator in a mute but distinct image is what it is at the basis of itself: an ark on the water. It is a perfect circle, as is the great cycle of paddles, mornings, and words which, each in turn, plunge into the currents of language and noiselessly draw from it the enchantment of stories.

It is curious to note that, for Foucault, this procedure is seen as an essentially "closed" one. The iconographic always turns back on the mechanical, the machine turns back on the procedure of writing, the woven cloth turns back on the text, and so on. Between each of these doublings there is a space of rupture, but there is an identity between them as well, just as there are spaces within and identities between the various manifestations and mutations of a single phrase. Foucault writes of the "hermetically sealed" space, and his image for it is that of the labyrinth and the Minotaur (102). The labyrinth is the ever-repeating, enclosed, and rigid space of the quest; the Minotaur is the phenomenon of transition, metamorphosis, chance—the instant of transgression. Foucault has here chosen an interesting image to represent the union of chance and plan, the found and the sought-after, the excessive and the regulated—for although the labyrinth was built around the Minotaur, and indeed presents him to the outer world, it nevertheless shelters him. "Communication" (the "tropological space" [24] or impossible point of union between chance and plan, represented by the sheltered Minotaur) is narrowly circumscribed and mediated; just as machines and textual machines "themselves create stories" (98) and in this way are self-sufficient, so too the entire Rousselian apparatus as Foucault presents it is (like the labyrinth and sheltered Minotaur) "hermétiquement fermé," circulating its reflexive doublings of text, illustration (the Ark represented on the woven cloth), and history in isolation.

This space of identity and repetition (and chance in repetition) is often referred to by Foucault as the "neutral space," the "neutral moment between double and double"—the space, finally self-sufficient, in which the doubles' knowledge and blind repetition meet. We might, however, ask this question: if the space is closed or isolated (since it is always surrounded by a labyrinth, a procedure), what in fact is exterior to it? The Minotaur—the phenomenon of communication, transgression, nonidentity, chance—would seem to indicate that all that is not of the closed space can somehow enter into it, and in that way can violate its integrity. But when Foucault finally analyzes the black box of Bedu's machine, a black box that in its isolation and seeming exteriority to the functioning of the machine might offer a heterogeneity to that closed system, we realize that this external box, like the Minotaur, is already at the heart of the machine, at its neutral or tropological space: "son vide insidieux, désertique et piégé" (24) ["its insidious void, desertlike and set with traps"]. The black box is a coffin; in it "ce dernier langage . . . n'y trouve que son échéance" (88) ["this last language . . . only finds its passing away"]. Through the black box, language is put into contact with what is radically exterior to it: death. The invisible has been visible all along in its invisibility, the exterior, internal all along in its externality. This is why Foucault can write:

Le langage est cet interstice par lequel l'être et son double sont unis et séparés; il est parent de cette ombre cachée qui fait voir les choses en cachant leur être. (154)

Language is this meeting point through which being and its double are unified and separated; it is akin to this hidden shadow that causes things to be seen by hiding their being.

Yet the reader cannot help but suspect that the "closed space" in fact makes something visible that is invisible in Foucault's text. At issue here are the extent and limits of what is exterior to the "closed"—but always radically "open"—movements of language and representation. Might the thematics of Roussel's novels reflect and double the mechanisms of language in a way that is not only exterior to those mechanisms, but is exterior to the mechanics of Foucault's explication itself? Might there be in that respect an externality, a "black box," that, while internal and essential to the movements of Roussel's textual machine, is in fact external to (or excluded from) the movement of Foucault's?

There is, of course, an aspect to the image of Noah's ark woven by Bedu's loom that Foucault does not touch on: its status as a mythical-historical account of the (doubled) origin of humanity. While this problem of the origin is certainly consistent with Roussel's presentations of language, at the same time the Bibical history introduces factors that are only treated with difficulty in the model of the loom and its black box.

Especially in the case of Noah's ark, which Foucault cites as a figure of the loom, we can see a process that is external to the closed space of Foucault's double procedure. Rather than as a meeting of chance and plan, the ark may just as easily be seen as a kind of vast encyclopedia in which a biological record of every living thing on earth is kept. In such a closed space, the mutations of language—indeed language itself—would only be another phenomenon to be classified within an ordered and subdivided universe. The kind of research with which we would associate such an encyclopedia must in fact be radically external to the repetitious textual knowledge (a knowledge that only opens out onto death) of the loom. It is a research that involves the possibility of confrontation exterior to the play of language: in other words, of natural, historical, economic, and social phenomena that would figure in an encyclopedic project. The double of the exteriority of death (even more external than death) may be, for this reason, a historical research that accounts for details in Roussel's text that would at first appear extraneous or irrelevant to the functioning of Foucault's textual machine. The only way that Foucault's machine can function, however, is by denying encyclopedic knowledge—a knowledge that it nevertheless indicates precisely by ig-norning the problem in its reading of the representation of Noah's ark.

There is an articulation indicated here, a neutral point, a juncture of the machine with the historical and mythical accounts that lie outside it. Identical to the articulation of chance and plan, elaboration and simple destruction, Minotaur and labyrinth, this point is different in that, when we attempt to examine it, we are confronted with problems before which the closed machinery of Foucault's text is impotent. Another example of this problem can be seen in the presentation of the severed head of Danton in *Locus Solus*. This head, floating in its special preservative water, electrically revivified, is even more problematic than Noah's ark. Why Danton and not Marat or Robespierre? Why the French Revolution? Somehow Roussel's textual machine has chosen and incorporated these events, just as Bedu's loom somehow was put in relation to the story of Noah's ark. But there would seem to be few connections between the "sealed" machinery of the text and possible explanations for the choice of Danton as hero of this episode. These explanations might involve the historical epoch in which Roussel wrote, his own status as an independently wealthy member of the "haute bourgeoisie," and so on. These problems would seem to be as external and hidden to Foucault's machine (and its dead spaces) as the black box was to the visible mechanisms of the loom; yet they cannot simply be forgotten. The task remains for us to see how they, as the "invisible," are as important for the functioning of the machine, and as heterogeneous to it, as was the black box that was seen to contain death itself. Indeed, just as the weaving machine could only be visible in its functions through a concomitant invisibility, it may be that Foucault's machine can only maintain its visibility through the invisibility of certain other questions: invisible for him, visible for us (and perhaps visible for us because of their invisibility for Foucault), his readers, his doubles.

We are perhaps making a distinction between hermeneutics and poetics. Because Foucault's problematic is in the end rigorously one of poetics—his versions of thematics, imagery, and myth always return and point to the originary rhetorical breakdown and reconstitution of language—the hermeneutic problem of interpretation escapes him. Why is one historical figure or episode or legend presented in the text and not another? It is to this sort of problem of interpretation (a problem that escapes or is invisible to the overriding question of language and its metamorphoses) that we now turn.

II

In Roussel's novel *Locus Solus* (1914),[3] Mathias Canterel, a fabulously wealthy and eccentric inventor, shows a group of friends around a special enclosed space—a "lieu solitaire" ["solitary place"]—in which a collection of incredible inventions is to be found. One of the most impressive of Canterel's curiosities is the actual severed head of Danton, somehow preserved for 120 years and contained in a giant diamond-shaped tank filled with a special "crystalline water." The head is periodically animated by a shaved Siamese cat that swims under water (the water's special quality allows land animals to breathe while swimming under the surface). The cat touches the head with an electrically charged funnel attached to its (the cat's) nose. The history of the possession of this head by Canterel is even more amazing; it was given to Canterel's ancestor, Philibert Canterel, through a subterfuge, arranged by Danton the night before his execution (74–75; 67–68). Philibert in turn attempted to mummify the head (he could not trust the job to an outsider), but since he was an inexperienced embalmer, the outer skin of the face decomposed in the intervening century, leaving only brain and nerve tendons.

Two details in this story immediately catch our attention. The first is that Roussel's version of the story apparently accounts for Danton's famous demand on the scaffold, addressed to his executioner: "Tu montreras ma tête au peuple, elle en vaut la peine" ["You must show my head to the people; it's worth the trouble"] (75; 68). According to the account in *Locus Solus*, Danton tells this to Samson the executioner (who is in collusion with Philibert) so that Samson has a pretext for first elevating the severed head, and then surreptitiously tossing it into another basket, from which the head can be spirited to safety. The other detail concerns the retention of the head itself. Fearing an unmarked grave, Danton wants his head to be preserved, and desires that it be kept in Philibert Canterel's family, passing forever from father to son. Their possession of the head is to be a remembrance of the mortal risk Philibert ran in order to procure the head.

Il [Danton] voulait que, si le complot réussissait, sa tête fut embaumée—puis transmise de père en fils dans la famille de son ami en souvenir de l'héroïque dévouement qui n'allait pas sans être entouré de risques mortels. (75; 68)

He [Danton] wished to have his head embalmed and transmitted from father to son in his friend's family, in memory of the latter's heroic devotion, which was not without danger to his life.

This all has a strangely circular quality. Danton's head is exhibited to the crowd only so that it can be preserved, and the reward for the risking of life (to preserve the head) is the indefinite possession of the preserved and exhibited head. The exhibition of the bloody fragment, and the risk of life to maintain that fragment, is repaid by the privilege of the indefinite possession of the fragment. Purposeful activity—the rescuing of the head and its embalming and preservation—is established as equivalent to the risk of life and the gruesome display of death. Purposeful activity and the negativity of risk and death enter into equivalence; indeed, even the expression "You must show my head to the people; it's worth the trouble'' indicates the meeting of purposeful labor (''it's worth the trouble'') and senseless, pointless, and morbid activity (''show my head'').

We might see a similar configuration in the personage of the mythic Danton known to all schoolchildren during the Third Republic. Danton had in fact by this time been rehabilitated and made a national hero, the man who rallied the nation in a time of crisis (whereas immediately after the Revolution he was known primarily as a swindler). Danton in popular mythology is the ''moderate'' of the First Republic, the forerunner of the middle-class man who enjoys food, wine, and sex. His opposite (and double) is the austere left-wing Robespierre, who believes primarily in abstinence and production. Danton predicted that his killer Robespierre would follow him to the guillotine, and when Robespierre faltered in his last attempt at a speech, a member of the assembly is said to have shouted: ''the blood of Danton chokes you!''[4]

This sacrificial couple, standing and dying at the almost official inauguration of the bourgeois epoch, can be seen to be in complicity with one another. Danton, in Roussel's account, seems to accept willingly the death Robespierre has decreed for him; the preservation and (albeit private) glorification of his severed head seems in continuity with the sacrificial public beheading ordered by Robespierre. (After all, Danton could have asked Philibert to bury his head after the execution.) A severed head is as much a commemoration of a beheading as it is of any earlier events in the victim's life. Danton could be said to be sacrificing himself by entering into an alliance with his enemy, Robespierre. At one and the same moment, at the moment of death, Danton is both himself— dissolute, defiant of Robespierre (and of his law)—and in complicity with Robespierre, involved in a labor that will preserve Robespierre's ultimate labor, the beheading of Danton. In fact the only way Danton can *be* Danton, can truly defy Robespierre, is by submitting to the beheading administered through Robespierre's law, by becoming Robespierre and his law. Once again, labor and the excessive (Robespierre and Danton) meet.

Yet Canterel's repetitive reenactment of Samson's sacrificial display of Danton's head (a head that is now electrified so that it literally mouths fragments of the heroic patriotic platitudes of Danton's career) would seem to refuse or exile rather than manifest the impossible union of production and consumption (or destruction). In this sense Canterel's reenactment, while trying to restage the original display, doubles it by negating it; rather than embodying labor and that which transgresses it (sexuality, excess, dissolution, and, as we saw in Foucault, death), Canterel's Danton is neither dead (dead men do not mouth platitudes), nor does he, or the machine he is in, labor (the senseless and mechanical repetition of words is not purposeful labor, nor is electrical stroking by a shaved cat). Clearly, then, Danton's head as preserved by Canterel is in a kind of negative or neutral space, neither laboring (i.e., alive) nor dead. What is the significance of this shift from double affirmation (the union, in sacrifice, of Danton and Robespierre) to double negation (neither labor nor death)? Instead of accretion there is subtraction; Danton is stripped of his face and scalp, leaving nothing but a nonhuman, nonmechanical construct. Might something beyond simple labor and death be negated in this configuration?

III

We now turn to the major movement of *Locus Solus*: the giant warehouse where Canterel has revivified a number of corpses—an enterprise, we are told, directly inspired by the success of the revivification of Danton's head (128–129; 118). What was previously negative (the gruesome remnants of a head mouthing incoherent fragments of political platitudes) is now positive: the unmutilated corpses of the recently deceased mechanically reenact crucial moments of their lives (which remain recorded in their dead brains), moments that are usually connected with, or that immediately preceded, their deaths. Perhaps the negative duality of Danton's head (neither dead nor laboring) can be resolved by pushing the corpses (so to speak) further in the direction of life. The corpses are dressed exactly as they were when the original events took place, and the settings have been carefully recreated. These bizarre *tableaux vivants* are nevertheless seen to have a positive value: for the family of the deceased, who want to remain close to their loved ones, as well as for investigators (in one case, the actions of a corpse help solve the mystery of his suicide). Thus, rather than a negation of life and labor (as in the case of Danton's head), here there seems to be an affirmation of these things. The corpses look alive, even though they are in a deep freeze, and they perform a useful labor, at least for their friends or for investigators.

But there is also a historical problem here. As well as recounting personal histories, the corpses, as the continuation of the Danton experiment, must be seen as at least a possible continuation of the problem that we saw in the conflict between Danton and his mortal enemy—a conflict that was by no means resolved. There is, however, a difference between the stripped-down Danton and this group of cadavers who are lavishly furnished in the utmost verisimilitude; it is a difference between mock-life and mock-death. In the same way, there may be a difference in the politics (or political fragmentations) of these corpses, a difference revealed by their stories (Canterel tells each one's story as he leads a guided tour through the warehouse).

The seventh life (and death) story presented, Lady Ethelfleda Exley's, appears to be in some fundamental way beset by problems of social and class relations. We know from the outset that Ethelfleda comes from a poor background, that she married a lord not because of social conventions but out of "love," and that she lost her father when, as a colonel in India, he was attacked and killed by a tiger. That bloody attack, witnessed by Ethelfleda, is the cause of her "neurotic horror" of the color red:

Son père, jeune colonel, était mort sous ses yeux au cours d'une excursion, la gorge broyé par la machoire d'un tigre dont l'attaque subite n'avait pu être prévenue. D'intarissables flots vermeils coulant de la carotide ouverte avaient, pour jamais, donné à Ethelfleda l'horreur nerveuse du sang et, jusqu'à un certain point, des objets de couleur rouge. (169; 158)

Her father, a young colonel, had been killed before her very eyes during an expedition, his throat crushed in the jaws of a tiger, whose sudden attack could not have been averted. The endless flood of vermilion pouring from the open cartoid had ever afterwards given Ethelfleda a neurotic horror of blood and, to some extent, of red-colored objects.

As a poor commoner, Ethelfleda must repress her blood to the point of covering the flesh under her nails with silver foil so that she will be spared even the color pink. That blood, however, keeps her alive now as a peeress, and in fact the same blood, her father's, was shed in India so that a society and an economic system that honors lords and ladies (members of a nobility that luxuriously consumes wealth produced by workers) can exist. Thus we can say that Ethelfleda's blood itself is double, to the extent that it is both an indicator of working-class status, and an indicator of nobility.

Bearing this duality in mind, we can examine the three appearances of red that cause Lady Exley to go mad and then die. Seeing her title ("pairesse") on a letter would, one would think, inspire confidence in Lady Exley, but exactly the opposite takes place, because the name is written in red. Startled, she inadvertently cuts herself with the thorns of a yellow rose she is holding and bleeds: a chance movement has caused her to turn an unlikely weapon against herself. Finally, chance again causes her to see red, this time in one of her silvered nails. A map of Europe, painted red to denote the greatest extent of Napoleon's military triumphs, is seen reflected—and reversed—in her silvered thumbnail. This map, on a sign displayed by her hotel, causes her even greater panic, because it suggests to her not only a red stain, but an entire red continent:

La jeune femme resta hypnotisée par cette brillante tache rouge, dont la forme caractéristique était pour elle nettement reconnaissable malgré l'interversion de l'occident et de l'orient.
Immobile, angoissée, elle dit, sans accent . . .
"Dans la lunule—l'Europe entière—rouge—toute entière—" (172; 161)

The young woman remained hypnotized by this brilliant red spot, whose characteristic shape she could plainly distinguish despite the inversion of east and west.
Motionless and in dread, she said in a flat voice . . .
"In the half-moon—all Europe—red—the whole of it—"

The final cause of Ethelfleda's madness comes when an old messenger, having dropped the letter addressed to her, calls a young servant to pick it up, and addresses him as "tiger," an outmoded slang word from the period of dandyism. This reminds Ethelfleda of her father's bloody death, and it is at this moment that she succumbs to madness.

Mais celle-ci [Ethelfleda], ayant, du fond de son hypnose douloureuse, perçu, non sans un frémissement, le vocable ["Tigre"] émis . . . avec une sèche puissance, crut à un cri d'alarme et, soudain hallucineé, vit devant elle . . . son père aux prises avec le fauve qui l'avait jadis égorgé. (173; 162)

But the latter [Ethelfleda], having heard and shuddered, from the depths of her distressing trance, at the word ["Tiger"] uttered with curt emphasis . . . fancied it to be a cry of warning and was suddenly hallucinated . . . by the vision of her father before her, grappling with the wild beast that had once slaughtered him.

Each manifestation of red is doubled or in some way involves doubling. The word "pairesse" written on the letter that Ethelfleda receives implies (in French) the word "pair" as well as "peer"; the letter, asking to borrow money (it is from a poor acquaintance of earlier years) clearly refers both to Ethelfleda as peeress and Ethelfleda as a woman with a background of poverty. Similarly, the wound caused by the rose not only shows a doubled violence (Ethelfleda as both unconscious attacker and victim) but reveals a blood that implies a genealogy that she would rather forget, a genealogy that is an inverted double of her husband's noble lineage. The red map of Europe is also doubled: on the one hand, it is the innkeeper's fantasy of Napoleon's triumph, since it marks in red the furthest extent of his conquest; on the other, it represents, in the historical period in which Ethelfleda lives, the phantasmic spread of the reds— the communists—to all corners of Europe. The red Europe thus serves

as a link between the era of Danton and Napoleon—the start of the bourgeois epoch in Europe—and the "present" of the story, the early twentieth century. The historical (blood) red of the beginning of bourgeois
history (the beheadings, Napoleon's conquests) quickly gives way and
reveals what lies outside it, and is opposed to it: a communist Europe.
The scene of this episode, then, shifts from the inauguration of a bourgeois epoch and its antinomies—Danton/Robespierre/Napoleon—to the
inauguration of a Marxist one, and *its* antinomies, labor/waste. Finally
Ethelfleda herself is double in that her stylish silver nails, meant to repress the color red, only transmit it, in the form of the reflected (and
reversed and intensified) map of Europe that she sees in them.

The appearance of the two tigers (the animal and the servant) not only
sets off the young woman's fatal madness, but indicates the context in
which the doubleness associated with the color red must be seen. The
tiger attacking the colonial representative and the stooping servant, when
conflated in madness, become the stooping servant (as "tiger") attacking
the colonial representative. In fact, each of these images of red, when
read critically, indicates a similar violence, a violence of the worker—the
servant, the poor producer of welath—against the noble or the bourgeois,
or the communist against the luxury-loving, wasteful ruler. Hence the
doubled letter, the politically reflected and reversed Europe and, between
them (in the diachronic movement of the story), the figure of this conflict, Ethelfleda mutilating herself with a rose. Her loss of consciousness,
her moment of death, is at the space of intersection of these conflicting
tendencies. It would seem that Ethelfleda's "neurosis" is only a painful
awareness of the duality of her genesis, of her automutilation as class
conflict.

We must recall, however, that Ethelfleda's corpse is revivified at the
request of her husband and that as a corpse she is now his property. He
is "heureux surtout de revoir Ethelfleda en pleine raison pendant les
rapides instants qui précédaient la remise du pli" ["glad above all to see
Ethelfleda in her right mind during the brief instants preceding the enve-
lope's delivery"] (175; 163). But he can only see her in this position, a
position in which her madness (the negativity of conflict between worker
and ruler, producer and wasteful consumer) is effaced, by watching again
and again her experience of the conflict, her crisis of madness and death.
The repetition of life in death—the opposite of Danton's death in life—
can only be attained by the exile of production and consumption, utility
and waste. These exiled terms, and the social conflict they entail, always
reappear, however, because they make the peaceful moments of Ethelfleda possible. Lord Exley cannot have the one without the other: the
images of conflict—the red "peeress," the reversed red Europe, the

rose's wound—in fact also make the repetition necessary, because each time the moment of peace before the attack occurs, it is immediately followed by the crisis of blood—and then the cycle must be gone through again. Revivified sanity is nothing more than a response or reaction to a prior mutilating madness.

Just as Danton's head situated itself in the space between death and labor, so Ethelfleda's self-mutilated corpse is in the space between the waste of the bourgeoisie and the productive labor—and revolution—of the workers. This neutral space, though repressing that tension (in the moment when, as a revivified corpse, Ethelfleda is in her "right mind"), nevertheless makes the tension apparent precisely through this very repression. The conflict, so to speak, appears as the negative image of itself every time Ethelfleda "revives," perfectly sane, but dead. (The ferocious strife of expenditure and restraint is pacified—and reversed—when transposed as the joyless union of sanity and death.) And it is a question of the bourgeoisie, not the aristocracy, in this conflict. Lord Alban Exley is doubled in his labors by Canterel, who has furnished the factory where the dead relive their experiences. Even though Lord Exley is a peer (Canterel's class origins are unclear), he has recourse to a mechanical, industrialized solution to his problems. This is why the building in which the corpses are housed—its architecture seems to be in a sort of functionalist Bauhaus style (102; 93)—must be seen as a factory as well as a theatre. The work of the corpses in this factory is certainly far from the work one would associate with a land-based economy, even if that labor too were performed by corpses.

The attempt to master this class conflict (Canterel is incessantly called "le maître" by the narrator) is an effort to occult a radical discrepancy of economies. The red and the brown—the red of production (communism) and the brown of fecal waste—is found even at the origin of Canterel's experiments with corpses, when the reddish fluid vitalium meets the brown fecal stick of resurrectine inserted in the back of the corpse's head. (The meeting of these two elements triggers the revivification of the corpse.)

We must now consider the exile of Ethelfleda's self-mutilation—the point of her death—in another context. If that mutilation represents a larger mutilation, a point of ideological tension or noncongruence, then the text—Roussel's—that represents the repetitive obfuscation (by Lord Exley and Canterel) of that mutilation will be in complicity with it. Roussel and Canterel are doubles. In Foucault's reading we saw how the textual machine both depended on death—the little external black box of the weaving machine—and was bound to be blind to it. So too, in Roussel's machine (a machine that doubles Canterel's to the extent that it mechanically revivifies dead romantic and symbolist "topoi" as well as political clichés) Ethelfleda's radical point of madness and death is exiled. She is now (momentarily, at least) sane but dead—the ideal phantasmic, passive citizen of a fascist state. That point of conflict between communism and capitalism, reappropriation and waste, the workers and the bosses, is repetitively forgotten in the mechanized structure of the text. Now the most obvious example of a modern ideology that attempts to establish itself as the radical negation or forgetting of the conflict between Marxism and capitalism is fascism. The fascist ideologies of the 1930s regularly presented themselves as neither Marxist nor capitalist, but as utopias in which the problems of both economic models were overcome. The oppressive rationalization in production and consumption of Marxism, and the waste and destruction of capitalism were supposedly transcended, but the result was only a system of horror. Roussel's text must be seen as a construct of nonknowledge that performs, as an avant-garde literary text, the same obfuscations that fascist propoganda performed under cover of more traditional modes of literature. Canterel's revivification factory, his dead utopia (the topographical mark of the space of this nonknowledge) is, after all, only the reverse image of a death camp, where the living dead work as slaves.[5]

Yet the conflict obscured by Roussel's text is not only one of political or ideological opposition; it is also a point of noncongruence of representation. Ethelfleda's self-mutilation comes at a point between two kinds of conflicting representation: the written (the name on the letter) and the iconographic (the map of Europe). Conflicting representational modes meet in Ethelfleda: her self-mutilation is a writing (inscription of thorn in flesh) as well as an indexical representation (her blood recalls her father's blood). The process of mechanical reproduction—Canterel's and Roussel's—would nevertheless forget this point of conflict in representation, just as it would forget the point of political and ideological conflict we examined earlier. It would seem that this neutral space, this point of conflict, is therefore itself double: it is both one of representation *and* of politics/ideology.

Chapter Four
Leiris's Unwritten Autobiography

I

We have already seen the importance of puns and double (or multiple) meanings in the writings of Raymond Roussel; Roussel's "writing machine" was made possible by the steadily elaborated mutations of words and by the "ordering" of those mutations into a narrative. Michel Leiris, in his four-volume series of autobiographical writings, takes Roussel's writing procedure one step further: rather than ordering his autobiography in a simple chronological progression (from his birth to the impossible recording of his own death), Leiris structures his memories around the experience of certain privileged words.[1] In Leiris, the various metamorphoses of a single word act as magnets that accumulate personal memories: these memories in turn illustrate the personal importance to Leiris of the word itself. Thus, quite often, the event recounted is Leiris's childhood memory of the oral permutations of certain words, and the free associations that these permutations generated.

An excellent example of this procedure can be found in the chapter entitled "Perséphone," in *Biffures* [*Erasures*], the first volume of *La Règle du jeu* [*Rules of the Game*].[2] Of course Persephone is the goddess of spring, who is yearly captured by Hades and brought to the depths of the underworld, and who yearly escapes and passes through the crust of the earth to cause the rebirth of nature. Leiris associates a number of images that involve piercing, spirals, "circonvolutions," and so on (I,

85–86) with the name—and sound—of "Perséphone." The twists of a corkscrew, the turns of a drunk, the spirals of the tendrils of a grape vine, as well as the spit curl on the cheek of a prostitute and the decorations of the entrances to the Métro—and many others—are conjured up by the idea of the spiraling growth of springtime, as well as by the penetration of the spiral through the earth, the passage from the subterranean realm of death and seed to the realm of solar illumination.

From "Perséphone" Leiris derives the word "perce-oreille," French for that most Joycean of creatures, the earwig. "Percer" means "to pierce," and the earwig is said to be able to pierce the ear of a sleeper and enter his brain. Indeed "perce-oreille" (literally "pierce-ear") is a kind of double play on "Perséphone": "perce" is derived from the identical sound—but different meaning—of the first syllable of "Perséphone," whereas "oreille" is different in sound from "phone," but related in meaning, for it is the ear that is sensitive to phonic signals. The transformation of "Perséphone" into "perce-oreille" indicates in itself the double aspect of the generation of the transformation of words in Leiris. One aspect is phonic, dependent on the ear (this is the association of "Persé"/"perce"); the other is figural, dependent on associations of elusive signifieds rather than signifiers (hence "phone" and "oreille" are associated, despite the fact that the two words do not sound the same). This second kind of association could be said to be essentially written, because associations on this level could best be fully developed through recourse to written compendia of definitions, histories, analyses, as well as dictionaries and encyclopedias.[3] Ironically enough, it is the syllables "Persé"/"perce," which indicate writing (for they indicate the piercing of paper by pen and pencil—see I, 107–8), that are linked phonetically, whereas the syllables that indicate sound ("phone"/"oreille") are linked through their meaning, and thus depart from the phonic.

This is certainly a significant variation on Roussel's writing machine, because here the whole problem of the relation of sound to writing in the mutations of words (in the constitution of narrative) is figured in the machine itself. In the "Perséphone" chapter Leiris presents us with a machine that—much like Roussel's weaving/writing machine—serves as a master metaphor for the constitution of his narrative. Leiris's machine, however, takes into account both the written and the phonic: it is his father's phonograph, or more properly, his "Graphophone."

When Leiris was a small boy his father owned a deluxe Edison "Graphophone," which had the capability of both making home recordings on wax cylinders and playing back either the home recordings, or commercially produced cylinder recordings. The process of recording, which Leiris recounts in detail, involves the same conjunctions of sound and writing, piercing and spiraling, above and below ground, that were associated with Persephone: "la trace, dans le cire, de cette longue hélicoide serrée en laquelle la succession des sons se transcrivait" (I, 97) ["the trace, in wax, of this long tight helicoid in which the succession of sounds was transcribed"]. As the recording needle pierces the wax, it leaves both the spirals of its sound/writing, and the spirals of the excess wax gouged out of the virgin surface of the cylinder.

When in turn a recording is listened to, the chthonian or underground realm is reached by the piercing needle: it is the sound track. The fact that Leiris's system of figural "turns" or spirals enables us to make the association "realm of the dead"/"origin of sound" indicates that it is precisely as an inscription that sound must be considered here. Indeed, Leiris presents the reproduced sounds from the inscribed roll as "cadavres resuscités" as well as "céréales mûres" (I, 95); the reproduced sound must always be considered as already a corpse, as well as a living grain. Death accompanies germination, just as writing accompanies sound in this "Graphophone," a device that seems to favor the "graph" over the "phone," contrary to the usual order of things ("phonograph").

Just as Roussel's weaving machine had an unknowable "black box" that both guaranteed its operation and was radically exterior to it, so Leiris's "Graphophone" is fitted with a "diaphragme" whose membrane both is the origin of the sounds emitted by the phonograph and is alien to them: "l'action de la membrane sensible du diaphragme semble incapable d'expliquer à elle seule le bourgeonnement de toutes ces notes vocales" (I, 99) ["the action of the sensitive membrane of the diaphragm seems incapable of explaining by itself the budding of all these vocal notes"]. Rather than being a mere passive receptor of sound, this mysterious diaphragm seems to conjure up out of its inner depths not only music, but the jarring crackles that common sense tells us are the result of interferences in the musical inscription of the cylinder; the diaphragm itself seems to be the origin of these crackles: "les tirant de ses entrailles plutôt que les recevant du dehors, se comportant ainsi en cause séparée de trouble plutôt qu'en instrument passif" (I, 99) ["tearing them out of its bowels rather than receiving them from the outside, acting thus as a separate cause of the disorder rather than as a passive instrument"]. In the diaphragm, then, in the space of "origin" of sound, the phonic and the crackles (products of the decay of the inscription) are coterminous. In the diaphragm the crackles and breaks of inscribed reproduction—the marks of the resuscitated cadaver of sound—appear simultaneously with the contours of the "original" sound.

The diaphragm/mechanical union of the continuities of sound and the fragmentary breaks of inscription is clearly a figure of the unknowable yet necessary mechanism behind Leiris's autobiographical project. As the impossible embodiment of irruption and constitution, the diaphragm is "in itself" a fragment: "J'ai quelque peine, en effet, à me représenter le mot 'diaphragme' sans le concevoir comme entretenant avec 'fragment' un rapport etymologique étroit, que l'existence d'un même bloc compact de sons dans l'un et l'autre de ces substantifs peut paraître démontrer irréfutablement" (I, 99) ["I have some difficulty, in fact, picturing to myself the word 'diaphragm' without imagining it maintaining a strict etymological link with 'fragment,' which the existence of the same compact block of sounds in each of these substantives seems to demonstrate irrefutably"].

Also associated with the diaphragm—and for that reason with the operation of Leiris's text—is the word "anfractuosité" (I, 102), defined by the *Petit Robert* dictionary as a "deep and irregular cavity."[4] While the phonic resemblance of this word to "fragment" is clear enough, it is also a kind of mirror image of "fragment," because it indicates not a discrete and solid entity, but instead a hollow that might remain after a fragment has been removed. Associated with "anfractuosité" are not only the cracks or hollows in rocks, but the cracking noises of splitting stone, the "fracas" that brings us back to the crackling of the diaphragm. And through "an*frac*tuosité"—through its associations with rocks, fracas, and the noise of cracking—we come not only to "dia*phrag*me" but to the ear:

Le mot anfractuosité—tel qu'il se situe dans mon vocabulaire—recèle donc un paradoxe, puisqu'il me sert ici à évoquer, en même temps que l'aprêté et la dureté impénétrable du roc, la brèche auriculaire par où je croirais maintenant volontiers que s'immisçait en moi le monde minérale, c'est-à-dire ce qui m'est le plus irréductible et le plus étranger. (I, 102)

The word "anfractuosity"—as it is situated in my vocabulary—thus hides a paradox, since it serves me here by evoking at the same time as the sharpness and the impenetrable hardness of rock, the auricular opening through which I would now believe that the mineral world interferes with me, that which is, in other words, the most irreducible and the most foreign to me.

We have now come full circle, from the crackling associated with writing (the interference in the diaphragm) to the primacy of the aural and phonic. But it is not that simple. The ear opens out, but not simply to sound; it opens itself to what is "foreign" or "irreducible," namely to the solidity of rocklike fragments, the sharpness and impenetrable hardness of a diamond stylus.

If the fragmentary diaphragm is opened to sound or if, conversely, the phonic ear of the diaphragm is opened to its opposite, sharp rock, then in both cases we have a metaphor for the functioning of the text: the diaphragm, offspring of Roussel's "black box," opens itself to what is *other* (solid/splitting writing is opened to sound, and vice versa).[5] The "neutral space" of Leiris's writing—if we can carry over this term from our discussion of the constitutent element of Roussel's machine—is not simply the point of incompatibilities of strata of writing, but is the point of interference between the written and the phonic, neither of which can be logically or temporally prior. The diaphragm in Leiris's textual machine signals a radical break indeed: it departs not only from simple writing or simple speech, but (impossibly) from what Derrida has called the "Western metaphysical tradition" of phonocentric and hence logo-centric thought.[6]

Without contemplating this radicality of *Biffures* as an "urtext" of deconstruction—we will return to the radicality of the writing/speech interference later—we might consider what the "radically exterior" is for Leiris as a theme in *Le Règle du jeu*. As figured in his autobiography, to what *other* is the textual machine—the ear—open? To what does the long arm of the diaphragm—the needle—reach? What does that stylus hear?

Leiris does not spell out the answer to this question, precisely because the answer is a function of a language that is not associable with a single, stable signified; the "bifur" (a pun on the title of the first volume of his autobiography, *Biffures*), the bifurcation that is a split and a knot in meaning or concentration, in turn refers to other splits, other doublings. The bifurcations generate an experience of being situated "en porte à faux" (I, 126), of losing one's footing, of finding oneself suddenly on another level: "l'individu [qui subit les bifurs] se sent jeté dans un état de particulière acuité et [les pertes de pied ou sautes de niveau] faisant craquer apparement les cadres, débouchent l'horizon" (I, 278) ["the individual (undergoing bifurcations) feels himself thrown into a peculiarly acute state and (the losses of footing and jumps in level) apparently making the limits crack, open up the horizon"].

A breaking of the limits of existence, an opening of the horizon; both of these expressions indicate the moving across, or piercing, of a barrier, and the reaching of what is beyond. It seems, however, that beyond this framework, there is only (always again) a heightened experience of other "bifurs," and so on to infinity. Is this a progression or a vicious circle?

Leiris over and over throughout the four volumes of his autobiography does provide one other "exterior" that should—indeed must—be reached: the realm of society, of other people. And the terms in which he presents the movement outward from elite aesthetic project to social concern are much the same as those used to indicate the movement through the breach in language—through the trace, through the auricular opening or solid fragment (which itself breaks open the smooth flow of sound)—to the "bifur" and beyond.

In the "Perséphone" chapter Leiris already broaches the problem that will become more and more important as one volume follows another of *La Règle du jeu*—the necessity of breaking open or piercing through the screen of words to the "reality" that lies behind it: "les mêmes écrans me separent de la realité" (I, 83) ["the same screens separate me from reality"]. In this context, "reality" is associated with "nature" (I, 84), but that nature, as we will see shortly, cannot be simply separated from a conception of society. In *Fourbis* [*Thingamabob*], the second volume of *La Règle du jeu*, Leiris writes of his intact body "qui, jamais aventuré, me paraît inachevé comme si, malgré mon age, j'étais encore un impubère" (II, 151) ["which, never risked, seems to me unfinished as if, in spite of my age, I were still a pre-adolescent"]. The fact that he has never been wounded—that the screen of his skin has never been pierced by a projectile—strikes Leiris as an indication of his isolation from the great social upheavals of his time, such as (and especially) the Liberation of Paris in 1944. Finally, in the third volume (*Fibrilles*) [*Fibrils*], Leiris reflects back on the opening chapter of *Biffures* and sees in it an event that represents the breaking out of a closed personal space and an attainment of the social realm through the accession to language:

J'avais découvert, apprenant que c'est "heureusement" et non " . . . reusement" comme venait de faire le bambin que j'étais alors, l'existence du langage en tant que réalité extérieure me dépassant, ce dont il faut déduire que *l'on ne parle pas tout seul* (les autres mêmes absents étant impliqués dans l'acte de parler puisque c'est leurs mots qu'on emploie). (III, 94)

I had discovered, learning that it is "heureusement" ["fortunately"] and not " . . . reusement" as the brat that I was had just said, the existence of language as exterior reality going beyond me: from which it is necessary to infer that *one does not speak completely alone* (the others, even absent, were implicated in the act of speaking since it is their words that one uses).

The "external" reality, the breaking open of frames, the penetration of limits or screens—all this recalls the image that we saw at the beginning of our reading of "Perséphone," namely the needle or pen piercing a surface and reaching, after traversing or chiseling a hollowed-out passage, a submerged or subterranean "pit" ("ce puits central" [I, 97]). Leiris presents this cavelike opening as belonging to a "chthonian deity" (I, 87), perhaps Hades himself, or one of the other earth deities who could be put in opposition to the brilliant (and reasonable) power of a monotheistic God.

Absurd as it might seem, this piercing through to the chthonian must be seen as a move to formulate a political strategy for the autobiographer and his text. Leiris was involved with Georges Bataille in a study group, the College de Sociologie in the late 1930s. Bataille (in the Acéphale group of the same period, to which Leiris did *not* belong) promoted a kind of political cult that would, he hoped, bring off a revolution in more than just the sphere of relations of production: he hoped that a subversive group, by reinstituting virulent myth in everyday life, would rejuvenate society. The myth of the headless man, like that of the chthonian earth deities, implied a "base materialism" of orgiastic expenditure and sacrificial dread. In opposition to the solar God of reason and conservation, the chthonian god embodied loss, death, and mutilation.[7]

In a letter to Bataille in 1939, Leiris objects that many of Bataille's formulations in his lectures for the Collège de Sociologie—and by implication, in his writing for the cult-organ *Acéphale*—deviated from the anthropological theories of Durkheim.[8] (It must be recalled that Leiris was a trained anthropologist, and Bataille was not.) Perhaps what Leiris objected to in Bataille was less Bataille's lack of theoretical rigor than his insistence on the need for a small, active revolutionary group that would light the fuse for a revolutionary rebirth of myth. In a text published in the *Nouvelle Revue Française* in 1938 (along with texts by Bataille and Caillois) entitled "Le Sacré dans la vie quotidienne,"[9] Leiris presents an intimate portrait of his childhood, using scenes that will reappear later in *La Règle du jeu*. These childhood scenes are meant to indicate that myth *already exists* in everyday life, that the subversion of Bataille's mythic chthonian figures can be seen in the linguistic experiences of a middle-class Parisian childhood. In opposition to Bataille's (at least theoretically) violent sect, Leiris presents himself, alone, as a singularly cerebral, nonphysical child, yet as a child whose verbal experimentation will (or already results) in chthonian mythical revolution.

In this early version of *La Règle du jeu*, then, we see a bizarre political project—the subversion by the chthonian or mythic—rewritten as an individual autobiographical experience. This is the central paradox of Leiris's project: how can the writing of an autobiography— necessarily an individual task played out between a writer and his language—move *beyond* words and have a constructive, revolutionary purpose in society? This is the final problem posed by the diaphragm as a metaphor for Leiris's text: how can the diaphragm embody not only the impossible interpenetration of writing and speech, but the conjunction of the writing/speech dyad—and its "subject"—with an external social "reality"?

II

Leiris's project specifically equates taking heroic risks in the realm of political action with the act of writing the autobiography itself. The auricular breach opens out to the bifurcations of language—hence to the text itself—as well as to the social realm "outside" the solipsistic literary games of the child or adult. In the (at least desired) unification of these two tendencies—or their complementary bifurcation—the heroic task of the individual writer supplanting the collectivity as the most subversive "mythical" revolutionary is brought off. Leiris alone in his room, writing, supplants the theatrical rituals of Bataille's Acéphale group. As we will see, however, the risk taken by the text, its breach, soon reverses itself into an extremely stable form of adaptability. It is the how and why of this reversal that we must now investigate.

One aspect of Leiris's project that critics seem to have ignored is its function as a confession. Leiris manages to fill his text with everything that has ever happened to him, down to the most minute and most recent detail. His writings are certainly the polar opposite of the narratives of Blanchot, from which virtually all narrative—and autobiographical—detail has been stripped. This will to say all must be considered as a confession and as a desire for absolution. As Leiris himself notes, "au fond de toute confession il y a désir d'être absous" ["at the basis of every confession there is the desire to be absolved"] ("De la littérature considérée comme une tauromachie" ["Of Literature Considered as a Bullfight"], 13).[10]

In "De la littérature considérée comme une tauromachie," written immediately after World War II and published as a preface to Leiris's autobiographical essay L'Age d'homme [Manhood], Leiris posits the act of writing an autobiography in which no details will be spared the reader —this as a kind of "engagement," analogous to the risk of death (or of being punctured by horns) faced by the bullfighter in the "corrida"—or, as suggested by its resonances with the term "littérature engagée" (15), by the politicized Sartrean intellectual when he takes a stand and refuses to relinquish his freedom and be appropriated by regressive political forces. This often-cited piece by Leiris is a strange amalgam of the continuation of, on the one hand, the valorization of solely individual experience (such as the various sexual experiences Leiris recounts in L'Age d'homme) and, on the other, an affirmation of the collective action that Sartre at the time was promoting as "engagement" (indeed, a chapter of

Biffures, "Dimanche" ["Sunday"] was originally published shortly after the war in Sartre's *Les Temps Modernes*). The way out of this potentially troublesome internal bifurcation (Leiris himself writes of his "mauvaise conscience" on p. 10) is to pose the writing of the autobiography itself as a kind of risk, analogous to the risking of life by the bullfighter (facing the "horn of the bull") and, by implication, by "l'homme engagé." Indeed, Leiris conflates bullfighter and autobiographer when he points out that they both follow strict rules, which in turn lead to greater risk (18) (although, of course, the nature of the risks run is different in the two cases).

Writing, that sedentary occupation par excellence, can be compared to fighting bulls or fascists to the extent that the writer takes a risk when he exposes *all* of his life in his work, even the most seedy or disgraceful details. By making this move, Leiris opens the hermetic activity of writing to the risks run in society and politics. By writing everything, Leiris's pen pierces the screen of writing and reaches society.

But there is a problem in this. What if the writer must confess not only his sexual peccadilloes and fears, but his own guilt in the form of the betrayal of a just political cause? Could he then claim that he is taking a mortal risk somehow analogous to political engagement by confessing his betrayal of that same engagement?

This is essentially what concerns Leiris in *Fourbis*, the second volume of *La Règle du jeu*, but with an added twist. Not only is his text an embodiment of risk through a confession of guilt, but it risks its isolation as an autonomous text by affirming its solidarity with progressive political movements. Thus it bifurcates, risking the security of its author in two opposing ways: it presents him as politically compromised and as a committed radical.

It should be noted, however, that if the confession of guilt and the proclamation of commitment are less than thoroughgoing, the status of the text as the author's total and even death-defying risk will be put into question.[11] "Un certain désir de dire le maximum" (I, 270) ["A certain desire to state the maximum"]: of all the chapters of *La Règle du jeu*, "Les Tablettes sportives" ["Sporting Notes"] is the most concerned with a frank portrayal of Leiris's inadequacies; the chapter opens with a description of the idolization of jockeys by Leiris and his brothers— and, of course, their fantasies of themselves as jockeys. Leiris then goes on to present himself as a completely nonathletic youth, the kind who fails at all sports after making only perfunctory efforts:

Me démettre dès l'origine, ne pas même essayer (par crainte de ne pas réussir ou simple nonchalance): mélange de pessimisme et de paresse, l'un fondant l'autre de sorte qu'il y a cercle vicieux. (II, 111)

To give up from the beginning, not even to try (from fear of not succeeding or from simple apathy): a mixture of pessimism and laziness, each one at the basis of the other, resulting in a vicious circle.

The great irony is that, while nonathletic, Leiris also imagines himself a great jockey; in fact his only resemblance to a jockey is that, like a true dandy, He wears colorful clothes, just as the jockeys wear the colors of their stables (II, 122). He even tries to play rugby as a youth after World War I, not because he wants to be an athlete but because he wants the image of an athlete: "je jouais, en somme, à celui qui joue au rugby" (II, 123) ["in sum I played at being someone who plays rugby"]. It would seem that behind this facade there is nothing genuine; a genuine physical development, perhaps the most authentic thing to the one who is incapable of achieving it, is replaced by a mere facade, a screen of dandyism that evokes not the substance of physical prowess, but merely its signs.

But coupled with this surface ornamentation, this "parure," there is a tendency in Leiris (according to Leiris) to absolute, withering honesty—an ability to see beyond the decorations, to see their uselessness, and finally to see their ultimate irrelevance in situations of extreme danger, of *real* physical risk: "attachement à la vérité, qui . . . m'ôte jusqu'à la certitude de tenir dans mon ultime retranchement si j'étais mis au pied du mur" (II, 122) ["attachment to truth, which . . . takes from me the certainty of my holding out if I were put against the wall"].

Later in this chapter Leiris transposes this paradigm (facade/honesty) onto his experiences in Occupied France. Beyond the facade, the screen, the "tricherie" ["cheating"] there is always the question: what is it to risk death, how would Leiris stop being a spectator, and become "engagé."

He recounts a number of his experiences under the Nazis, and in the liberation of Paris. At the outset he makes it clear that he never really risked the smooth surface of his skin in the war and that this lack of involvement is reminiscent of his refusal to involve himself in physical activities (II, 151). Indeed, each incident that he recounts indicates goodwill toward the forces fighting the Nazis, but a complete lack of physical involvement in the struggle. He joins a partisan group but his sole act is giving some bullets (left over from his father's gun, which he gave to the German authorities at the beginning of the Occupation) to a man named "Marc"; he occupies the Comédie-Française briefly, then leaves it to occupy the Musée de l'Homme (the museum of ethnography where Leiris worked). He fails to carry out an adventurous mission involving a pickup of arms at the Place de la République; finally, hoping there will be more action in the sixth arrondissement where he lives, he returns home, but never quite gets involved in the project of moving a garbage truck that blocks the street (II, 154–55). His conclusion: "Ainsi, durant l'insurrection comme durant la guerre, je me serai borné à quelques gestes, dont aucun n'eut de suite et que j'accomplissais, d'ailleurs, comme des formalités pures" (II, 155) ["Thus, during the insurrection, as during the war, I limited myself to a few gestures, none of which led to anything, and which I carried out, moreover, as pure formalities"]. He explicitly compares his activity to his performance in the gym as a child, when he made only a show ("de mimique rituelles") of doing the exercises that had been assigned to him. Even in the war, then, he wore a facade—and now it is his critical, ruthless gaze that pierces through it (beyond it there is impotence and guilt) as he writes his autobiography.

As in "De la littérature considérée comme une tauromachie," the grave risk that is never confronted under the Occupation is encountered here, in the act of confessing. The revelation of one's own guilt is the true risk, the true "horn of the bull" faced by the matador.

One of the most striking things about Leiris's guilt, however, is its innocuousness. If Leiris is not heavily involved in the Resistance, it is not out of sympathy for the Germans, but out of fear of being tortured or killed—certainly a fear with which any reader can sympathize. Indeed, in the postwar notes to *L'Age d'homme*, he writes: "Il me reste . . . la certitude que, si je m'étais mis dans le cas d'être torturé, je n'aurais jamais eu . . . la force de ne pas parler" (*L'Age d'homme*, 209) ["I am still . . . certain that, if I had ever been put in the position of being tortured, I never would have had . . . the strength not to speak"]. The only time under the Occupation when Leiris actually faces death is when, on his bicycle, he is inadvertently caught between a squad of Germans and their bleeding victim (II, 151); here, however, he is once again an innocent bystander whose worst crime is a certainly justifiable self-preservation, as he quickly pedals away.

It hardly seems that one will risk death, or even censure, for the kind of details Leiris recounts. If there is no risk in recounting them, and if, as is the case, Leiris does not indicate that (after the war) his "indecision"—thus his refusal to get involved, his clinging to facades—is behind him (II, 138), it is likely that his confession is less a mortal risk, the opening up of his skin or screens to fenestration, than it is the alternative to risk, that is, another facade, another jockey's costume.

What is beind this facade? In the very act of confessing and recognizing a guilt, Leiris has made it minor; the recognition of one (petty) guilt implicitly rules out the possibility of another, all-corroding but still passive, guilt. Caught for a moment on his bicycle between victim and

Nazis, Leiris can feel threatened, his life in the balance, his skin vulnerable to a hail of gunfire. Then he rides away. The point here is certainly not to see in Leiris (or Leiris as he has written himself, for we are not analyzing or judging here the "actual historical Leiris: we are not writing a biography) any active guilt—it is no crime to have survived the Occupation. And no one could or should argue that he or she would have behaved differently in this emblematic and terrifying situation. Perhaps Leiris's very innocence, and concomitant moderation, is itself guilty. The paradox, which is probably as painful today in contemporary America as it was in Occupied France, is that one's moderation, one's simple attempt to continue living, becomes guilty through the very fact that working, eating and sleeping cannot be dissociated from collaboration. Perhaps there is no real way to resist effectively. One does not resist, one only continues to go reluctantly along with things, and in this one is profoundly guilty. This deeper but still passive guilt is never recognized or admitted in Leiris's text, except perhaps in the very hollow of its elision, through the recounting of these events.[12]

By recognizing and affirming minor guilt, then, the text elides this other more general and thoroughgoing guilt. The same phenomenon occurs toward the end of "Les Tablettes sportives" as well, but on the opposite end of the political spectrum. At this point we are exposed not to Leiris's guilt, but to his liberalism. He finds himself in Dakar, Senegal, on V-E Day (II, 161). To condense a long story: wanting desperately to celebrate the end of the war, Leiris breaks away from a stodgy group of whites and, by now very drunk, decides to impose himself on three blacks (whom he does not know) and walk with them. Leiris is full of noble sentiments: "j'affirmai mon désir d'une compréhension meilleure entre les races, mon amour pour l'Afrique . . . et les Africains, gens plus proche de la vraie vie que les Européens" (II, 170) ["I affirmed my wish for a better understanding between the races, my love for Africa . . . and the Africans, people closer to the true life than are the Europeans"]. These sentiments are rewarded when Leiris is beaten by the blacks; his shoes and wallet are stolen as well. Finally he punches not one of his assailants—who have disappeared—but a white seaman who can only imagine that Leiris was looking for sexual relations with his assailants (II, 171). Leiris is finally knocked out by the white.

Once again Leiris must tell all; his mea culpa consists of exposing the liberal naïveté in what, in another context, might have been a resolute "engagement," a willingness to risk injury fighting for what one believes in (the rights and dignity of blacks). But Leiris (at least as he portrays himself, in 1945) has not made the effort to understand why the blacks might resent the aggressive drunken friendliness of a white stranger.

Just as Leiris would present himself as an innocent bystander whose guilt is passive and innocuous, so he now presents himself, ironically, it is true, as a liberal whose politics are well meaning but naive and harmless. By getting into fights, Leiris certainly risks his skin to prove he is liberal. But what is he risking through his confession? Certainly not his political beliefs; throughout *La Règle du jeu* he has proclaimed himself a "progressive" who is nevertheless opposed to forms of left-wing dogmatism. Nor is Leiris risking his position in society, let alone his life; there is nothing risky about confessing that one is naive.

If there is no risk, once again we face the possibility that this confession is a façade. Just as before an innocuous guilt displaced a deeper and perhaps more universal one, so here ineffective liberalism replaces a more thoroughgoing and rigorous—but also more threatening and dangerous—politics. In the presentation of China (vol. II) or Cuba (vol. IV) Leiris displays his sympathy for the regimes of Mao and Castro without ever risking a "dogmatic" statement that might discredit him. Instead, his appreciation of these regimes is largely sentimental and aesthetic. In much the same way as the nineteenth-century novel tended to both exile or condemn the police while at the same time embodying the functions of the police in its narrative strategy,[13] so Leiris both exiles any pretense of innocence, while at the same time embodying innocence in his text through his endless confessions of harmless guilt or innocuous liberal "radicalism."

Leiris in "Les Tablettes sportives" has managed to cover both ends of the political spectrum: the left and the right. Between these two alternatives there is a "bifur" that is not a "bifur," a simulacrum of saying all that can be said, of finally reaching an absolute knowledge of confession (no matter how "contradictory" it might be) from which, nevertheless, all the really gulty or dangerous positions are implicitly exiled and through which the author is vindicated because he is a moderate. Indeed it is the exile of these dangerous positions that makes the safe confession—the screen, the façade—possible. Leiris's confession is for that reason still dependent on those more radical positions, but only negatively. The outline of those missing positions is indicated through their very rejection, when Leiris is read critically.

Interestingly enough, the same exile of radical alternatives takes place when Leiris confesses his impotence in the writing of his autobiography. Writing of his method of writing—the elaboration of a complex network of associations and contraries ("bifurs"), which he builds up through the coordination of a vast collection of notecards—Leiris argues for a freedom of experience that the interplay of his notecards makes possible:

Tout ce qui peut entrer de libre et de vivant dans mon travail [deviendra], en somme, question de liaisons ou de transitions et celles-ci [gagneront] de l'epaisseur à mesure que j'avance, jusqu'à représenter les véritables expériences. (I, 282)

Everything free and living that can enter into my work [will become], finally, a question of links or transitions and these will [gain] density as I advance, to the point where they represent the true experiences.

On the other hand, *Biffures* ends on something of a note of defeat because the project of coordinating notecards and writing the autobiography has become little more than the work of an archivist, the review of the fragmentary remains of once vibrant experiences and associations:

Il ne m'est bientôt plus resté des *bifurs* que le nom. . . . Je me suis donc enlisé dans ma besogne de raboteur de fiches et trouve un goût de plus en plus amer à ce ressassement perpétuel d'observations. (I, 287)

Soon nothing was left of the "bifurs" but the name. . . . So I bogged down in my job as polisher of notecards, and I find a more and more bitter taste in this perpetual reexamination of observations.

In these metastatements on his own writing, we once again have a kind of false "bifur" between two alternatives. Leiris covers here the entire spectrum of his writing—from its radically liberating side to is stuffy, archival, and egocentric side. Yet each of these sides by its recognition or confession of a phenomenon manages to bracket something else that is more excessive. Recognizing the liberating aspect of the play of associations, he neglects precisely what we saw to be the most radical implication of his writing: the interpenetration of the phonic and written, and the corresponding possibility of an "originary" *writing*. Similarly, in recognizing himself as guilty of the mere collecting of dead cards, he sets aside the more serious guilt that may arise from his (confessed) indecisiveness. He "says all" concerning his guilt when it comes to writing boring confessions; we are meant to excuse him because he has been honest, he has taken his risk. . . .

In attempting to write everything there is to write about his own writing, Leiris exiles its most excessive gestures: its radicality as writing, and the implicit threat of its radicality as a doubled political position (in complicity with right and left) that could only be seen as a betrayal from the point of view of the reigning "moderate" or "commonsense" political alternatives. (This latter radicality is indicated only negatively, by a text that outlines certain extreme political realms by rejecting them—just as, perhaps, the outline of the "fragment" can be determined by examining the surfaces of the "anfractuosity.") But the coming together of these excesses was implied in the "Perséphone" chapter when the stylus pierced a surface and came into contact with a chthonian revolutionary underground. It was there that writing acceded to a mythical political position based not on conservation but on death, the excessive element in any closed economy. In order for it to constitute itself as a total, honest confession, however, Leiris's autobiography had to omit any text that touched on the interpenetration of the realms of writing and chthonian politics. This is not to say that Leiris never wrote such a text, but only that his autobiography had to exile anything that would call into question its integrity, its completeness as the account of the *life* of a comfortably excessive, moderate man.

III

We must now look in more detail at what Leiris's text has excluded in order to constitute itself; perhaps we can imagine an "impossible" moment in which all the excluded elements come together.

First and most simply, Leiris's autobiography has exiled the death of the writer. This of course is a fundamental fact of *all* autobiography, and its paradox: the author who would write his own life—his entire life—cannot record the moment when he comes to face death, when he experiences it. Strictly speaking, no autobiography can be an autobiography unless it records both what the author lives to experience, and the passage to what is no longer life.

Leiris's text has also exiled, as we have seen, the most rigorous, as well as the most horrifying and unthinkable political alternatives. We might imagine the conjunction of the two political extremes in question in an individual (since autobiography treats the life of an individual) at the moment of his death (the moment that is necessary but impossible for autobiography): for example, a rigorous, rational, and collective political orientation coming up against the passivity of the traitor who executes, at the order of the fascists, one of his countrymen. Because both extremes (collective action/passive individualism) are embodied in the same individual, the person he executes will be himself.

To continue with our conjunction of elements, we recall that another thing excluded from the metastatement on the problem of writing in *La Règle du jeu* (see I, 282 and 287) was the radicality of the interpenetration of writing and speech, and the concurrent "originary" *writing*, as embodied in the "diaphragm." We may imagine such a diaphragm (conjoining written and phonic, above-ground and chthonian) somehow grafted onto the self-sacrificing revolutionary. Such a diaphragm would contain, as its *written* side, the account of the death of the autobiographer.

Finally, a diaphragm must be conceived, and seen to be working in the text, as an impossible conjunction of all the elements which the autobiography needs to constitute itself (conjunction of political extremes, conjunction of writing and the phonic), but which must be excluded from it if it is to be written by a living, moderate man. This diaphragm is both necessary to the machine of the autobiography and irreconcilable with it: it is a kind of missing element, the complex knot that cannot simply be integrated into the system of "bifurs," but on which they are dependent.

Leiris published a collection of dream records—with some records of lived incidents—which were, significantly enough, never incorporated in his autobiography. This sub- or para-autobiography, recording a "second life" (according to the epigraph), is *Nuits sans nuit et quelques jours sans jour* [*Nights without Night and a Few Days without Day*] (1961).[14]

There are two dreams, recorded during the Occupation and separated by two years, that convey Leiris's fear of being executed by the Germans. The first, "19–20 Mai 1942" (143–44), after describing the fear of someone who realizes that nothing stands between himself and death, goes on to recount the (phantasmic) publication of the last words of Anatole Lewitzky, who in waking life was an anthropologist-colleague of Leiris at the *Musée de l'homme* and who was executed by the Germans for his work in the Resistance on February 23, 1942.[15] In the dream, Lewitzky's execution becomes a kind of religious-sacrificial rite. What is most interesting, and most unlikely, is that Lewitzky's last words are somehow his writings, recorded "jusqu'à la dernière minute" ("up to the last minute") before the guns are fired:

Lewitzky rapporte que, devant la porte de la case qui lui tiendrait lieu de poteau d'exécution, il y avait sur le sol un poulet ou une squelette de poulet (comme on peut voir en Afrique, sur des autels domestiques . . .). (144)

Lewitzky reports that, before the door of the hut which for him replaced the execution-stake, there was on the ground a chicken or the skeleton of a chicken (as one sees in Africa, on domestic altars . . .).

A week later Leiris has another dream about Lewitzky; this time Leiris visits Lewitzky just before the latter's execution, and in a "religious" ceremony (the kind of ceremony they would study as anthropologists), Leiris, Lewitzky, and their friends from the Musée all eat together (145–46).

Two years later ("16–17 Mai 1944," 162–63) Leiris has a very similar dream. Now, however, *he* is the victim—but his is also associated with the executioner. As he walks to the place where he is to be executed, he is not under guard, and he is welcomed by the crowd. Unguarded, he is at least passively collaborating with his executioners:

Aucune garde autour de moi; en apparence, je suis tout à fait libre. Devant mes amis massés en un double haie comme les spectateurs d'une arriveée de Tour de France, je passe accompagné de Z. (162)

No guards around me; from the look of it I am completely free. Before my friends, grouped in two rows like the spectators on the last day of the Tour de France, I walk, accompanied by Z.

Leiris becomes frightened when he hears approaching horses or troops. Finally he introduces himself into another dream by dreaming that he is awake and that he is explaining to someone that he can wake himself up through a "voluntary fall." Then he has the same dream again, with variations:

Toujours endormi, je repasse ce rêve dans mon esprit et j'en refais certaines parties, avec d'autres détails. Dans cette seconde version intervient, notamment, un rectangle de papier blanc qu'on donne à ceux qui vont être mis à mort. Il leur est permis d'y inscrire leurs dernières paroles, et au moment de l'exécution il sera collé, non sur leurs yeux, mais sur leur bouche à la manière d'un bâillon. (163)

Still asleep, I play this dream back in my mind and I revise certain parts, with other details. In this second version there appears, notably, a rectangle of white paper that is given to those who are going to be put to death. They are permitted to inscribe their last words on it, and at the time of execution it will be fastened not on their eyes, but on their mouthes like a gag.

The last words of the victim are now stuck in or over the mouth like a gag. It is also interesting to note here that this execution scene is repetetive: it is interrupted by a fall, starts again, and, we suppose, might be indefinitely repetitious, as dreams often are.

This dream is clearly a repetition of the Lewitzky dream, only now Leiris himself is Lewitzky, the Resistance fighter. But he is also the German police who take him away, since he is leading himself. In the victim the two extremes (Resistance fighter and German guards) are joined, in a religious sacrificial ceremony (the crowds applaud Leiris's entry). What is at stake here is clearly the mythical, chthonian politics we mentioned in the context of "Perséphone";[16] now, though, it is possible for the individual as writer to take part in a collective political/ mythical experience. He does so by embodying two extremes that necessarily see each other as betrayals.

Sacrificial death is accompanied by an account of that death (Lewitzky's last words are a description of his last moments). This account is placed over the mouth or in it, both as a gag to stop or close the mouth (and speech) and as a kind of opening through which what would be said is still expressed—only now through writing, not speech. The diaphragm (the resonating sheet) is outside the body and in plain view (rather than hidden in the body's mechanisms); it reverberates with the last speech as last writing. As a gag it is a solid fragment, blocking access to the interior of the victim's body, to its cavelike tubes and depths; as a gag it opens the mouth, keeping itself inserted, doubling the words (in writing) that the open mouth would say. And as a gag it keeps the victim silent, preparing him for death, for the opening of his inner caves and tubes. The word "bâillon" ["gag"] itself suggests its opposite, "bâiller" ["to yawn"]; the mouth covered (or stuffed) with a gag is also a yawn, opening into the chthonian recesses of the body. Like the diaphragm, "bâiller/bâillon" indicates both sound (yawning) and what covers sound and rewrites it (the written gag). But as the yawn opens to the cavelike depths of the body, "bâillon" also suggests a rising into the sunny air: "bâillon" suggests "ballon," the balloon that rises not only because of helium, but because of words that are spoken/written on it (the balloon of comic strips). ("Bâillon" also suggests "baionette," that military version of the piercing needle or pen.)

"At the time of execution"—at the time of his death—the victim speaks through writing (or, looked at another way, he at least makes sounds through it, with his yawns or groans). Life and death, the phonic and the written are conjoined in the repetitious moment of the victim's sacrifice (the last written words will always already be there when in the repetition of the dream the victim comes alive and is once again put to death).

We must face the curious fact that the autobiography that confesses all—even its own ultimately lovable naïveté, impotence, and guilt— precisely cannot say (or write) everything. Yet the second, doubled autobiography—the diaphragm (like the "black box")—had to be written as well, but could never be a part of the autobiography. The very heterogeneity of this second autobiography ("Le rêve est une seconde vie")[17] is perhaps founded on the fact that not only do elements seemingly banished from La Règle du jeu come together in it, but that they come together in a repetitive *point*; the autodestruction of the author at the moment of the meeting of the phonic and the written. Unlike the "main" autobiography that continues to grow by accretion as its author slowly grows older, this para-autobiography "says" everything in a point, in an impossible and repetitive instant—which is a "bifur," and also a canceling or erasing, a "biffure" (to the extent that the "main" text must always cancel it, or make it unknowable, in order to go on).

Chapter Five
Ponge's Photographic Rhetoric

Light plays a central role in the writings of Francis Ponge; his poetry is inconceivable without it. But light—and its ultimate though problematic source, the sun—is more than just one theme or metaphor among many in Ponge's poetic universe; it is, in fact, the central metaphor around which all others turn. When we have understood light (and its contrary, dark) in Ponge, we will be able to understand the status of Ponge's own writings as objects within his light- and object-filled cosmos: we will understand what the writings describe and, perhaps more importantly, what they cannot describe.

Of Ponge's writings, "Le Soleil placé en abîme" ["The Sun Placed in the Abyss"] (1928–54) is surely the most central—not only because it was elaborated over a quarter of a century, but also because of its subject matter. The sun itself is so central that it is "la condition formelle et indispensable de tout au monde. La condition de tous les autres objets. La condition même du regard" (III, 162; 49) ["the formal and indispensable condition of everything in the world. The condition of all other objects. The very condition of the glance"].[1] But if the sun is inescapable, at the same time it cannot be fully observed, because of its blinding glare; it is thus the least likely object that Ponge could describe in a poem: "[Le soleil] repousse le regard, vous le renfonce à l'intérieur du corps!" (162;

49) ["(The sun) repels the glance, it pushes the glance further into the interior of your body!"]. Nevertheless it must be admitted that everything we see is the sun; we ourselves are merely parts of it, exiled and "envoyés à une certaine distance pour [le] contempler" (163; 50) ["sent a certain distance away in order to contemplate (it)"]. All we can do is contemplate the sun, not directly (for that is impossible), but in its surrogates, its metaphors: in all other things.

The sun must be, yet cannot be, represented; in the same way, the sun is the origin both of life and death. It allows us to live and die on this planet, keeps us somewhere in a middle zone between freezing and burning, keeps us warm for a while and then lets us—along with all other living things—turn cold. Life is a lukewarm mediocrity, "the degradation of solar energy": "Songez combien plus proche de la mort est la vie, cette tiédeur, que du soleil et de ses milliards de degrés centigrades!" (163; 50) ["Imagine how much closer life, so lukewarm, is to death than it is to the sun with its billions of degrees centigrade!"]. The sun can neither be avoided nor confronted; it is the origin and condition of both life and death, and therefore is neither. This is the "oui et non" of the sun; it is heterogeneous, for that reason, to human understanding or logic to the extent that it embraces contradiction in itself: it is, as a philosopher would say, both A and not-A. It is a logically impossible object: "Le Plus Brillant des objets du monde n'est—de ce fait—NON—*n'est pas* un objet; c'est un trou, c'est l'abîme métaphysique" (162; 49) ["The Most Brilliant of the world's objects is not—for this reason—NO—is not an object; it is a hole, it is the metaphysical abyss"]. The sun is not a usable object like all others in the world; it is "sans doute en deçà de la Vie et de la Mort" ["doubtless beyond Life and Death"] and for that reason it cannot serve as an ultimate grounding for man's meanings—as can the Word of God, for example. "Tu[le soleil] es la seule personne (ou chose) au monde qui ne puisse jamais avoir (ou prendre) la parole. Il n'est pas question de te l'offrir" (170; 55) ["You (the sun) are the only person (or thing) in the world that can never speak or have (or take) the right to speak. It is not a question of offering it to you"]. A little later, again writing of the sun, Ponge asks: "Mais LUI qu'aurait-il donc à dire? Quelle faiblesse, quel manque à avouer ou compenser? Non, il n'a rien à dire!" (172; 56) ["But what would IT have to say? What weakness, what lack would it have to avow or compensate for? No, it has nothing to say!"]. The sun, not simply an object or a thing (because it is outside the play of signification), and for that reason not a guarantor of deathless meaning (as it is usually presented) nevertheless lacks a lack ("un manque") precisely because it is so totally removed from the (human) play of substitutions and replacements that constitutes both language and the world.

But this creates a certain problem for Ponge. As a perfect, faultless (or lack-less) being, the sun becomes something not only outside the system, but something associated with the success of the system and the happiness of those within it. A moral or ethical meaning is assigned to it. Thus Ponge writes of the "remontée du soleil," the reappearance of the sun after the winter solstice, as something to be celebrated through language: "Recommencer volontairement l'hymne. Prendre décidément le soleil en bonne part. C'est aussi là le pouvoir du langage. Nous en féliciter, réjouir. L'en féliciter" (166; 52) ["To willingly restart the hymn. To take the sun positively and well. That is also the power of language. To congratulate ourselves, to rejoice in it. To congratulate it"]. This honoring of the most important cog in our universe takes on an ethical dimension: "Changer le mal en bien. Les travaux forcés en Paradis" ["Change evil into good. Forced labor into Paradise"]. Darkness is the lack of the sun, the shadow thrown by each individual on his neighbor: light is joy, shadow is unhappiness, and those who receive more light, and thus block out more light, will be happiest: "Dans la joie, hierarchie" (168; 53).

Even though Ponge's sun is in itself alogical, a "metaphysical abyss," at the same time by the very fact that it is so removed from the earth, the earth can only see the sun in terrestrial terms—terms of good and evil. Writing on the earth, removed from the sun, can only laud the sun. Since it would seem to be so removed from the sun, however, the attitude of writing, even after lauding the sun, becomes one of indifference. Writing lauds—and thus represents—a sun whose perfection puts it outside the realm of what can be represented. Thus indifference: "Puis finir dans l'ambiguité hautement dédaigneuse, ironique et tonique à la fois" (166; 52) ["Then to end in a highly disdainful ambiguity, ironic and tonic at the same time"]. This healthy indifference on the part of Ponge's "objeu" ["obgame"]—that is, on the part of a writing that incorporates the "liaisons formées au niveau des racines et les significations bouclées à double tour" (156; 45) ["connections formed on the level of roots and meanings that double back on themselves"]—becomes a simple form of amorality. Once the sun is made whole or is elevated, writing is distanced from it and becomes either homage or indifference to the sun and its moral qualities. (Indeed, writing must be indifferent to the difference between these alternatives.)

But why does Ponge write as he does? The painstaking descriptions of objects, the compacted paragraphs in which the etymologies of words and the shapes of letters are crucial for the understanding of the poem—

what are the origins of these poem-objects? Is their origin the sun, that most fundamental nonobject? If so, how did they derive from it? Is their celebration of the nonanthropomorphic simply a function of indifference? Could their relation to solar light be more fundamental than mere homage or indifference? Could the *confusion* and *profusion* of the poems (see III, 155; 44) be more than simply analogous to the structure of the sun? In other words, how does the totally heterogeneous sun exit from its sphere and come to the earth as light? What are the manifestations of this heterogeneous light on earth?

"Scvlptvre," a short piece written in 1948 on the sculpture of Germaine Richier, establishes a more fundamental link between light and writing. In this text the sun, as light, comes violently to earth. We are told at the outset that SCVLPTVRE, "ce mot de foudre" (I, 76) ["this word of lightning"], is only a memory of "la première fulguration":

Lorsque la conscience à la lueur de son propre déchirement se conçut à la fois elle-même comme un amoncellement de nuées et le monde avec évidence autour d'elle comme un Temple ou un Forêt peuplée de formes blanchies par l'arc électrique qui s'éteignit aussitôt. (76)

When consciousness by the gleam of its own rending conceived itself at the same time as an accumulation of clouds and the world clearly around it as a Temple or a Forest peopled with forms whitened by the electric arc which was soon extinguished.

This first blast of light, this big bang, is not necessarily a mythical gleam (even more "originary" than the sun) that starts the universe and is then forgotten (or celebrated); instead it is a gleam of light of the sundering of consciousness itself in the act of conceiving itself as clouds and as landscape of Temple and Forest. "Le mot de foudre SCVLPTVRE" ["The lightning word SCVLPTVRE"] is itself created in memory of this brilliant self-conception, by and under the light of a self-rending. Rather than writing of an unattainable mythic sun and its generation of light, Ponge now imagines an originary light as the accompaniment of the impossible self-genesis of consciousness in (or out of) a self-destruction or laceration ["son propre déchirement"].

The next two paragraphs of "Scvlptvre" go on to demonstrate the relation between writing itself and the sudden gleam of self-recognition/self-destruction sketched out in the first paragraph.

It is clear from the second paragraph that it is the lightning itself, the "foudre," that has inscribed the word SCVLPTVRE on the "tables de pierre de la loi" (76) ["the stone tables of the law"] or on the "fronton du petit monument logique que je prévois" (77) ["the pediment of the little logical monument that I foresee''']. The inscription has evidently been suddenly etched on the stone; this lightning-inscription in fact *precedes* the ''Parole,'' the spoken word, which is then nothing more than the repetitive and degenerating echo of the original rending inscription: "mais la Parole, contrairement à ce que l'on croit, ne se fit entendre qu'aussitôt ensuite comme un craquement interminablement repercuté depuis lors en proclamations de plus en plus indistinctes et lointaines des INSCRIPTIONS mysterieuses'' (76) ["but the Word, contrary to what is commonly believed, only makes itself heard immediately after as an interminably reverberating cracking since then in more and more indistinct and distant proclamations of mysterious INSCRIPTIONS''].

We can understand now the word SCVLPTVRE and why it is ''imprononcable'' (77): the two v's not only reflect the fact that this word is inscribed and not pronounced (its pronunciation is only the degenerating sound of its inscription), but the v's represent both the chiseling and dividing point of the lightning, and the cross-section of the surface of the stone, with its inscription.

The next paragraph is a meditation on the fact that the word SCVLPTVRE is an impossible conjunction of the instantaneousness of its inscription and the eternity of its self-presentation on the pediment of the ''monument logique'':

La sculpture contient dans son principe une contradiction absurde puisqu'elle propose . . . d'instituer à la lumière du jour des formes éternelles . . . tandis que son idée . . . tient d'ailleurs non de l'éternel mais de l'instant le plus fugitif. (77)

Sculpture contains in its principle an absurd contradiction since it proposes . . . to institute in the light of day eternal forms . . . whereas its idea . . . comes moreover not from the eternal but from the most fugitive instant.

The inscription is now an impossible union of the instantaneous and its eternal remains. In the process light has changed poles, so to speak: daylight (''la lumière du jour'') is now representative of the stable, clear, and eternal, while night is closest to the ghastly light (''formes blanchies,'' ''le monde blafard du plâtre'') (78) [''whitened forms,'' ''the pale world of gypsum''] of the lightning of consciousness/laceration. The last parenthetical statement of this paragraph underscores the point and finds a ''solution'' to the ''contradiction absurde'': ''(Et peut-être en déduirai-je par suite que son état de prédilection est la photographie sur fond noir dans un recueil par l'orage rapidement feuilleté)'' (77) [''(And perhaps as a consequence I will deduce that its preferred state is the photograph on a black background in a collection rapidly leafed through by the storm)"]. The light inscription, the photo-graph, is not read or viewed in the clear light of day, but instead it is "leafed through" by the storm itself and its lightning-light. The photograph is now severed from the light of day: its "taking" and its "viewing" are now both functions of the light of the night storm, of the consciousness of the rending of consciousness.

This does not mean, however, that the inscription is not in some way permanent, but instead that it is so permanent that it presides over the mutation of human consciousness into other forms. Thus the rending consciousness as inscription is the awareness of animals and plants that make their home in the ruins of the inscription: "les insectes-branches et les femmes-mantes ont pris corps dans le monde de la balafre, dans le monde blafard du plâtre" (78) ["the insect-branches and the woman-mantises have taken shape in the world of the scar, in the pale world of gypsum"]. The inscription is now so permanent that it has overshot the "daylight" of human consciousness entirely; *in* the inscription a meeting takes place between man and that which is radically other—namely Things. It is a "chemin déjà parcouru de part et d'autre par l'Homme et par les Choses vers leur prochaine étreinte" (78) ["a road already followed on one side and the other by Man and by Things toward their next embrace"], a union that will lead to a "mutation brusque (révolution)." Thus when the storm "leafs" through the collection of photographic inscriptions, the "leafing" is a process whereby leaves and branches, along with insects and animals, come to make their home in (and finally impossibly merge with) the inscription, the photograph, the word SCVLPTVRE.

At the end of "Scvlptvre" Ponge invokes "la foudre," "la priant impérieusement de se reproduire" ["imperiously imploring it to reproduce itself"] and demanding that it somehow replace or tear apart ("déchirer") his own writing, "l'informe ébauche des paragraphes ci-dessus" (79) ["the formless sketch of the paragraphs above"]. The very fact that he can invoke lightning in this way is an indication that it is the consciousness of the writer himself that, in the first paragraph of "Scvlptvre," is said to "create" the word as a "memory" ("souvenir") of self-genesis through the mutilation of consciousness. Lightning is invoked to memorialize the rending genesis of a writer's consciousness by rending the language of "Scvlptvre" itself ("pour la déchirer de son jour blafard" ["to tear it from its pale day"]), by somehow radicalizing the writing and inscribing SCVLPTVRE at its base ("pour inscrire sur le socle le mot imprononcable de SCVLPTVRE" ["to inscribe on the pedestal the unpronouncable word SCVLPTVRE"]).

The violence of the inscription is therefore inscribed on the pedestal of Ponge's text; "Scvlptvre" comes under the sway of SCVLPTVRE, the text itself becomes a photograph of the inscription (itself a commemoration of the rending origin of consciousness). "Scvlptvre" memorializes SCVLPTVRE as SCVLPTVRE memorializes the "original" lightning of consciousness; this regress is itself reminiscent of the decay of the inscription, its reuse in other contexts (as when various animals or creatures come to inhabit it).

Ponge's poetry, as in "Scvlptvre," (and as in the self-referential SCVLPTVRE) is a contradictory conjunction of the lightning bolt (the heterogeneous sun come to earth) and its perpetual, dead but fecund, memorialized inscription. "Texte sur l'électricité," a piece written for a French Electrical Company brochure (1954) (I, 143–182; 156–213) considers the problem of the rhetorical status of this light-writing. After we consider this text and its theory of rhetoric, we will be able to understand why Ponge writes the "objeu" as he does.

Ponge has recourse to a figure in order to condemn traditional figures. The "old figures," "ellipses, hyperboles, paraboles" are figures of a Euclidean rhetoric, somehow analogous to the rigid and unique parallel lines of Euclid's geometry. Opposed to these old forms, Ponge posits "les nouvelles Figures, qui nous permettront de nous confier à la Parole pour parcourir l'Espace courbe" (163; 185) ["the new Figures, which will allow us to trust in the Word in order to explore curved space"]. What Ponge means by "curved space" is perhaps explained a few pages later, when the new rhetoric is conceived in the context of electricity: "une certaine rhétorique: celle de l'étincelle jaillissant entre deux poles opposés, séparés par un hiatus dans l'expression. Seule la suppression du lien logique permettant l'éclatement de l'étincelle" (172; 199) ["a certain rhetoric: that of the spark shooting between two opposite poles, separated by a hiatus in expression. Only the suppression of the logical link permitting the explosion of the spark"]. Ponge here perhaps betrays the origin of his theory in the surrealist theory of metaphor. The idea, or the figure used to convey it, is still important, but the new rhetoric involves a connection between two elements whose linkage is not logical. This connection is not the famous sewing machine and umbrella, but is instead light: the instantaneous juncture of "figural" and "literal," of "signifier" and "signified," is a spark of light, a momentary and impossible linkup of two things that cannot be put into a useful, coherent system or a dictionary of meanings. If this spark of light itself has any ultimate referent, it is the heterogeneous sun, the photographing sun come to earth that we saw in "Scvlptvre."

But as in the case of the photograph or SCVLPTVRE, there is another side to this electrical rhetoric. We must recall that SCVLPTVRE was ultimately inscribed on the front of a "logical [hence useful, we would suppose] monument" (I, 77). Here too the electrical burst of light leaves a remainder that becomes a dwelling for creatures: just as the mollusk leaves behind its shell, which then is taken over by other creatures, so man leaves behind something, which is then taken over by other men or other creatures. In man's case, however, what he leaves behind is an extension of himself that has never been an unconscious "natural" outgrowth (like a shell or web), but is instead a fabricated tool or dwelling. He leaves behind something he can always come back to and use; this "différence caractéristique" (179), the externalized artificial body part, is in fact linked to man and put to use through the electrical spark, the current that drives household appliances: "Il donnera donc toujours la préférence à ce qu'il peut commander à distance, et du geste le plus facile. Eh bien, l'électricité à cet egard n'a pas sa pareille, puisque c'est la force qui se transmet le plus vite" (179; 209) ["He will thus always prefer to command from a distance, and with the least movement. Well, electricity in this respect has no equal, since it is the most quickly transmitted force"]. Electricity allows man the greatest freedom *from* his tools and dwellings; it therefore does the best job of preventing him from confusing himself with those things, from thinking that he is those things. In the realm of writing, the same thing is true: it is now the non-Euclidean rhetoric, the spark, which links naked (and agraphical) man to the ossified dwellings or tools, the hardened shells of inscriptions, that are his language.

Electricity and non-Euclidean rhetoric as forces join things together and at the same time keep them separate. Tools, dwellings, and language are always *different* from man. The recognition of this difference, in addition to the force of operation at a distance, is what separates man from the animals.

What might at first seem a characteristic of the "old" rhetoric—the linkage of man to his useful language and tools, by which he defines himself—is in fact a function of the alogical figuration of the spark. The tools in themselves might be logical, but when they are seen as different from man they are no longer anthropomorphic; instead they are simple residues that could be used or taken over by any beings. The spark of the new rhetoric jumps when man recognizes that he cannot simply be identified with his tools, logic, or writing, but that, since he is also dependent on his tools or his writing, he himself is not anthropomorphic. The short-circuiting of a rhetoric or language that is taken for granted as an integral part of man is the same as the short-circuiting of a self-conception of man whereby his tools or dwellings are simply himself. The lightning of the new rhetoric is a realization that man's words are separate and dead at the instant of their generation (in lightning). We are back to lightning-generated SCVLPTVRE, which, when read by the light of lightning, is an inscription so different from man that it has come to be the dwelling place of nonhuman creatures.

This is all ultimately about Ponge's own writing, of course. The middle ground of writing, the supposed naturalness, appropriateness, logic, usefulness, and permanence of signification (in rhetoric, in denotation) is done away with: on the one hand we have the spark of meaning or figuration that is momentary, ephemeral, a shock; on the other we have a permanence of signification that is so exaggerated that it has become a petrified tomb of language, a crumbling shell that, taken over by other creatures, refers to its artificiality and its difference from man. (Both the spark of inscription and the ossification of the tool (or text) are functions of duality: the spark is the momentary union of different and irreconcilable elements, as well as the self-conception of consciousness in rending or laceration ["déchirement"], whereas the ossification is the remainder of that spark, which may be useful but which is ultimately recognized as fundamentally *different* from man.) Between the extremes of spark and ossification, joining them in their radical difference, is, as we learn in "Texte sur l'électricité," the spark of light of the new rhetoric, of the new process of reading—and writing.

Ponge admires writers like Malherbe and Mallarmé "parce que leur monument est fait de la véritable sécrétion commune du mollusque homme" ["because their monument is made of the true secretion common to mollusk man"] ("Notes pour un coquillage," 77). These authors as well see language in their poems as a stratification of dead layers of meaning to be mined in the dictionary, the shells of meaning thrown off by centuries of human life. The poem itself becomes a "Louvre de lecture" ("Louvre of reading"), a word box or gallery that is as much an object as the objects—man-made or natural—that it describes. In a way, the question of the status of the externality of the world and of the objects described in Ponge's poems is pointless, because the middle ground of language where internal human word describes external natural object has been destroyed in a blast of light. The de-anthropomorphicized objects that Ponge describes are figures for the residue-text as object. All that remains is the gleam of the rhetoric of curved space (where birth and death of meaning impossibly join) and the remains of a language that soon will be inhabited or read by the nonhuman, and then will slowly erode—like shells—when all life is gone:

O Louvre de lecture, qui pourra être habité, après la fin de la race peut-être par d'autres hôtes, quelques singes par example, ou quelque oiseau . . . .

Et puis, après la fin de tout le règne animal, l'air et le sable en petits grains
lentement y pénètrent, cependant que sur le sol il luit encore et s'érode, et va
brillament se désagréger.

(''Notes pour un coquillage,'' 77)

O Louvre of reading, which can be inhabited, after the end of the race perhaps by other guests, some apes for example, or some bird . . . .
And then, after the end of the reign of the animals, air and sand in little grains
slowly penetrate it, while on the ground it still gleams and erodes, and brilliantly
disintegrates.

(''Notes toward a Shell,'' 66)

Under the brilliant sun, the text slowly disintegrates.

The text as Pongian object, the ''objeu,'' the text as non-Euclidean
rhetoric, displaces the text as predictable (and denotative) useful object,
as political diatribe, as sentimental collection of traditional tropes:

Il y a le monde des objets et des hommes, qui pour la plupart, eux aussi, sont
muets. Parce qu'ils remuent le vieux pot, mais ils ne disent rien. Ils ne disent
que les lieux communs.

(''La Pratique de la littérature,'' II, 276)

There is the world of objects and of men, who for the most part themselves are
mute. Because they stir the old pot, but they say nothing. They only say com-
monplaces.

Men think that language is a natural part of themselves and that it can
be used to meaningfully change things in the world. Ponge on the other
hand holds that man is enslaved to a certain type of language—or rhetoric—and that if a revolution is to take place, it must first be a revolution
in the realm of rhetoric itself. Men must conceive a new relation to themselves, by conceiving a new relation to their words. Thus, to the con-
sternation of his friends, although Ponge was an active communist for
many years, he never wrote political tracts or poems. For Ponge, writing
has to reach a point at which it is no longer naive as to its origins in a
process of inscription that is alien to any guarantee of transcendental
reference (be it the sun, God, self-reflexive consciousness, or whatever)
before it can attempt to consider how ''external'' events could be represented: ''il faut que [le texte] atteigne, lui, à la réalité dans son propre
monde, dans le monde des textes, qu'il ait une réalité dans le monde des
textes'' (II, 276) [''it is necessary that (the text) reach reality in its own
world, in the world of texts, that it have a reality in the world of texts''].

The curved space of rhetoric turns on itself, eternally returning to the
blinding flash of the initial inscription because the only way this act of

inscription survives and is reproduced is through its betrayal, its ossification as crumbling ruin. The momentary flash of light can only be represented by its double and betrayer, the dead inscription.

Nietzsche's positions toward rhetoric and language can be seen in Ponge's position; Nietzsche's 1873 essay "On Truth and Lie in a Nonmoral Sense"[2] puts forward the idea that all language is essentially a lie because no two referents are, strictly speaking, identical. Thus we lie when we call two different leaves "leaves"; we ignore some (different) characteristics and focus on others that are the same. We notice traits held in common only because it is useful to do so. Language is made possible only by what Nietzsche calls a "residue of metaphor" (85), the dead, "bony" remainder of a metaphor, that is, of a word that was initially unique and referred only to a single referent. The momentary, unique (and hence impossible) conjunction of two different elements (what Nietzsche calls "metaphor") is codified and petrified by language and that perfection and petrification of useful language, science. Thus Nietzsche can write of science as an "edifice of concepts" that is finally a "columbarium" (85)—a structure that houses dead metaphors, metaphors removed or abstracted from their original and stunningly unique— but not necessarily useful, logical, or anthropomorphic—significations.

Only by forgetting this primitive world of metaphor can one live with any repose, security, and consistency: only by means of the petrification and coagulation of a mass of images which originally streamed from the primal faculty of human imagination like a fiery liquid, only in the invincible faith that *this* sun, *this* window, *this* table is a truth in itself . . . does man live with any repose, security, and consistency. (86)

This brilliant "fiery liquid," and this sun, as well as all other objects, are tamed and become useful. Here Ponge goes further than Nietzsche: he pushes the dead anthropomorphic object so far in the direction of death that it is no longer even anthropomorphic; nonhuman beings come to inhabit language or writing, and in the process the ecstatic danger of the "original" metaphor (or inscription) is reinscribed. In a *graphic* way in Ponge, then, and in a graphically dead text, there is a demonstration of what Nietzsche's language can only state: dead useful writing becomes "aware" of its own death and *returns* to represent, not life, but a light that is an impossible momentary blast of rent consciousness, an originary different (and self-differentiating) metaphor.

That originary metaphor (as we know from Ponge) is the sun, but not a useful sun that can serve as a stable grounding for metaphysics, morality, or even indifference. Jacques Derrida has analyzed, in his "La Mythologie blanche" ["The White Mythology"][3] the sun as the ultimate metaphor in Western philosophy. Derrida argues that there are finally two suns: the stable sun of knowledge is mimed and subverted by a sun that is its written constructed destruction (320; 268). The sun is double and turns like any trope; its visible face—the face that guarantees the vision of all things—is also the blindness of vision and the night of logic. According to Derrida, this curved trajectory of the sun is accompanied by a curved movement of rhetoric; stable metaphor, the clear distinction between figurative and literal levels of meaning, is mimed by a rhetoric whose most basic and most singular trope is catachresis—a problematical figure (a "forced metaphor") through which no "literal" meaning can be isolated (302-8; 253-58).

The sun (and its light) is, in Ponge, such a catachrestic metaphor; the sun is also *the* metaphor in Ponge. The very subject matter of Ponge—his objects—as well as his written matter—his object texts ("objeux")—are, as we have seen, the petrified residue of the intervention of light. This light is therefore the ultimate referent in Ponge; at the same time, the sun's light (and its earthbound double, illuminated electrical force) is the sign of a rhetoric that is not "natural," that cannot guarantee the "truthful" parallel (Euclidean) conjunctions and adequations of figurative and literal levels of meaning. For this reason, any reading that attempts to account for the strata of meaning in the descriptions of Ponge's objects, his shells and oysters and oranges, or that would ground the meaning of these descriptions in extratextual "hypograms,"[4] must come to terms with the catachrestic sun under which Ponge's objects are photographed.

II

We might return at this point to a problem that appeared in our exposition of the political status of Ponge's writing. If his writing consists of an articulation of the two extremes of writing—and thus excludes the middle ground, the constative, the sentimental, or the political—then how, after language is somehow reformed, and the taken-for-granted elements of language are stripped, will Ponge repoliticize it? How will Ponge move from the old political writing to the new political writing? And what will the configuration of that new political writing be?

For an answer to this question, we turn to Ponge's 1948 memorial to his friend Bernard Groethuysen, "Note hâtive à la gloire de Groethuysen" (I, 39-47) ["Hasty Note to the Glory of Groethuysen"]. Groethuysen, a social historian who wrote on Rousseau and on the rise of the French bourgeoisie,[5] was an important figure in French intellectual life of the 1920s and 1930s. In looking at Ponge's "Note," however, we will restrict ourselves to what Ponge writes of Groethuysen.

Ponge starts his memorial by noting that Groethuysen's name, when broken down, rhymes with two words: "loup" (for "Groeth") and "buisson" (for "huysen"). Groethuysen is "le loup dans ce buisson, à l'oreille ne se prononcé pas comme il s'écrit" (I, 40) ["the wolf in this bush, to the ear not pronounced as it is written"]. This wolf in the bush soon becomes, in the next paragraph, the sun in the bush—not such a strange mutation if we recall that "loup" means not only "wolf," but, in typographer's jargon, any "lacune dans une copie" ["lacuna in a copy"] according to the *Petit Robert* dictionary.[6] The wolf is what is missing from this text to the extent that it is soon replaced by the sun; nor can the sun, as we saw in the previous section of this chapter, be said to be simply "present."

Ponge goes on to associate "Groeth-buisson" both with the burning bush of the Bible and with the "soleil dans les buissons" (40) ["sun in the bushes"]. This sun in Groeth (as Ponge calls him) makes him a great painter—or at least a great light-artist. Ponge ascribes to Groeth the remarkable ability to assimilate himself to all types of thought: "Il se met à l'intérieure de Votre Pensée pour la débrouiller" (41) ["He puts himself within Your Thought in order to straighten it out"]. If systems of thought are like forests or bushes, Groeth can adapt himself to them, living in them or through them to illuminate them with a flash of light:

Il est toutes les forêts. Il est tout dans la forêt, sauf le bûcheron. Ne détruit rien. Il dispose les pièges (et d'abord, ceux de la lumière), dispose les éclairages, les projecteurs. (42)

He is all the forests. He is everything in the forest, except the woodsman. Destroys nothing. He arranges the traps (and first of all, those of light), arranges the lighting, the projectors.

This light, we learn in the next paragraph, is a light associated with Marxism: "Marx y a installé une sorte d'éclairage axiale" (42) ["Marx installed there a kind of axial lighting"]. The bushes, then, are both Groeth himself, bushes as physical entities examined from within, and bushes as ideological systems or constructs that Groeth as a Marxist ["Groeth était marxiste"] somehow comes to inhabit and examine, only to defeat nonviolently (using the arms of his opponents).

Il faudrait se faire fourmi—ou soleil—et suivre patiemment [les] contours [des buissons] y compris ceux de leurs épines. . . .
    Reprenons de l'intérieur chaque buisson. Réinventons chacune de ses pousses, ses moindres propos ou manières. Il deviendra alors tout à fait inoffensif, imbécile. (43)

It is necessary to make oneself an ant—or the sun—and to follow patiently [the] contours [of the bushes], including those of their thorns. . . .

Let's start again from the inside of each bush. Let's reinvent each of its shoots, its slightest utterances or manners. It will then become completely inoffensive, imbecile.

Thus Groeth, using Marxism, "la philosophie qui jette une lumière aveuglante, et se montre si dangereuse pour l'ordre établi" (45) ["the philosophy that casts a blinding light, and shows itself so dangerous for the established order"], somehow at the same time "mimait le philosophe" (44) ["mimed the philosopher"] and mimed his ideological adversaries as well, "entr[ant] dans le jeu de l'adversaire et le bat[tant] (en lui-même) avec ses propres armes" (44) ["enter(ing) into the adversary and beat(ing) him (in himself) with his own weapons"]. Like light, which falls on everything and shows it warts and all, Groeth's philosophy conforms to a philosophy and in the process defeats it by showing its weapons: "la fausse prétention, le sectarisme, l'assurance aveugle" (47) ["false claims, sectarianism, blind assurance"]. Working not only within groups of adversaries, but "à l'intérieur de chacun" (46) ["within each one"], Groeth defeats them all, but at the same time shows them "sollicitude." The defeated philosophy is not destroyed, but is left to "sa place dans la forêt, à son époque dans l'histoire, l'histoire des caprices du soleil" (43) ["its place in the forest, to its epoch in history, the history of the caprices of the sun"]. Unlike the conventional writing that Ponge condemns, that is taken to be a "natural" part of man in its substance and in its themes, Groeth's writing is merely a kind of textual attachment that does not add some pompous theory to a universe of ideas, but only mimes or parodies the ideas of others. In the end it is the sun that is both the origin of these dated philosophies and their termination, through the blinding light of a solar Marxism. The sun's radiance is somehow both a scientific tool (in the form of Marxism) and a capricious jester that engenders and then defeats philosophies.

In "Faune et flore" in *Le parti pris des choses* ["Fauna and Flora" in *The Voice of Things*] Ponge elaborates the idea of a tree—or bush—that can only "express" itself by adding more leaves, more branches: "Oisifs, ils passent leur temps à compliquer leur propre forme . . . ils ne s'occupent qu'à accomplir leur expression: ils se préparent, ils s'ornent, ils attendent qu'on vienne les lire" (82; 64) ["Lazy, they spend their time complicating their own form . . . they are only occupied in accomplishing their expression: they prepare themselves, they ornament themselves, they wait for someone to come and read them"]. Without a doubt Groeth's bushes are similar texts that lack a center, that grow by accretion or multiplication. In his piece on Groeth, however, Ponge goes beyond the earlier "Faune et flore" to the extent that the text is now read not just as a text-tree describing a tree-text, but as an "illuminated" Marxist text-tree (Groeth) reading other political/philosophical text-trees. It would seem that Ponge has finally settled the problem as to how to join his own revolutionary textual method to a revolutionary political method of reading and writing.

Unfortunately, however, Ponge is not Groeth. He doubles Groeth, perhaps, just as Groeth doubles others; at the same time he is not simply Groeth, nor does he practice what he "glorifies" in Groeth. Perhaps the basis of this can be found in Ponge's remarks on Groeth's silence just before he died:

Quelle pensée alors aurait-il pu mimer? Nous le savions marxiste. . . . Les marxistes ne se donnent pas la mort à penser. Il se borna à vivre (ou à mourir) la sienne, sans paroles. (41)

What thought then could he have mimed? We knew him to be a Marxist. . . . Marxists do not give themselves death to think. He limited himself to living (or dying) his own, without words.

Yet we know that Ponge precisely does "give himself death to think." He thinks the moment of consciousness in its own rending; he thinks inscription outside the context of human survival or existence, both in the flash of the (impossible) originary metaphor and after the demise of man. Ponge's nonanthropomorphic inscription clearly is "death to think," both as thinking death and as death to thought.

Thus in a fundamental way Ponge is different from a Marxist, or at least from a Marxist intellectual. But he would clearly like to be a writing Marxist. That, as we saw in the previous section, is a long-range, albeit perhaps utopian goal of Ponge's writing: to fuse the textual and the social revolutions. Ponge apparently cannot wait: he has a compulsion to write the revolution—as does Groeth—but he cannot, because a Marxist by definition thinks labor and production, and not death.

But what kind of political/textual solution can Ponge find to this dilemma? Can he write a text that is both political and at the same time a *text*, moving beyond the simply anthropomorphic and into the realms of the sun and the shell (or the bush)? Such a text may be "Baptême funèbre" ["Funereal Baptism"] (I, 36–38), a memorial piece whose main concern is to think and situate death.

The crucial question raised by the death of René Leynaud, a Resistance fighter executed by the Germans in the area of Lyon on June 13, 1944, is this: "FACE A UN TEL SUJET QUE PUIS-JE?" (37) ["BEFORE SUCH A SUBJECT WHAT CAN I DO?"] This question applies to Ponge, who finds himself wordless before the death of his friend, and it applies to the German executioners, who, try as they might, cannot kill René, whose very name signifies the incessant rebirth of the hero. Ponge identifies with the executioners because, at the end of the question "QUE PUIS-JE?" there is a question mark that indicates both the impotence of the author who questions himself and the impotence of the soldiers whose rifles' smoke (in the shape of a question mark) comes to point back at and question its authors.

Oh cette fumerolle ce point d'interrogation, Oh déjà par ce JE suivi de sa fumerolle ce leger empuantissement de l'atmosphère Oh FACE A UN TEL SUJET comme si je faisais partie du peloton ennemi. (37)

Oh this wisp of smoke this question mark, Oh already by this I followed by its wisp this light stench of the atmosphere Oh FACING SUCH A SUBJECT as if I were a part of the enemy squad.

Before the *subject* of his piece, Ponge is impotent, and can say nothing; facing the *subject* they must execute the soldiers are impotent, even if they kill him. Ponge cannot write about René's death because, as we know, he is committed not to write a sentimental political screed; the soldiers cannot execute René because he is a natural force, like the ever-flowing rivers or, ironically enough, like the always reused words of a language: "Et les ruisseaux de l'Ardèche comme ceux de notre langue maternelle coulent et couleront toujours" (37) ["And the streams of the Ardèche like those of our mother tongue flow and will always flow"]. But Ponge also turns on himself, question marks himself, to the extent that before his subject he can do nothing, write nothing; the soldiers' guns turn on them to the extent that they too can do nothing: "LES CANONS DES FUSILS HORIZONTAUX S'INTERROGEAIENT ENCORE" (38) ["THE HORIZONTAL RIFLE BARRELS STILL INTERROGATED THEMSELVES"]. Thus Ponge and the executioners, because they share the same words, the same question, *turn* into each other: the circulation of René in life and death is doubled by the circulation of the writer and the killers.

The central figure for this turning is the "fumerolle," the wisp of smoke that appears over a volcano before it erupts. Where there's smoke there's fire: the light of the fire, though not directly invoked in "Baptême funèbre," nevertheless is implied and its presence is questioned by the circulating question mark of smoke.

Rolling fumes replace inscribing fire ("le feu," by the way, can also mean "gunfire"). But does smoke obscure fire? Is its obscurity related somehow to the unanswered question the writer faces? As does Groeth,

Ponge uses the same weapons—the same words—as his enemies: "QUE PUIS-JE FAIRE?" But these same weapons reveal the weakness of silence (following the unanswered question) rather than the strength of Marxism, and therein lies Ponge's difficulty.

Both the stench of the smoke ("ce léger empuantissement") and its unanswered question cause the narrator to be afraid: "Mais ressaississons-nous. . . . Oui, rasserenons-nous. Et réprimons ce tremblement devant les paroles" (37) ["But let's get a grip on ourselves. . . . Yes, let's calm ourselves. And let's repress this trembling before words"].

Ponge, doubling the trembling of the victim before the executioner, trembles before the question—or not so much the question as the fact that Ponge's question is the same as the enemy's, the executioner's ("comme si je faisais partie du peloton ennemi"). Unlike Groeth, Ponge has used the weapon of the enemy—his words, his question—but the result has been not Marxist mastery but the weakness of the victim. Ponge cannot answer the question because to do so would be to start to write propaganda—to betray his writing practice. Yet not to answer the question is to risk complicity with the other side, to betray his political beliefs through silence and through mimicking the enemy. The very effort needed to "repress" his tembling before the words that threaten to condemn him indicates the tenacity of the problem.

Ponge is not Groeth—Ponge thinks death—yet he would use the tools of the enemy, their words, their question (his question mark doubles the smoke from their guns). He becomes the double of the enemy exactly at the point when he questions what he can say in the "face" of such a subject—the very elision of the answer to this question already establishes his identity with (through his mimicking of) the enemy. Ponge's writing practice—his silence before political events, his use of the various strata of his opponents' dead words—leads him into unwilling complicity with those he would struggle against.

The only solution to this difficulty is to posit a rebirth of the victim—so that, just as the enemy's words can be reborn in the writing of the poet, so the life of the hero can reappear in another guise: "TOI DEJA ET POUR TOUJOURS AU PARADIS DE NOS MEMOIRES PUR HEROS IMMEDIATEMENT RENE" ["YOU ALREADY AND FOREVER IN THE PARADISE OF OUR MEMORIES PURE HERO IMMEDIATELY REBORN—RENE"]. The rebirth of the fighter (at least in part through the memorial of Ponge's writing) is the defeat of the enemy: celebrating the rebirth, the poet can distance himself from complicity with the enemy.

A problem still remains. The triumphant rebirth of the victim/hero/Resistance fighter, his position in a circular history, presupposes the necessity of those who kill (or sacrifice) him. If, as the title of this memorial indicates, "Baptism" and "Funeral" are intimately linked, the presence of the executioner is as necessary (in the myth) as the heroic status of the victim. Once the thematic political position of the text is excised—as we saw it must be in Ponge's "curved-space" rhetoric—the politics of the enemy is excised as well: he becomes instead a necessary member of the victim/sacrificer dyad, and is thus indispensable.

Yet even if the text—in its most basic problem ("FACE A UN TEL SUJET QUE PUIS-JE?")—is apolitical, at the same time it is still clearly a memorial to a fallen political hero. René's death and rebirth are significant because of his participation in a political (and military) struggle. But the political commitment (on the part of Ponge) that this significance implies precisely cannot be written in the text.

If we consider "Note hâtive à la gloire de Groethuysen" for a moment, it becomes apparent that the Marxism put forward there was an imaginary solution to the problem that Ponge faced as a consequence of his "curved-space" rhetoric. With the practical-political writing excluded from his textual universe, Ponge still faced the question of what a Pongian political text would be in a utopian future in which the textual and political revolutions had both been brought off. The resolution of the contradiction between nonanthropomorphic text and humanistic political revolution is not Marxism in general, but Groethuysen's Marxism. Onto his dead friend Ponge could project the ideal solution, a Marxism that fought and built with the remains of the weapons of its enemies—just as Ponge writes with the ruins of alien or dead languages. But the impossibility of this ideal solution becomes evident when we realize that the sun or light of Marxism is not identical with Ponge's light, that the identification of Groeth with wolf and sun already indicates that a Groeth-sun will not necessarily be the same as a Ponge-sun. (Ponge as writer or inscriber is, necessarily, the sun of his own text.) Ponge's light (and glory) projected onto Groeth becomes something else entirely, a light that is beautiful in theory but that Ponge himself cannot write.

This is borne out by our reading of "Baptême funèbre." Ponge's light becomes a curling smoke cloud, a question-mark perhaps predicting the fiery revolutionary eruption of the volcano, but just as easily announcing the salvo of fascist guns—and, as another alternative, possibly raising the question as to which of these alternatives lies behind the smoke-screen of the text. Without Groeth, Ponge has no screen on which to project a solution; what we have instead is a space of obfuscation, an unanswered question. Ponge, trembling before his words as he would tremble before guns, is able to do away with a complicity with the executioners only by positing the eternal rebirth of the victim—a rebirth that would negate the destructive force of the executioner and reaffirm the constructive politics and regenerative power of the text. By advancing a theory of cyclical history, however, Ponge only makes the executioner necessary for the rebirth of the victim—and thus he once again is in complicity with the executioner. Rather than an ideal Marxism, "Baptême funèbre's" solution to this is simply to pass over the problem in hazy silence, to affirm the heroism of the incessantly reappearing and metamorphosed hero/victim.

What is behind this silence or this Marxism projected as an ideal solution? On one level, it is the refusal to recognize—and affirm—the painful and self-lacerating identity of the victim and his executioner, of the revolutionary and his enemy. On another, perhaps more profound level, this dualistic identity must be seen in the text itself, as the impossible identity of two warring textual factions: the tendency of the text to be a useful political document, and the equally necessary tendency of the text to be a postanthropomorphic object, and as such, to be an object that will betray any political position, that will be, strictly speaking, useless. Perhaps this duality could already be found in light as Ponge presented it in "Scvlptvre," where the constructive activity of consciousness could only be conceived "by the gleam of its own rending," under or by a gleam of light that was an indication and an offshoot of its own betrayal and laceration. When this light illuminates the political future of the text, however, smoke gets in Ponge's eyes.

Chapter Six
Betrayal in the Later Bataille

It at first seems that after World War II Georges Bataille lost his Marxist convictions. Whereas before the war he contributed to a Marxist review (*La Critique Sociale*) and took part in a militant left-wing group with the surrealists (Contre-Attaque), after the war he criticized Stalinism—and praised the Marshall Plan—in his 1949 collection of essays on economics and history *La Part maudite* [*The Cursed Share*]. Although this work, like the prewar essays ("La Notion de dépense," Le Sacré," etc.), focuses on expenditure and sacrifice as the bases of society and the motors of history, it does not attempt to found a theory of "base materialism" that could eventually be coordinated with dialectical materialism—a major goal of the prewar work.

But in 1950 Bataille published a rather strange novel, *L'Abbé C.*, in which the problem of the betrayal of Marxism—so prominent in *Le Bleu du ciel*—enters by the back door, so to speak.

In *L'Abbé C.* the main character is a village priest in Occupied France rather than a Marxist intellectual. But his problem—his embodiment of an absolute truth and his inevitable betrayal of that truth—is very similar to Troppmann's in *Le Bleu du ciel*. As luck would have it, L'abbé C. (Robert C.) is shaken in his faith by his identical twin brother, Charles C., who has devoted his life to debauchery rather than devotion. Robert, who is in any case something of a hypocrite—his favorite slogan is "Say it with flowers" (in English), and his oily "good humor" covers over an "angoisse au fond du coeur" (*L'Abbé C.*, III, 255; 33) ["dread in the innermost region of the heart"][1] finds his belief shattered when his brother lures him to the top of the village church's tower one windy night. At the instigation of Charles, Eponine, the local "garce," is waiting there for Robert. Robert experiences the death of God when Eponine opens her coat and reveals her nude body.

Rather than simply giving in to temptation, Robert reacts in a most unexpected way: he refuses Eponine. Robert's betrayal of the Church, the loss of faith instigated by Charles, is immediately doubled by Robert's betrayal of Charles and Eponine. This betrayal of friends sets the tone of the novel, in which what is betrayed is not—as in *Le Bleu du ciel*—a Marxist party or political platform that foresees a future rationalized society. Instead, it is a secret society of complicitous friends, devoted not to justice and reason but to expenditure and defiance, that is betrayed. In effect, they betray themselves; Charles and Robert are after all doubles, identical twins, and throughout the novel expenditure is always embodied in their mutual betrayals.

From the beginning, Robert's betrayal of Charles and Eponine is in complicity with language or with the silent lack of language. After Robert experiences the death of God through Eponine's nudity, his silence toward her changes radically. Before the incident on the tower, Robert was silent toward Eponine, but his silence was mere hypocrisy, the priest's need to show that he is somehow superior to those who sin. After the incident, Robert is silent but his silence is a betrayal of the beliefs of Eponine and Charles. Robert transforms Charles's betrayal of the Church into a betrayal of Charles's "beliefs." He refuses their impious language as something that is too easy: "nous ne pourrions parler de choses indifférentes" (278; 62) ["we could not go on talking of things that do not matter"], Robert tells Charles. Robert must betray a comfortable little group that can forget about the death of God by enjoying garrulous sex.

Yet Robert's new silence cannot be pure. Just as Robert and Charles betray themselves in their identity—"cette opposition avait le sens d'une identité parfaite" (291; 77) ["this opposition was tantamount to a perfect identity"]—so Robert's pure but now unbelieving silence is immediately betrayed, through signs. The sign is the betrayal of silence, and the signs that betray Robert's silence only contribute further to the betrayal of Charles and Eponine.

Robert one night silently leaves "filth" ["une saleté"]—apparently a smudge of excrement—under Eponine's window (309; 98). His nocturnal comings and goings, his dirty "traces," his "soutane" which is nothing more than a mask (277; 60) but which he continues to wear—all these signs betray and defy Eponine's desire. "La soutane aggrava la comédie. Ce déguisement fut pour Eponine la plus irritant des provocations" (268; 50) ["The soutane made the comedy worse. This disguise was, to Eponine, the most irritating of provocations"].

Robert's silence is also betrayed by a sign that he does not even fully believe in his own "comedy." Robert, offering his last Mass before a congregation that includes Eponine and her friends Rosie and Raymonde, collapses just before singing the "dominus vobiscum" (290; 76). As he is attended by doctors and nuns, he pinches Charles (292; 79). His collapse and unconsciousness are feigned, are a trick; he is physically able to carry out the sacrifice of the Mass. Charles writes:

Sous le regard vide de Robert, jamais le monde ne m'avait paru plus faux, il commandait une aberration silencieuse, un glissement à la tricherie. Dans un mouvement d'ironie mauvaise, je me trouvais mis à l'envers, et l'envers a sur l'endroit l'avantage de ne pouvoir paraître vraie. (300; 87–88)

Under the empty gaze of Robert, the world had never seemed to me more false; it commanded a silent aberration, a sliding into trickery. In a movement of bad irony, I found myself inside-out, and the inside, compared to the outside, has the advantage of never appearing true.

Without God (or with God, if God is a total traitor) even absolute silence cannot be guaranteed. Thus Robert's silence (which itself is a defiance of Charles and Eponine) is contaminated by a sign, a pinch; even silence is a trick that forbids any final establishment of truth.

Betrayal, however, implies complicity as well. Robert and Charles as twins, and Robert's total identification with Eponine (when he writes, calling himself "Chianine"), must be conceived of as unities as well as dualities. Thus Robert is inevitably a part of Charles's and Eponine's secret society, even if (and when) he betrays it. Speaking again (to Charles) of the reasons why he should refuse to speak, Robert says:

Naturellement, j'aimerais te dire ce qui m'arrive, mais je ne pourrais te parler que de choses indifférentes. . . . Si nous parlions de choses indifférentes, je finirais par te prendre pour un autre et maintenant. . . . Pour être sûr d'une complicité aussi grand, il me faut me taire. (301; 89)

Naturally, I'd like to tell you what's happening to me, but I could only speak to you of indifferent things. . . . If we spoke of trivialities, I would end up taking you for someone else and now. . . . To be sure of so great a complicity, I must be silent.

Trivialities—things having to do with utility and survival (including, one must conclude, the transgressive sexuality of Charles and Eponine)—would only defeat the two brothers' betrayal of each other, their insertion of a radical negativity into the placidity of a sibling identity or rivalry. And thus these indifferent things would defeat the complicity that is inextricably linked to that betrayal.

This differentiating identity between betrayal and complicity involves, once again, the phenomenon of language. Like betrayal, language is not unitary or simple; language betrays not only silence, but it betrays and silences itself in the very act of autocitation. Thus Charles presents, at the end of the novel, a series of texts written, incongruously enough, by the silent Robert. They were found under Robert's pillow after he was arrested by the Gestapo for clandestine Resistance activities. Charles defends his gesture of publishing (the now dead) Robert's obscene and incoherent texts by stating that the recopying and publication of the texts is, in fact, the only thing that can silence them. Charles writes:

Le seul moyen de racheter la faute d'écrire est d'anéantir ce qui est écrit. Mais cela ne peut être fait que par l'auteur; la destruction laissant l'essentiel intact, je puis, néanmoins, à l'affirmation lier si étroitement la négation que ma plume efface à mesure qu'elle avança. . . . C'est ainsi que, Robert mort, parce qu'il laissait ces écrits ingénus, . . . il me fallut . . . par le détour de mon livre, l'anéantir, le tuer. (336; 128)

The only way to atone for the sin of writing is to annihilate what is written. But that can only be done by the author; because destruction leaves the essential intact, I can, nevertheless, tie negation so closely to affirmation that my pen effaces as it advances. . . . Thus, with Robert dead, because he left these artless writings, . . . it was necessary for me . . . through the detour of my book, to annihilate him, to kill him.

Just as Robert and Charles defy each other in their identity, so silence and the staining word or sign destroy themselves. The mutually assured destruction of language and silence takes place through copying, the repetitious writing that both destroys and preserves, betrays and is an accomplice of its identical twin, another writing.

But Robert does more than simply betray Charles through silence or through sneaky signs that betray that silence. Robert plays the ultimate dirty trick on Charles and Eponine: he betrays them to the Gestapo. Robert's squealing on Charles and Eponine, however, is entirely of his own choosing; he reveals their names *before* being tortured by the Gestapo. As is their wont, the Gestapo agents distrust him and torture him anyway, but they get nothing more out of him. Exhausted, "de guerre lasse," they give up, end the torture, and accept the names that Robert gave them at the outset (363; 155).

Robert freely admits to a cellmate, after his torture, the crime he has committed. What most strikes this cellmate, a young, silent Calvinist who later reports to Charles on his meeting with Robert (ironically, it is Charles who survives the war, but Robert who dies in a camp), is the fact that Robert has betrayed those he loves, but has remained silent about his friends in the Resistance. He is courageous under torture, but at the same time from the outset he is guilty, dishonorable, cowardly. Robert has told the Calvinist after being tortured:

Je n'ai pas fait preuve d'un courage insignifiant, mais enfin, malgré tout, je meurs déshonoré. Finalement, si j'ai refusé de donner les noms des résistants, c'est que je ne les aimais pas, ou les aimais loyalement, comme il faut aimer ses camarades. . . . C'est qu'il m'était facile d'endurer [la torture] s'il s'agissait d'hommes auxquels je suis étranger! Tandis que j'ai joui de trahir ceux que j'aime. (365; 157)

I did not prove to be lacking in courage but, finally, in spite of everything, I die dishonored. Finally, if I have refused to give the names of the Resistance people, it is because I did not love them, or loved them loyally, as one must love one's comrades. . . . It was easy for me to endure [torture] if it was a question of men to whom I am a stranger! Whereas I experienced great pleasure in betraying those I love.

Robert, betraying his friends, betrays himself. The torture he undergoes—and which in a strange way he enjoys—is merely a prolongation of autobetrayal, and as such is a link between autobetrayal and automutilation.

But at this point we can see how Bataille attempts to solve a problem that has haunted him since *Le Bleu du ciel*: how can one embrace a violence so subversive that it is inevitably a betrayal, without allying oneself with the fascists? The solution here is very neat: one betrays one's friends—they are one's true society, the subversive or secret society of lovers—and one refuses to betray one's political comrades, because betrayal (like eroticism or death) has nothing to do with (or is beyond the bounds of) the rational society for which one struggles, along with those comrades. Indeed the gratuitousness of torture—and self-betrayal—is even linked to the refusal to betray political friends: Robert's torture, which is really a kind of automutilation, goes on *while* he refuses to give the names of Resistance friends. Automutilation and commitment to a just cause are thus indivisible.

II

While it might seem that at this point Bataille has solved one set of problems, others emerge. First there is the question of silence: up to now we have seen silence incessantly betrayed—by an excremental trace, by a pinch, by another silence. Here, however, the silence of Robert before the Gestapo is comfortably maintained; one silence may be risked and violated (the silence as to his friends' identities) but another (the secrecy concerning his Resistance comrades' identities) remains intact. There is a realm, then, that is outside the betrayals of language and silence, of writing and copying. The question of a rational revolution—of the Resistance, or of communism—is untouched by the problem of language and (re)writing.

In order to isolate the rational struggle for a just society from the excessive violence of mutilation and betrayal, Bataille must distinguish between two different types of violence. Thus in a 1947 essay on Camus's *La Peste* ("La Morale du malheur: *La Peste*" ["The Morality of Misfortune: *The Plague*"] in *Critique* 13/14, June–July 1947), Bataille takes Camus to task for simply condemning violence and for linking the irrational violence of sacrifice with the violence utilized by the Nazis. Camus does value what he calls "la révolte," but this revolt is a refusal of a Dionysian or even Christian order, and is, instead, a demand for a tolerable, just, and human(e) order that does not have recourse to violence. The violence of Camus's "révolte" tries to *eliminate* both "nihilistic" (sacred) and "totalitarian" violence.[2]

Bataille as a Nietzschean first rejects Camus's call for a new peaceful morality—"Combien tout ceci est loin d'une morale de révolte . . . c'est la morale de tous les temps, c'est, avare et sans vie, une morale de malheur" (13–14) ["How far all of this is from a morality of revolt . . . it is the morality of all times, it is, avaricious and lifeless, a morality of misfortune"]. He then makes a fundamental distinction between a totally unusable violence ("the sacred"), which is to be affirmed, and (for example) the violence of the Nazis, which they attempted to put to use, and which, of course, is to be refused. In Bataille's view, in a strange way, Camus and the Nazis, from their opposite viewpoints, make the same mistake concerning violence. Camus collapses the violence of the sacred and the utilized violence of the Nazis together, and sees them as the same phenomenon; the Nazis ignore sacred violence and assume that all violence is useful. Both Camus and the Nazis ignore the possibility of an autonomous sacred violence.

Bataille would separate the two violences, affirming one (sacred, useless violence) and denying the other (violence that is seen as useful). Thus Bataille is against capital punishment, because it attempts to use human sacrifice to teach people a lesson. Bataille distinguishes between two separate realms, "revolution" and "revolt": "revolution" is the legal, rational, and moral sphere, from which violence should be exiled;

"revolt" is the sphere of the only violence that is worth recognizing in a human context—the violence that cannot be used or restrained. When the two are confused, one gets either Camus's morality or the Nazis' barbarity.

But Bataille himself did not respect these distinctions. In *L'Abbé C.*, there is a certain kind of confusion between the two types of violence: after all, in betraying Charles and Eponine, Robert goes through repressive political channels—he betrays them to the Gestapo. Thus even if the two realms—the legal and the passionate—are rigorously separated, they nevertheless come in contact. Even if the Gestapo men misunderstand it, they are the embodiment of death and betrayal, unlike the other elements of a moralistic society. Robert, in complicity with them, therefore crosses the line and confuses the two kinds of violence ("the sacred" and "the useful"), as well as "revolution" and "revolt."

We see this line crossed—and everything betrayed—in an article written in 1947, three years before the publication of *L'Abbé C.*: "Réflexions sur le bourreau et la victime: S.S. et déportés" ["Reflections on the Executioner and the Victim: S.S. and Deportees] (in *Critique* 17, October 1947). This article, a book review of David Rousset's *Les jours de notre mort* [*The Days of Our Death*] (an acount of life in the Nazi concentration camps), attempts to analyze the phenomenon of Nazi evil. Bataille starts his review in the same vein as in the Camus article: the executioner is ignorant of the force of death that he attempts to use.

Le bourreau s'avilit, avilit sa victime, surtout il ne frappe que lâchement, par ignorance (. . . un tortionnaire ignore qu'il frappe lui-même, il ajoute à la souffrance de la victime l'anéantissement de l'idée humaine). (339)

The executioner degrades himself, degrades his victim; above all, he only strikes as a coward, through ignorance (. . . a torturer does not know that he strikes himself, to the suffering of the victim he adds the annihilation of the idea of man).

But soon the direction of the argument shifts: if we are to avoid being Camus-like moralists who refuse everything that is not ordinary comfort and satisfaction, we must recognize that we are the doubles not only of the victims of the S.S., but of the S.S. themselves. We must recognize in ourselves a cowardliness, a despicable nature, a betrayal that goes beyond all bounds:

Mais nous ne sommes pas seulement les victimes possibles des bourreaux: les bourreaux sont nos semblables. . . . Notre possibilité n'est donc pas la seule douleur, elle s'étend à la rage de torturer. Les Toni Brüncken, les Heinz, les Popenhauer, tant de tueurs bottés et matraquant, tous lâches et inexorables, sont là pour nous dire avec leur irréfutable rage, que souvent la lâcheté seule est la limite de la violence et qu'il n'est pas de limite à la lâcheté. (341)

But we are not only the possible victims of the executioners: the executioners are our fellow men. . . . Our possibility is thus not only pain, it extends to the rage of torture. The Toni Brünckens, the Heinzes, the Popenhauers, so many clubbing, booted killers, all of them unrelenting and cowards, they are all there to tell us with their irrefutable rage that often cowardice alone is the limit of violence and that there are no limits to cowardice.

At the moment when all is lost—when, perhaps because of the death of God, there is nothing to guarantee man's nobility—even the stable distinction Bataille established between kinds of violence breaks down. Man then truly betrays himself, and *as man* and in his "essence" he is despicable and inhuman. Writing of the camps, Bataille states:

Il n'est rien en nous d'isolable, que nous puissions mettre à part et qui nous permette fermement de dire: c'était impossible, de toutes façons. (341)

Nothing in us can be isolated, that we can set aside and that permits us firmly to say: it was, in any case, impossible.

Bataille is not implying that all people are Nazis, but rather that the total evil those Nazis represent is—as much as anything else—human. In a short review of Sartre's *Réflexions sur la question juive* [*Anti-Semite and Jew*] (*Critique* 12, May 1947, 471) Bataille writes: "comme les Pyramides ou l'Acropole, Auschwitz est le fait, *est le signe* de l'homme. L'image de l'homme est inséparable, désormais, d'une chambre à gaz" ["like the Pyramids or the Acropolis, Auschwitz is the fact, *is the sign* of man. The image of man is, from now on, inseparable from a gas chamber"] (emphasis added).

Perhaps not in *L'Abbé C.*, then, but in other writings of Bataille from this period, betrayal spreads and saturates everything: unfathomable and inhuman cruelty becomes the *sign* of the human: "Nothing in us can be isolated."

But what then of language or writing in relation to this guilt? Robert, whether he likes it nor not, is guilty of collaborating with the Gestapo when he gives them *anyone's* name. Robert's "lâcheté" (a word often used to describe him—a word that means both cowardice and villainy) cannot be clearly distinguished from the "lâcheté" of the S.S. or Gestapo. Robert cannot, in a gesture of bad faith if there ever was one, somehow be innocent of collaboration, and at the same time have the Gestapo do his bidding. Thus a second reading of the scene in which Robert reveals his friends' names must envision the necessity of Robert's *total* collaboration, up to the point of turning in his Resistance friends: likewise, it must be able to indicate how (because betrayal itself is in complicity with language and ultimately writing, the doubled sacrificial violence of inscription) this boundless betrayal *collaborates* with the phenomenon of rewriting.

III

Clearly we have already started this process of rewriting, to the extent that we have reread and rewritten Robert's collaboration with the enemy in the context of the recognition of a total "human" cowardice or betrayal that appears in some of Bataille's essays of the postwar period.

But our rewriting is doubled by another, crucial rewriting/silencing: Bataille rewrites Sartre.

To see how this comes to pass, we might look at a work by Bataille that was not completed and that was intended as a sequel to *La Part maudite—La Souveraineté* [*Sovereignty*] (1953). Bataille in this work approaches a problem similar to the one just discussed, but now he approaches it from the perspective of communism: is the unspeakable evil of Nazism human? If so, how can communism constitute itself, since it sees itself as a defense of humanity in the face of an inhuman Nazism?

In the chapter entitled "L'Equivalence et la distinction" ["Equivalence and Distinction"] (VIII, 365-74), Bataille poses the question: how egalitarian is communism, really? Communism in Bataille's view can only liberate man and make him human (i.e., do away with his alienation) by rejecting as *inhuman* certain forms of behavior, most notably fascism:

Pour [le communisme], le mot humain, impliquant la dignité humain, est également applicable à tous les hommes, mais il ne l'est pas à ceux d'entre eux qui exploitent leurs semblables. L'exploiteur est lui-même un homme, mais il s'est excepté de cette qualité que le communisme accorde également à tous les hommes. . . . [Le communisme] apprécie à son tour les individus, les gouvernements, ou les classes selon le respect accordé à l'interdit, formulé par lui, qui s'oppose à l'exploitation. (372)

For [communism], the word *human*, implying human dignity, is applicable equally to all men, but it is not to those who exploit other men. The exploiter is himself a man, but he has denied himself the quality that communism accords to all men. . . . [Communism] assesses in turn individuals, governments, or classes according to the respect that they grant to the interdiction (formulated by communism) that opposes exploitation.

Communism thus faces a paradox: while it condemns elitism, distinction, discrimination, and so forth, it itself establishes a hierarchy in which it is superior to other forms or modes of human life. Thus its belief in equivalence or equality is something of a myth:

Le principe de l'équivalence est contraire à l'essence d'une espèce, constituée dans l'exclusion incessante, dans la malédiction, de ce qu'elle situait plus bas que le palier qu'elle atteignait. (373)

The principle of equivalence is contrary to the essence of a species, which is constituted through incessant exclusion, in the cursing of what it situates below the level it has attained.

Of course Bataille here is not arguing that this "essence of a species" is the only option open to man. On the contrary: he argues for an "equality" even more equal than that of the communists. In his view communism must lower itself, betray itself, and embrace what is radically opposed to it.

This characteristic Bataillean move—the autodestructive and impossible embrace of what one has rejected or shunted beneath oneself in order to constitute oneself—is presented in this essay as a problem for the communist or leftist intellectual. These intellectuals are caught in a kind of unhappy consciousness, or bad faith: they affirm a doctrine of rigorous equality, rationality, and utility (as communists) while at the same time devoting themselves to an "avant-garde" writing that is, strictly speaking, *useless*.

Une sorte de timidité, de mauvaise conscience, de honte, s'empare des esprits, à l'idée de peu de valeur, du peu de poids—comparé à l'enjeu de la politique communiste—de ce qui les séduit personellement . . . la seule véritable valeur est celle qui touche un ouvrier. (365)

A kind of timidity, of guilty conscience, of shame, takes over men's minds, at the thought of the lack of weight or value—compared to what is at stake in communist politics—of what appeals to them personally . . . the only real value is the one having to do with a worker.

Bataille then goes on to condemn this "guilty conscience." But since, as we have seen, communism for Bataille is not something that can rigorously exclude what it finds odious, the result for the leftist intellectual will not be a rejection of wasteful and useless avant-garde art or writing, but instead will be its embrace. Nor will communism be rejected: Bataille at no point rejects the "human" tendency of communism to push for equality through the exclusion of inequality and exploitation. He merely wishes to push communism to its logical end, to the point at which it betrays itself and embraces what is radically different and unassimilable.

Nous faisons une comédie de notre vie, un tissu de mensonges et de prétentions. Nous n'en sommes pas moins condamnés au mépris des autres, en de violentes prises de parti contre eux. La cause inéluctable est le désir d'être plus humain. Mais il est facile d'y céder en condamnant *chez l'autre* ce que nous jugeons *inhumain*. (373)

We turn our lives into a comedy, into a tissue of lies and pretensions. We are no less condemned to despise others, by taking violent stands against them. The ineluctable cause is the desire to be more human. But it is easy to give in by condemning *in the other* what we judge to be *inhuman*.

The human, then, must embrace the inhuman: communism can no longer see itself as superior to fascism or to useless (and thus fascistic?) avant-garde writing—but that does not mean that these opposing terms (human/inhuman, communism/fascism) simply melt into each other. In other words, the leftist intellectual *as leftist* betrays himself; if he did not remain a leftist, his self-betrayal could not "take place." In this light, we can see that, rather than rejecting or doing away with the guilty conscience (or bad faith), Bataille advocates a Nietzschean embrace of its impossible difference.

We can argue, then, that pushed to its logical end, Robert's betrayal becomes the affirmation of, a saying "yes" to, the guilty conscience and the double bind of the leftist intellectual. The excessiveness of betrayal is the radicality of this dilemma. But the conflict must be envisioned on the much larger scale of society as a whole, as well as on a personal scale: implied in all this is a utopian (or dystopian) vision of a communist society that somehow embraces what it finds most repugnant. (We will return to this problem shortly.)

Of course, all of this implies an audacious rewriting of Sartre. Sartre condemns the bad faith of the artist who hypocritically affirms both revolution and his own useless and elite modernist art. Bataille on the other hand would embrace this duplicity (this "lâcheté," this dishonor) as the most revolutionary—and self-destructive—act of the intellectual.

Sartre in "Qu'est-ce que la littérature?"[3] for example, condemns the surrealists for their attempt to merge an elitist revolt with a proletarian revolution:

L'originalité du mouvement surréaliste réside dans sa tentative pour s'approprier *tout* à la fois: le déclassement en haut, le parasitisme, l'aristocratie, métaphysique de consommation et l'alliance avec les forces révolutionnaires. (225; 187)

The originality of the surrealist movement resides in its attempt to appropriate *everything* at the same time: unclassing from above, parasitism, aristocracy, the metaphysics of consumption, and alliance with the revolutionary forces.

According to Sartre, this alliance with the communists is a sham, meant only "pour la tranquilisation de [la] conscience [des surréalistes]" (225; 187) ["for the tranquilization of (the) (surrealists') conscience"]. Refusing to fully ally themselves with the proletariat, the surrealists merely create a kind of ideal or phantasmic region where the contradiction they embody—between decadent bourgeois revolt and proletarian revolution—is effaced. Bataille, incidentally, according to Sartre, is a "feeble echo" of the surrealists: "les gloses sur l'impossible de Georges Bataille ne valent pas le moindre tract surréaliste, sa théorie de la dépense est un echo affaibli des grandes fêtes passées" (241; 211) ["the glosses on the impossible of Georges Bataille are not worth the slightest surrealist tract, his theory of expenditure is a feeble echo of the great bygone festivals"] [translation modified].

If Bataille rewrites Sartre by affirming the sundered consciousness, the bad faith of the surrealists that in different ways both the surrealists and Sartre refuse (the conscious affirmation by the intellectual of both the useless or excessive *and* the constructive), at the same time he rewrites, through Robert's betrayal of his friends, Sartre's condemnation, in the same essay, of both torturer and tortured. Again, Sartre:

Vient un instant où tortureur et torturé sont d'accord: celui-là parce qu'il a, en une seule victime, assouvi symboliquement sa haine de l'humanité entière, celui-ci parce qu'il ne peut supporter sa faute qu'en la poussant à l'extreme et qu'il ne peut endurer la haine qu'il ne porte qu'en haissant tous les autres hommes avec lui. Plus tard le bourreau sera pendu, peut-être; si elle en réchappe, peut-être que la victime se réhabilitera: mais qui éffacera cette Messe où deux libertés ont communié dans la destruction de l'humain? (247–48; 218–19)

A moment comes when torturer and tortured are in accord: the former because he has, in a single victim, symbolically gratified his hatred of all mankind, the latter because he can bear his failing only by pushing it to the limit, and because the only way he can endure his self-hatred is by hating all other men along with himself. Later, perhaps, the executioner will be hanged. Perhaps the victim, if he recovers, will be redeemed. But what will blot out this Mass in which two freedoms have communed in the destruction of the human?

The tortured *and* the torturer are in bad faith: by eventually talking the victim refuses his human freedom and "applique sa volonté d'homme à nier qu'il soit homme" (247; 218) ["applies his will as a man to denying that he is a man"].

It would seem then that Sartre is the base of Bataille's text; Bataille rewrites him, silences him, affirms him while betraying him. Bataille's rewriting of Sartre's refusal of the guilt of the victim and the guilt of the leftist intellectual must be seen together: Robert's final "Mass," his naming names, implies a betrayal of not only what is human for Sartre, but necessarily of Sartre's progressive political dialectic as well. The rewritings of these two Sartrean positions are complementary: the rewriting of Sartre's diatribe against the surrealists affirms the *inner* betrayal of the intellectual, his or her self-sundering in a dual position; the rewriting (in *L'Abbé C.*) of Sartre's position on tortured and torturer affirms an outward betrayal of coherent and rational social structures—of what is human.

This is not to say, however, that a rewriting of Sartre implies a simple rejection of his theory. Instead, his theory could very well be identifiable with the Marxist position that Bataille's sundered intellectual simultaneously affirms and turns against. (Nor is this to imply that Sartre is at the "origin" of Bataille's concerns at this time; after all, Sartre's writing is already a rewriting—a repetition and silencing—of the surrealists' double bind. Bataille's position in rewriting Sartre is thus a re-rewriting, a reflexive or self-conscious return to the surrealists' "position"—itself a split rather than a simple "origin.")

Indeed "communism" could be replaced in the dyad of mutilation by the "Sartrean dialectic" or, finally, by a State that somehow recognizes Bataillean "excess." The latter is an option put forward in a collection of Bataille's essays on history and economics, *La Part maudite* (1949). In this work, in mock-Hegelian fashion, Bataille reads history not as the progress of Spirit or as a series of progressive changes in modes of production, but instead as a chronicle of the development of modes of waste. The end of history for Bataille is a "State," to be founded in the near future (VII, 174), that promotes production so that all people have a minimum level of well-being (it thus embodies the "absolute knowledge" of a communism that would rationalize production) and at the same time recognizes excess to the extent that the surplus that remains after all are fed and housed will somehow be "consumed," rather than be "used" in the production of dangerous weapons. A mad, utopian dream, perhaps; then again the arms race is even more mad (VII, 179).[4]

Or, as in *L'Histoire de l'érotisme* [*The History of Eroticism*], another sequel to *La Part maudite*: at the end of history there could very well be another, "minor" history, not of major revolution and cataclysm, but of private eroticism (VIII, 163).

Bataille can very well progress from the total rationalization of Stalinism, to a more liberal Sartrean dialectic, to his own "utopian" State in which the tendency to expend would be fully recognized through legislation; the problem of betrayal remains the same. Each one of these futures—and they may be linked in a progression—will always again be defied by the guilty one in revolt. Thus these futures are not different in kind. Writing of Nietzsche in *La Souveraineté*, Bataille states:

Il n'est de résolution que le tournis, où jamais la conscience n'est satisfaite, où le jeu paraît pauvre à la mesure d'une souveraineté évidente, mais inaccessible et inconcevable qui n'appartient qu'à la totalité. D'où une sorte durable de mépris pour soi-même, non moins que l'outrecuidance inévitable. (VIII, 417)

The only resolution is in a vertigo in which consciousness is never satisfied, in which the game means little when compared to an obvious but inaccessible and inconceivable sovereignty, which belongs only to the totality. This leads to a kind of permanent despising of oneself, no less than to the inevitable presumptuousness.

If "sovereignty" is "obvious," if excess—and betrayal—have in one way or another been recognized or posited as the cornerstone of a future presumptuous era of human history, there will nevertheless be an incessant revolt of the intellectual against his or her own utopia, accompanied by an inevitable exaltation and abjection. The other alternative, however, is by itself no more satisfying: a sovereignty "of the totality"—completely beyond the constraints of understanding or utilization—inevitably leads back to the "obvious" sovereignty because it is so formidable, and because by its very nature it cannot be "grasped" or maintained.

As criminal and god, the Bataillean writer bears within the inscription of a repetitious complicity and defiance. The utopian future society, rational in its irrationalism, and the useless inhuman revolt of avant-garde writing or crime, square off in the constitution of this cursed figure's "being."

It would seem that at each step in his postwar writing Bataille works to situate a betrayal. There seems to be little concern in these writings for a resolution or expurgation of this betrayal, as there was in the prewar *Le Bleu du ciel*. Or, put another way, if there is an attempt at safely situating this betrayal in a utopian future, this future is itself betrayed. Bataille is willing to defy Sartre, who, in his examination of bad faith, analyzed the problem of how individuals could shirk responsibility and betray their own freedom. But for Bataille the guilt of betrayal is the most extreme freedom.

We saw, at the end of *Le Bleu du ciel*, how a self-mutilating writing could be a powerful analytic tool. The vision of Dorothea in her Nazi-red dress at the close of the novel underscores the ability of the writer (the narrator) to criticize his own betrayal. Nothing comparable seems to happen in Bataille's postwar writings; even though there might be an opposition in these writings between, say, the cynicism of Robert's betryal (in

L'Abbé C.) and the self-righteousness of the State as presented at the end of *La Part maudite* (in works published one year apart), there is not the kind of reciprocal analysis and attempt at a working out of a problem that was so evident in *Le Bleu du ciel*. Perhaps this is why the postwar works appear to be less "political" than the prewar ones. This does not mean, however, that the postwar works are "depoliticized"; Robert's naming of names is a profoundly political—and repulsive—gesture.

What then of the critical analysis of the avant-garde and its utopia? Bataille himself affirms the guilt of useless avant-garde art, but he does not analyze it. Is it possible to formulate a method of critical reading that does not simply lose or ignore the doubled position that evolves (or devolves) in Bataille's writings, but that at the same time can turn and read not only Bataille's utopia (the written realm of the intersection of rationality and mindless expenditure) but the utopias of other avant-garde authors as well? We will return to this question (after a detour through Derrida and Foucault) in our last chapter.

Chapter Seven
Derrida, Foucault, and Their "Precursors"

I

In this chapter we will attempt to place in historical and textual perspective two critics who have come to be called "poststructuralists" in the United States: Jacques Derrida and Michel Foucault. We will attempt to see them as the continuers of a tradition in French thought that was largely ignored for many years in the English-speaking world. We will restrict this "tradition" here to Bataille and Blanchot; these two have probably been the most immediately influential, through their rereadings of Hegel and Nietzsche, and through their stress on transgression (especially in Bataille) and language (especially in Blanchot). Our project is clearly a walk on an intellectual tightrope, to the extent that as soon as we postulate "influence" or "filiation" we have returned to a straightforward Hegelian model of struggle and succession (between master and slave, for example) questioned in different ways by Bataille, Blanchot, Derrida, and Foucault. The paradox of our approach, then, will be to situate Derrida and Foucault in a historical context; the notion here of history, however, will have less to do with fathers and sons, rivalries and the resolution of rivalries (on a "higher level") than it will have to do with doublings, betrayals, and the *return* of moments of a recalcitrant negativity. Indeed in the preceding chapter we already saw, in the conflict between Bataille and Sartre, a phenomenon of betrayal rather than one of simple "influence."

Hegel and Nietzsche are crucial here; if we consider for a moment Bataille and Blachot in the context of the 1940s and 1950s, we realize that what separates their approach from that of existentialists such as Sartre and Camus is precisely *how* they read Nietzsche and Hegel.[1] In the cases of Sartre and Camus, Nietzsche's value as a "precursor" is primarily due to his announcement of the "death of God." In other words, many of the most characteristic aspects of Nietzsche's thought are avoided by Sartre and Camus: the "eternal return," the "superman," the notion of "force," and so on. Instead, the "death of God" and the "transvaluation of all values" are seen by the dominant French philosophers of this period to be a call for man to choose his own life, to take responsibility for it, to refuse subservience to any illusory God or dictator. Camus in particular distanced himself from other aspects of Nietzsche's thought (such as the emphasis on force), which for many in the immediate postwar period smelled strongly of Nazism.[2] On the other hand, for Sartre especially, the triadic dialectical movement that we associate with "Hegel" was valued in itself, even if the larger trappings of the *Phenomenology*—or the trappings of mechanistic Marxism—were jettisoned. One can see this not only in Sartre's theoretical writings, but in plays like *Huis clos* [*No Exit*], in which "hell" is a dualistic circular structure from which the third person is always excluded; the escape from hell, if at all possible, starts to come when the dualistic, repetitive, and reversible power structure is abandoned, and when the third person is included in the minisociety. From that point on the vicious ahistorical circle can perhaps be left behind, and progress—and history—can be made.[3] Finally, a reliance on a triadic and progressive dialectical movement entails for Sartre the embrace of a notion of scarcity: just as the slave in the master/slave dialectic produces objects out of unformed matter and thereby fulfills his own—and his master's—needs, so the committed man in Sartre must always face the fact of scarcity, of a need to be filled.[4]

The readings of Nietzsche and Hegel carried out by Bataille and Blanchot were very much at odds with the contemporaneous existential readings. We have already mentioned (in chapter 4) Bataille's Acéphale group of the late 1930s.[5] We might consider, then, Bataille's advocacy of elements of Nietzsche's thought generally ignored by the existentialists: force, expenditure, repetitious time, and the death of God (the meaning of God's death for Bataille, however, is different from its meaning for the existentialists).

The "symbol" of the Acéphale group was the headless man, the man who "échappera à sa tête comme le condamné à la prison" (I, 644) ["will escape from his head just as the condemned man will escape from the prison"].[6] This man who ends man, who represents the death of man through the force that exceeds the boundaries of man's head—of his reason, his consciousness, his establishment of himself at the top of a hierarchy—is also Nietzsche, who, before the pyramid-shaped rock of Surlei, experienced the vision of the death of God and of the eternal return.

Ce que Nietzsche eprouva quand le cours de sa réflexion, tout à coup, lui donna du retour éternel une vision extatique ne peut être comparé avec les sentiments liés d'habitude à ce qui passe pour réflexion profonde. . . . Le caractère toxique du "retour" est même d'une importance si grande que s'il était un instant écarté, le contenu formel risquerait de paraître vide. . . .

C'est le TEMPS qui se déchaine dans la "mort" de Celui dont l'éternité donnait à l'Etre une assise immuable. Et l'acte d'audace qui représente le "retour," au sommet de ce déchirement, ne fait qu'arracher à Dieu mort sa puissance *totale* pour la donner à l'absurdité délétere du TEMPS. (I, 510)

Nietzsche's thought, resulting in the sudden ecstatic vision of the eternal return, cannot be compared to the feelings usually linked to what passes for profound reflection. . . . The *toxic* character of the "return" is even of such great importance that, if for an instant it were set aside, the formal content of the "return" would run the risk of appearing empty. . . .

TIME is unleashed in the "death" of the One whose eternity gave Being an immutable foundation. And the audacious act that represents the "return" at the summit of this rending agony only tears from the dead God his *total* strength, in order to give it to the deleterious absurdity of TIME.

It is not that God simply does not exist, or that we no longer believe in him; instead, his *death* exists (and always existed, even in the days of Heraclitus and his meditations on time), liberating a force that cannot be used for constructive purposes. This helps us understand "deleterious," "toxic" time: time is not the progressive, constructive phenomenon in which and through which we do a job; instead it is the fall, the irrecoverable expenditure of God's control of power, of control by the head, of control by God's proxy, man.

The "death of God" in Bataille is thus far from being an invitation to redefine man, or to take responsibility for that meaning, now that the hope of a transcendental meaning is lost. Instead it is a call for us to face up to the death of man. Excess rather than scarcity, the fall of catastrophe rather than the erection of production, are now the central problems that must be faced by the (non)philosopher who repeats or doubles Nietzsche.

Yet for all this Bataille does not simply reject Hegel. Instead, he doubles Nietzsche and betrays him by accepting Hegel, or at least the reading of Hegel by Kojève that did so much to rekindle interest in Hegel in the 1930s in France.[7] In a letter to Kojève dated December 6, 1937 (and thus written during the Acéphale period), Bataille posits the existence of an "unemployable" negativity, at the end of history, after the ultimate "solution révolutionnaire du communisme" envisaged by Kojève's Marxist Hegelianism has taken place:

> Si l'action (le "faire") est—comme dit Hegel—la négativité, la question se pose alors de savoir si la négativité de qui n'a "plus rien à faire" disparaît ou subsiste à l'état de "négativité sans emploi" (je ne pourrais me définir de façon plus precise). . . . J'imagine que ma vie—ou son avortement, mieux encore, la blessure ouverte qu'est ma vie—à elle seule constitue la refuatation du système fermé de Hegel. (V, 369-70)

> If action ("doing") is—as Hegel says—negativity, the question then arises of knowing whether the negativity of one who "no longer has anything to do" disappears or whether it remains as a "jobless negativity" (I could not define myself in a more precise manner). . . . I imagine that my life—or its abortion, or better yet, the open wound that is my life—by itself alone constitutes the refutation of the closed system of Hegel.

Just as Hegel in his person embodies the end of history, so Bataille, in the "abortion" of his life, embodies the opening of a wound in the closure of history. At the Hegelian end of history, all negativity is recognized and used—except the unemployed (and unemployable) negativity that *cannot* be used. This Nietzschean negativity is the blind spot where the all-seeing eye of consciousness looks and loses itself, where the exiled unemployable negativity—exiled precisely so that a homogeneous field, a closed circle of employable negativity, can be established—is recognized *as* unemployable, *as* nonrecuperable: "dans la mesure où l'on envisage dans l'entendement l'homme lui-même, je veux dire une exploration du possible de l'être, la tache [aveugle] absorbe l'attention: ce n'est plus la tache qui se perd dans la connaissance, mais la connaissance en elle" (V, 129) ["to the extent that one envisages in understanding man himself, in other words an exploration of the possibility of being, the (blind) spot absorbs the attention: it is no longer the spot that is lost in knowledge, but instead it is knowledge that is lost in the spot"]. Consciousness recognizes nonrecognizable negativity, but in that way it endlessly loses itself by entering into a vicious circle, where this recognition—a really *final* absolute knowledge—can only know what definitively cannot be known: a recalcitrant negativity, a toxic *non-savoir* ("non-knowing").[8] The highest knowledge immediately and incessantly reverses itself and becomes the lowest: "Dieu, s'il 'savait', serait un porc" (III, 31) ["God, if he 'knew', would be a pig"].

Thus in Bataille's doubling of Hegel the circular completion of the dialectic, its final closure, is undermined; absolute knowledge becomes a vicious circle, or, to put it another way, an eternal return.[9] Nietzsche therefore always already infects the Hegelian dialectic: the point of dialectical finality, of the *Aufhebung*, is a moment of expenditure or toxic time. The dialectic automutilates to the extent that the two sides of the Nietzsche/Hegel combine are in violent conflict, yet are conjoined; Nietzschean negativity re-turns "in" the dialectic.

Bataille, in his letter to Kojève, sees a kind of Nietzschean, parodic counter-history running parallel to but subverting or perverting the official Hegelian-Marxist history; this second history is one of excess, sacrifice, death, and art. (The constitution of this second history is not simply Nietzsche infecting Hegel; it is also Hegel's temporality infecting the sheer repetition of Nietzsche.) But Bataille criticizes these earlier forms of expenditure—and especially art and religion—becuase they do not recognize themselves as *simply empty*, as empty as "toxic time": "Il [l'homme dans l'histoire] a compris que son besoin d'agir n'avait plus d'emploi. Mais ce besoin, ne pouvant être dupé indefiniment par les leurres de l'art, un jour ou l'autre est reconnu pour ce qu'il est: comme négativité vide de contenu" (V, 371) ["He (man in history) understood that his need to act no longer had a job to do. But this need, no longer indefinitely duped by the traps of art, is sooner or later recognized for what it is: a negativity emptied of content"]. At the end of history negativity will somehow impossibly be recognized as empty, without its artistic, religious, or metaphysical trappings. At that point the two ends of history—the history of modes of consciousness and production (Hegel/Marx) and the history of modes of empty force—will join.

This is the project of *La Part maudite*, written some ten years after the letter to Kojève. We have already seen, in the preceding chapter, the problems ultimately faced by Bataille in this conjoined Hegelian-Marxist/Nietzschean history: what will be the *social* manifestations of this "empty toxicity" at the doubled end of history, when the eye of knowing focuses on nonknowing, when the reason of the State perhaps unknowingly puts forward the nonreason of sexuality or the death of God? It is clear that Bataille was never able to see only the "abortion" of *himself* as the ultimate repetitious end of history: just as Hegel had his State, the ultimate incarnation of reason, so too Bataille, repeating Hegel, attempted to think a political realm in which annihilating expenditure— war—would be done away with, and in which empty toxicity could somehow be put forward. We would argue that this realm itself, however, was liable to be betrayed, to forget itself and become unknowable, to mutilate itself and its embodiment, the victim-writer.

Bataille was not alone in his attempt at thinking a conjoined Nietzsche and Hegel in opposition to the Nietzsche and Hegel of the existentialists. Leiris and Klossowski, both involved in the Collège de Sociologie, had kindred projects.[10] But perhaps the most important fellow traveler with Bataille, and the most important friend of Bataille,[11] was Maurice Blanchot. After a brief period as fascist propagandist (see chapter 2), Blanchot's writings of the 1940s show a reading of Hegel—and a concomitant reading of death—that in many ways are close to Bataille's Hegel.[12]

Blanchot, like Bataille, sees in Nietzsche's death of God, not the mandate for a redefinition of man or freedom, but instead the opportunity for freedom to *fall*. Freedom "recognizes" itself as a negativity that has no boundaries, that cannot be used to (re)establish God.

La Négation de Dieu est donc bien liée à quelque chose de positif, mais ce positif est l'homme comme négativité sans repos, pouvoir de nier Dieu sans fin: liberté. . . .

L'effondrement infini de Dieu permet à la liberté de prendre conscience du rien qui est son fondement, sans faire de ce rien un absolu (car le néant n'est que néant de Dieu, rejet de l'absolu).

(La Part du feu, pp. 285, 287)[13]

The Negation of God is thus well tied to something positive, but this positivity is man as negativity without rest, the power to endlessly deny God: liberty. . . .

The infinite collapse of God permits liberty to become aware of the nothing that is its foundation, without making this nothing an absolute (for nothingness is only the nothingness of God, the rejection of the absolute).

This is a movement that is quite reminiscent of the movement of the dialectic in Bataille: "liberty" becomes "aware" of itself, but instead of attaining in the process some positive knowledge, it only attains its own nothingness.

When Blanchot rewrites Hegel, however, we see more clearly how Blanchot differs from Bataille and from Kojève. Blanchot sees the movement of the master/slave dialectic as the most fundamental movement in Hegel's philosophy. Blanchot, in his seminal 1949 essay "La Littérature et le droit à la mort" ["Literature and the Right to Death"],[14] first sees the possibility that a work of literature, a book, might be like the labor of the slave in the master/slave dialectic in that it "réalise l'être en le niant et le révèle au terme de la négation" (305; 33) ["realizes being in denying it, and reveals it at the end of the negation"]. But it soon becomes clear that the writer of "imaginary" fiction in his "mastery," in his writing a book, masters everything "immediately," and in this way "il discrédite, par cette action, toute action, en substituant au monde des choses détermineés et du travail défini un monde où tout est tout de suite donné et rien n'est à faire qu'à en jouir par la lecture" (307; 35) ["he is also discrediting all action by this action, because he is substituting for the world of determined things and defined work a world in which *everything* is *instantly* given and there is nothing left to do but read it and enjoy it"]. Everything, immediately, implies not the useful labor and the self-objectification of the slave, but the implacable and abrupt appearance of death.

Blanchot goes on to note that Hegel, in a work anterior to the *Phenomenology*, had written of Adam's naming of the animals as an "annihilation" of them "in their existence" (312; 42). Blanchot, pushing Hegel beyond Hegel, sees this "annihilation" in language as a death that precisely cannot be utilized or put to work: "la mort parle en moi. Ma parole est l'avertissement que la mort est, en ce moment, lachée dans le monde" (313; 43) ["death speaks in me. My speech is a warning that at this very moment death is loose in the world"]. This death or negativity is in fact not only "loose in the world," but is in some sense anterior to the formation of language as well, even when it is a word that is "un moment de l'anonymat universelle, une affirmation brute, la stupeur du face à face au fond de l'obscuriteé" (317; 47) ["one moment in the universal anonymity, a bald statement, the stupor of a confrontation in the depths of obscurity"]. Significantly enough, this literature as literature is deanthropomorphized; it comes both before and after man: "elle [la littérature] est la présence des choses, avant que le monde ne soit, leur persévérance après que le monde a disparu" (317; 46) ["it (literature) is the presence of things before the world exists, their perseverance after the world has disappeared, the stubbornness of what remains when everything vanishes"].

This deanthropomorphization, similar in some respects to the movement of writing in Ponge, is nevertheless quite different from Bataille's transgressive "end of history."[15] Blanchot grounds this radicality entirely in literature and language; the political aspect that so concerned Bataille (in his rewriting of Kojève's Marxist Hegel) has been lost. Hegel's problem of the "slave's" labor immediately becomes, for Blanchot, the problem of the labor of the author writing a book; "death" for Hegel becomes for Blanchot first death in language, and then pre- and posthuman (non)existence as literature.

In fact what distinguishes Blanchot's reading of Nietzsche and Hegel from that of Bataille is not so much Blanchot's move to depoliticize their interaction, but rather his attempt to see Nietzsche and Hegel complementing each other. For Blanchot, Nietzsche's "liberty" grasps its foundation in nothingness; Hegel's conception of language points to a death behind—and in front of—all language. If Hegel and Nietzsche are in some ways pointing to similar problems, then there is no automutilation in a Nietzsche/Hegel entity rewritten in Blanchot's text. Put another way, Blanchot as Nietzsche/Hegel is not a doubling of philosophies as automutilation, but rather the affirmation of a single philosophy, albeit one that affirms transgression in and through literature and language.[16] In Blanchot, Hegel and Nietzsche no longer disrupt each other, with Hegel supplying a constructive social model of knowledge that Nietzsche disrupts, or with Nietzsche providing a pure disruption that Hegel disrupts with a constructive social model of knowledge; instead they become strangely alike, with both presenting a negativity that orbits language and literature.

Thus the loss of a political moment in Blanchot is a function of a loss of a Hegel and a Nietzsche who cannot be simply set aside or bracketed, or seen as minor.[17] If, on the other hand, neither Hegel nor Nietzsche in his negativity could be set aside, the result would be an automutilation as political moment—political even in its reflexively impossible refusal of constructive politics.

In turning to Derrida and Foucault at this point, we will want to see not only how they continue the reading of Hegel and Nietzsche put forward by Bataille and Blanchot (in opposition to the existentialists), but how they rewrite the political problem inherent in the Hegel/Nietzsche opposition. This is an important undertaking, for it will give us some insight into the vexed problem of the "politics" of Derrida and Foucault: we may, in fact, want to reconsider the usual classification of Derrida as somehow "apolitical," in contrast to the "political" Foucault.

II

Sartre, writing immediately after the war,[18] declared that Bataille's—and by implication Blanchot's—concerns were essentially outmoded products of the prewar period. According to Sartre, interest in myth and sacrifice would be replaced in the postwar period with a more vital and "constructive" concern with "engagement." But when Derrida and Foucault started writing in earnest in the early 1960s, it became clear that Bataille and Blanchot were more than a dead fad: Derrida's invocation of Hegel and Nietzsche clearly owes more to Bataille and Blanchot than it does to the existentialists. In an early critique of structuralism—a 1964 review of Jean Rousset's *Forme et signification*, entitled "Force et signification"—Derrida affirms a Nietzschean force over the structuralists' concern with form: "La *forme* fascine quand on n'a plus la force de comprendre la force en son dedans" (11; 4) ["Form fascinates when one no longer has the force to understand force from within itself"].[19] But Derrida is not affirming a force outside the context of any other philosophy, nor is he affirming it as an absolute, sufficient unto itself. To do so would be to reaffirm force as a simple philosophical concept, albeit one that replaces other philosophical concepts. The net result of this move would be to make Nietzsche another philosopher, proffering yet another concept in the marketplace of intellectual history. Instead, Derrida sees this force as a movement of interference, working in the interstices of other philosophical movements, doubling them and undermining them. It is a force "se propageant à travers tout le système, le fissurant dans tous les sens et en le *dé-limitant* de part en part" (34; 20) ["that spreads itself throughout the entire system, fissuring it in every direction and thoroughly *delimiting* it"].

In this *force* we can clearly see Derrida's method of reading, which avoids the simple positing of new philosophical concepts, and which instead *reads* the work of other philosophers and "sees" to what extent the elements that those philosophers refuse return to both make possible and undermine their systems.[20] Thus certain terms used by Derrida—like "écriture" or "différance"—are not positive concepts, but rather are nonconcepts that are necessary and impossible in the systems of others. To try to escape metaphysics by elaborating a new concept would be as "metaphysical" as straightforwardly elaborating another metaphysics. The alternative is to *double* metaphysical systems, never simply "escaping" them, but subverting them by repeating them.

This is clearly a strategy that is "inherited" from Bataille, although what is inherited is the subversion of simple inheritance or dialectical filiation. Bataille does not "escape" Hegel, for that would itself be an eminently dialectical move; instead Nietzsche doubles Hegel in Bataille, "producing" at the end of history a "non-savoir" that parodies and reverses absolute knowledge, without simply escaping or refusing it.

In his reading of Bataille, "De l'économie restreinte à l'économie générale" ["From Restricted to General Economy"],[21] Derrida reads Bataille's repetition of Hegel. In our reading of Derrida, we must attempt to understand not only what Derrida affirms in Bataille, but also what he strips from him.

Derrida's reading of Bataille is one of the few places where Derrida confronts Sartre. He does not do so directly, however; instead he cites Sartre's critique of Bataille ("Un Nouveau mystique" ["A New Mystic"], in *Situations I*) at a number of points where his reading goes directly against Sartre's. These quotes from Sartre are given in footnotes as if to emphasize the weakness of the Sartrean reading of Bataille—and hence of Hegel. In opposition to Sartre's reading there is, by implication, the crucial importance of Bataille's reading of Hegel and now of Derrida's reading of Bataille, bringing to "light" what Sartre chose to obscure or confuse.[22]

The passages cited from Sartre (see *L'Ecriture et la différence*, pp. 377, 382, 393, 394, 395; *Writing and Difference*, pp. 335 and 336, notes 11, 16, 28, 30, 31) all indicate that, for Sartre, Bataille was simply a Hegelian ("Mais le rire est ici le *négatif*, au sens Hegelien" [377; 335] ["But laughter, here, is the *negative*, in the Hegelian sense"]) or an anti-Hegelian ("De la trinité Hégélienne, il [Bataille] supprime le moment de la synthèse" [382; 335] ["Of the Hegelian trinity, he (Bataille) suppresses the moment of synthesis"]). Bataille according to Sartre is either falsely scientific when he attempts to see transgression at work in history (394, note 1; 336, note 30) or deluded when he thinks his own experience of "non-savoir" cannot be situated in history (395, note 1; 336, note 31). Sartre can only conceive of Bataille as one who unwittingly situates himself in a dialectic, and who dishonestly attempts to escape from a dialectic; in either case Bataille refuses the freedom one must recognize and the responsibility one must take when one sees oneself in a historical dialectic.

Derrida does not accuse Bataille of attempting to "escape" from the movement of history or of attempting to posit a reified mystical negativity; instead, he sees Bataille *as* Hegel, repeating him, but somehow situating a nonrecuperable negativity at the very points of articulation of the Hegelian system:

La réinterpretation est une répétition simulée du discours hégélien. Au cours de cette répétition, un déplacement à peine perceptible disjoint toutes les soudeurs du discours imité. Un tremblement se propage qui fait alors craquer toute la vieille coque. (382; 260)

Reinterpretation is a simulated repetition of Hegelian discourse. In the course of this repetition a barely perceptible displacement disjoints all the articulations and penetrates all the points welded together by the imitated discourse. A trembling spreads out which then makes the entire old shell crack.

But what happens once this "trembling," this "disjunction," takes place? Between the realms of sense and sheer non-sense—between the two totally hostile extremes—there is a space of transgression, of "sovereignty." Derrida explicitly associates this "neutral space" of incompatibility with Bataille's "general economy" (the theory of economy put forward in *La Part maudite*, in which wealth is expended rather than conserved). For Derrida, however, the really determining, overarching (non)concept of this general economy is in fact *writing*. "Major" *writing* impossibly links the dialectic with the completely adialectical realm of non-sense; as rewriting it deconstructs the Hegelian dialectic, putting discourse *in rapport* with absolute non-discourse:

L'espace qui sépare la logique de maîtrise et, si l'on veut, la non-logique de souveraineté . . . devra s'inscrire dans l'enchaînement ou le fonctionnement d'une écriture. *Cette* écriture—majeure—s'appelera *écriture* parce qu'elle *excède* le *logos* (du sens, de la maîtrise, de la presence, etc.). (392; 267)

The space which separates the logic of lordship and, if you will, the nonlogic of sovereignty . . . will have to be inscribed within the continuous chain (or functioning) of a form of writing. This—major—writing will be called *writing* because it *exceeds* the *logos* (of meaning, lordship, presence, etc.)

This "major" writing brings us back again to the text we are reading and rewriting, and away from the crucial problem of the status of the dialectic to be deconstructed (i.e., which dialectic is to be deconstructed—the idealist or the materialist?), and the political and social consequences of that deconstruction. If we deconstruct an idealist dialectic of "sense," we need not worry about the social or political consequences of that deconstruction. But if we consider the deconstruction of a materialist dialectic (since Bataille was a Marxist as well as a Hegelian), we must ask ourselves what the *material* manifestation of the dialectic's deconstruction will be: a question calling for the writing of a utopia if there ever was one. That is the sort of question Bataille himself incessantly posed, from the earliest Marxist texts[23] to the later essays on Stalinism and its limits.[24]

Derrida therefore changes the priorities of Bataille's project when he sees "une révolution qui réorganiserait seulement le monde de travail et redistribuerait les valeurs dans l'espace de sens" (397, note 1; 337, note 33) ["a revolution which would only recognize the world of work and would redistribute values within the space of meaning"] as only a "phase" in the "strategy of the general economy" (a "general economy" that Derrida equates with a "general writing"). This is not to say that Bataille is exclusively concerned with the "world of work," but rather that he is concerned with opening out the world—and the materialist dialectic—of work to non-sense, and prefiguring as a utopia the neutral space (of mutilation) between the realms of work and non-sense. By relegating the social and political world of work to the status of a soon superseded "phase" in a general economy, and by seeing Bataille's attempt at transgressing that world of work in the fifth (and final) part of *La Part maudite* as simply "brouillé" (397, note 1; 337, note 33) ["muddled"]—and then by shifting from a notion of a "general economy" to one of a "general writing"—Derrida has made a decision *not* to read certain of Bataille's texts and to highlight others (Derrida discusses "écriture" in Bataille's *Méthode de méditation* "De l'économie restreinte . . . —see 391; 266). But Derrida provides no justification derived from Bataille for this refusal to read. In short, the problem of the simultaneous repetition of Nietzsche and Marx-Hegel here remains unexamined. (This, however, is not to say that the problem of writing in Bataille should be ignored, but only that it should be seen in conjunction with, and in implacable opposition to, social, economic, and political transgression.)

In an essay written some twelve years after the one on Bataille, Derrida comes to the point of confronting the problem of the deconstruction of a social order grounded in an absolute knowledge. In this essay—on Blanchot's *La Folie du jour* [*Madness of the Day*][25]—it seems at first that Derrida considers more directly the consequences of the "death" of not only "man," but of the scientific, political, and sexual hierarchies that man has used to construct himself.

In many ways Derrida's essay, entitled "La Loi du genre" ["The Law of Genre"][26] and first presented at a conference devoted to the theory of genre in 1979, puts forward a number of themes by now familiar to readers of Bataille and Blanchot. Above all the reading of *La Folie du jour* is concerned with underscoring the transgression of the limits of the law—most notably the laws that establish the independence and legitimacy of various genres of writing (and not necessarily "literary" genres), the law of the clear distinction between sexual genders ("genre" in French is also "gender"), and the law of the autonomy of the text itself, the clear separation between contents and title, the legal (copyright) status of that title, etc.

Blanchot's "récit" is about a man (the narrator) who, having almost lost his sight, is treated in a medical institution by specialists who are also representatives of the law and who then require from the narrator an account— a "récit"—of what happened to him (188; 216). This the narrator is incapable of—so he tells us, at least, in a récit that affirms his total inability to write récits. This "mise-en-abîme" (see p. 190; 218) is a situation in which the first-person narrator ("je") *as* the narrative voice of récits both engenders the law and legal writing (they too are based on récits) and violates them, eluding their power. Derrida writes of the medical-legal specialists:

Or voici le paradoxe essentiel: d'ou tiennent-ils, et de qui, ce pouvoir, leur pouvoir-voir qui leur permet de disposer de "moi"? Eh bien de "moi," du sujet plutôt qui leur est asujetti. C'est le "je" sans "je" de la voix narrative, le je "dépouillé" de lui-même, celui qui n'a pas lieu, c'est lui qui leur donne le jour, qui engendre ces hommes de loi en leur donnant à voir ce qui les regarde et ne devrait pas les regarder. (196; 224)

Now herein lies the essential paradox: from where and from whom do they derive this power, this right-to-sight that permits them to have "me" at their disposal? Well, from "me," rather from the subject who is subjected to them. It is the "I"-less "I" of the narrative voice, the "I" stripped of itself, the one that does not take place, it is he who brings them to light, who engenders these lawmen in giving them insight into what regards them and what should not regard them.

In Blanchot's récit, the narrator, when examined by the men of science and law, thus violates their law and eludes their grasp. Blanchot's narrator states:

Sous leurs yeux en rien étonnés, je devenais une goutte d'eau, une tache d'encre. Je me réduisais à eux-mêmes, je passais tout entier sous leur vue, et quand enfin, n'ayant plus présente que ma parfaite nullité et n'ayant plus rien à voir, ils cessaient aussi de me voir, très irrités, ils se levaient en criant: Eh bien, où etes-vous? Où vous cachez-vous? Se cacher est interdit, c'est une faute, etc. (197; 224)

Under their unblinking gaze, I became a water drop, an ink blot. I was shrinking into them, I was held entirely in their view and when, finally, they no longer had anything but my perfect nullity present and no longer had anything to see, they, too, ceased to see me, most annoyed, they rose, shouting: Well, where are you? Where are you hiding? Hiding is prohibited, it is a misdeed, etc.

It is the narrative voice, then, that both generates the law (as récit) and violates it, maintains it while going beyond it, transgressing it, and eluding it. The violation of that law would seem to be much more specific here than in Derrida's reading of Bataille: Derrida writes of the disturbance of the legalistic "psy-" doctors (who demand of the patient a coherent narration, a récit) and of the unity of the "I think" that they command (198; 225).

This may seem similar to Foucault's historical and political critiques of legalized power, but Derrida precisely avoids the kind of specific detail that has made Foucault's analyses of power institutions so influential. In Derrida's reading, the transgression of some laws can be represented more clearly than others; the law of the text itself is the comprehensive "law of the law": "le mot 'jour', en son abîme disséminal, c'est la loi, la loi de la loi" (199; 227) ["the word 'day', in its disseminal abyss, is law, the law of the law"]. The very title of Blanchot's récit—*La*

Folie du jour—indicates the importance of this narrative "day" in which law and its night are engendered, and which leads to a kind of metalaw that is also transgressive madness.

Il n'y a pas de folie sans la loi, on ne peut penser la folie que depuis la folie, par rapport à la loi: c'est la loi, c'est une folie, la loi. (200; 228)

There is no madness without the law; madness cannot be conceived before its relation to law. Madness is law, the law is madness.

These terms enter into a "dissemination," reversing into each other, violating and engendering one another. Even the dialectic as law is engendered by the narrative "I," only to be violated by it:

Tout est récit et rien ne l'est, la sortie hors du récit reste dans le récit sur un mode non-inclusif et cette structure est si peu dialectique qu'elle inscrit la dialectique dans l'ellipse du récit. (191; 219)

All is account [récit] and nothing is; the acount's out-gate remains within the account in a noninclusive mode, and this structure is itself related so remotely to a dialectical structure that it even inscribes dialectics in the account's ellipse.

Yet in the "ellipse" of the text some terms are more privileged than others. The invisible but omnipresent *narrative* "I" engenders and transgresses law, but there is a difference between the law of genres, the law of the boundaries of the text, and the law of the medical and psychiatric police. The law of genres and texts seems to enter into this vast Möbius strip of engenderment and violation, but civil and psychiatric law does not. Derrida privileges one type of law and sets aside the other. He does not consider, within the récit or outside of it, what the consequences are of the violation of civil and psychiatric law; instead, he incessantly considers the consequences of the violation of the limits of the récit. This is the law engendered by Derrida's text; a law of selection and exclusion, the one law that is not violated within his text. It is, ironically enough, Blanchot who is here more forceful than Derrida, because he at least imagines, in his récit, the astonishment of the scientists and investigators as their subject matter evaporates before their very eyes. But Derrida's subject matter—the récit—never evaporates before him; instead, it always reappears, inescapable and all-inclusive, even (and above all) in its noninclusiveness ("the account's out-gate remains within the account in a noninclusive mode"). We could stand Derrida's "mise-en-abîme" on its head and state that it is the all-inclusive yet noninclusive social and political law—which cannot be reduced to a transcendent narrative voice, the "I" or eye—that generates Derrida and that evaporates under his clinical gaze. This is not to say that this material law and its effects, its economy, cannot be transgressed or does not engender its own transgression; it is only to say that Derrida, as the embodiment of the law of the récit and its examination, must be blind to the larger laws and transgressions that have given birth to him. Part of the text does a disappearing act under his eye, and the very absoluteness of the all-inclusive noninclusiveness of his analysis puts him in complicity with the straw men (doctors, psychiatrists, police) of Blanchot's récit.

We find ourselves in a strange situation: the texts that "engendered" Derrida—Bataille and Blanchot—find their law in him (more clearly enunciated than in their own texts, else why would Derrida write?) but at the same time they escape and transgress him. He consistently holds up what is to be the *true* concern of their text (above all, when the very notion of truth is violated), in opposition to other elements that may be "weak" or "muddled" and are therefore not worthy of consideration (as in the case of Bataille's presentation and critique of the Marshall Plan in *La Part maudite*);[27] but those very elements, those concerns with the violation of the "laws" of societal and economic models, *return* to violate Derrida's law. Derrida, repeating Bataille, might infect Hegel with Nietzsche, but he refuses even to consider the problem of infecting Marx with Nietzsche, or himself with Marx. Certainly Derrida "inherits" this privileging of language, of textuality, and perhaps even of writing, from Blanchot.[28] Even Blanchot, however, returns to the problems of State power (as in *Le Très-Haut*) or scientific or legal power (as in *La Folie du jour*), if only once again to exile them.

Thus the violence of nonrecuperable and "empty" (Nietzschean) negativity is kept within textual bounds in Derrida, even when those bounds are presented as "noninclusive," and even (and especially) when the notion of textuality implies a simultaneous but incompatible movement of material loss.

But what of Foucault? Does he not attempt to link a Nietzschean conception of force to a critique of the concentration of power in societal, political, and philosophical institutions? Can we not see in his critique of humanism and the modes of discourse associated with it an attempt to deal with the problems that Derrida avoids?

III

We have already seen, in our consideration of Foucault's writing on Blanchot (see chapter 2) and Roussel (chapter 3) the somewhat strange fact that Foucault, so well known for his analyses of social, political, and scientific institutions and their histories,[29] does his utmost to *avoid* such readings when he turns his attention to literature. The fractures and disruptions of language as read by Foucault are neither engendered by, nor point to, specific political or social conjunctions. Instead, language turns on its own impossibilities, reflecting to infinity the impossibility of a perfectly faithful reflection on the part of a transcendent writing subject. Foucault's reading of Bataille, "Préface à la transgression,"[30] manifests similar concerns. In this essay, Foucault stresses the idea, developed in works by Bataille such as *L'Erotisme* and *La Part maudite*, that transgression in any culture ("primitive" or modern) or economy cannot be seen as completely escaping, or existing independently of, the limits of law and discourse. Foucault, however, situates this transgression not within and against the articulation points of a Hegelian-Marxist dialectic, but within and against the limits of a literary and philosophical language. Transgression replaces dialectical contradiction (767; 50); Bataille's language transgresses itself.

Ainsi ce langage [de Bataille] de rochers, ce langage incontournable auquel rupture, escarpement, profil déchiré sont essentiels, est un langage circulaire qui renvoie à lui-même et se replie sur une mise en question de ses limites. (762; 44)

Essentially the product of fissures, abrupt descents, and broken contours, [Bataille's] misshapen and craglike language describes a circle; it refers to itself and is folded back on a questioning of its limits.

Indeed even sexuality itself, that crucial problem for Foucault, is finally absorbed in a language, in the "spoken" (but not necessarily in writing).

La sexualité n'est décisive pour notre culture que parlée et dans la mesure où elle est parlée. Ce n'est pas notre langage qui a été, depuis bientôt deux siecles, érotisé; c'est notre sexualité qui depuis Sade et la mort de Dieu a été ábsorbé dans l'univers de langage, dénaturalisée par lui, placée par lui dans ce vide où il établit sa souveraineté et où sans cesse il pose, comme Loi, des limites qu'il transgresse. (767; 50)

Sexuality is only decisive for our culture as spoken and to the degree it is spoken. It is not that our language has been eroticized now for nearly two centuries; rather, since Sade and the death of God, the universe of language has absorbed our sexuality, denatured it, placed it in a void where it establishes its sovereignty and where it incessantly sets up as the Law the limits it transgresses.

Only by becoming language can sexuality be more—or other—than simple reproduction. It seems that once again we confront a situation in which language and its disruptions absorb everything, leaving concrete legal, social, and historical problems literally without any status at all.

Foucault clarifies the connections between language and the "material" sociohistorical realms in his essay *L'Ordre du discours* [*The Discourse on Language*], given as his inaugural lecture at the Collège de France in 1970.[31] Language here is presented as "discourse," that is, as all the various societal language practices and most specifically the various discourses that lay claim to scientific truth. In a move that owes much to Nietzsche's notion of "ressentiment" (a resentment that "refuses" force or power only hypocritically to channel it and use it for its own ends against the forceful or powerful), and to Gilles Deleuze's reading of Nietzsche,[32] Foucault stresses the "volonté de vérité" ["will to truth"] in the modern sciences. This will to truth seemingly exiles desire and power, yet it uses them ever more forcefully to exile the very terror and enunciatory power which, according to Foucault, characterized the "ritual" truth of the sixth-century B.C. Greek poets (17; 218). Foucault in his own work clearly wants to give us a modern version of this primitive ritual truth, which was beyond good and evil; his own methodology, recognizing chance, discontinuity, and materiality (61; 231) becomes a discursive event rather than an eternal verity.

This discontinuous discursive power, which by its very nature cannot be totalized, utilized, or separated from a unique event, inevitably questions the "will to truth" when that truth desires to justify interdiction and define madness. Certain authors, such as Nietzsche, Artaud, and Bataille (23; 220) are among the first to turn the "will to truth" against itself in their language.

Discourse is thus more than just "language"; it must be seen as "ensembles d'événements" ["ensembles of events"], and the event is *not* immaterial to the extent that "c'est toujours au niveau de la matérialité qu'il prend effet, qu'il est effet" (59; 231) ["it takes effect, becomes effect, always on the level of materiality"]. Thus the disruptions of Nietzsche or Bataille are not limited to an isolated sphere of language, because *as* discontinuous discursive events they "remould" the larger material consequences of the "will to truth."

And yet this is all somehow unsatisfying. Questions inevitably arise: given the undermining of this unfortunate "will to truth" and its effects, what social formations will arise in their wake? And if the modern writing Foucault affirms is subversive on a social and cultural level as well as on a purely literary one, why do Foucault's readings strive so hard to exile any recognition of the social or political problems refused or worked out in those texts? Might not these texts be utopian, and somehow indicate or betray the direction a future society is to take?

Foucault, in a 1971 interview with a group of high school students,[33] provides some possible answers to these questions. When a student asks the obvious question: "What replaces the system?" (230), Foucault refuses to authorize any other system, any other social manifestation of a "will to truth": "I think that to imagine another system is to extend our participation in the present system." In other words, a social experiment that attempts to substitute one system for another will simply extend the tyranny; this happened in the 1920s in the Soviet Union. The "effects" of Nietzschean discontinuity and fragmentation preclude all systematization. And theory—as in a social or philosophical utopia—must be discarded along with the system:

It is possible that the rough outline of a future society is supplied by the recent experiences with drugs, sex, communes, other forms of consciousness, and other forms of individuality. If scientific socialism emerged from the *Utopias* of the nineteenth century, it is possible that a real socialization will emerge, in the twentieth century, from *experiences*. (231)

Despite the fact that he denies it, however, Foucault is still presenting a utopia here;[34] there is still a model of a social system, and a rather banal one at that. The revolutionary discontinuous drives of "experiences," and the concomitant destruction of the notion of "man," turn out to be nothing other than the absolute knowledge of hippie liberalism.[35]

Our statements here should not be construed as a denial of the importance of Foucault's analyses—especially in books such as *Surveiller et punir* [*Discipline and Punish*]—but instead only as a questioning of the system of positive values inherent in his work. (Indeed why should we accept uncritically any collection of values, no matter how benign it might be?) That Foucault precisely *denies* that there are any overarching values only intensifies the problem. It can be argued that a close reading of certain of Foucault's writings would reveal, through the very space left by its excision, a perfectly coherent morality, which only appears explicitly in Foucault's "informal" statements (such as interviews). An analysis of Foucault's work would first have to consider in detail these statements.[36]

At this point we must question whether Foucault's entire project is not—in spite of appearances to the contrary—simply a repetition of the Hegelian movement of history. In works such as *Les Mots et les choses* [*The Order of Things*], Foucault would relegate the Hegelian diachronic conception of history to a specific niche within European history; the changeover in "epistemes" replaces the dialectical "Aufhebung" and the very possibility of a totalizing "will to truth"—or absolute knowledge—is apparently discarded. Yet at the same time Foucault proposes new names for a final absolute break in history and knowledge: they are Nietzsche, Artaud, and Bataille.[37] Discourse as event is self-transgressing; but it is complacent in its own transgression, and Foucault never foresees how it might itself be transgressed by elements heterogeneous to it. Foucault's new history, then, may very well be as absolute and as inexorable as Hegel's, and even more so because it owes so much to a conception of a discontinuous history going beyond Bachelard's and Canguilhem's: a history not of production but of sacrifice, madness, and excess, put forward by Bataille in *La Part maudite*. (Bataille's method can be "used"—but only at the cost of making it simply *useful*.) Most important for Foucault now are sexuality, madness, and the force that exceeds legal systems and prisons; the disruptions of modern literature are finally relatively minor by comparison ("I am referring to all those experiences which have been rejected by our civilization *or which it accepts only within literature*" [*Language, Counter-Memory, Practice*, p. 222; italics added]).[38]

It may be that what presents itself as a thoroughly Nietzschean project may be (and may have been all along) a completely Hegelian one. While invoking Nietzsche, Foucault nevertheless strips him from his system; the difficulties of Bataille's Hegel—who was both impossible to escape and yet who opened out to non-sense in the very articulation point where the *Aufhebung* reigned supreme—are not to be found in Foucault.[39] Those difficulties, as we saw in the interpenetration of Hegel and Nietzsche in Bataille, took the form of the automutilation of the Nietzsche/Hegel-Marx philosophical, social, and textual combine. Yet that automutilation, and that betrayal, is a long way from Foucault's stable utopia of "drugs, sex, [and] communes."

This, finally, may explain why literature in Foucault is read completely outside the context of social and political conflict, and why (as in the interview with the students) it turns out to be very minor. What Foucault strips from the writings of authors such as Bataille and Blanchot—and especially Bataille—is not the inscription of politics in their texts but the internal textual and political violence that is re-presented there. Foucault may be capable of deriving a coherent model of defiant "events" from his system, but he is incapable of re-presenting how such events would themselves be defied or betrayed.[40] This, as we have seen a number of times, is the significance of automutilation in writers like Bataille or Blanchot: it is not so much the betrayal of reactionary systems that is important in their works, but instead *the betrayal of progressive systems that attempt to incorporate or somehow recognize or utilize automutilation or betrayal* that is really crucial—and really trivial, aborted, and abject.

For very different reasons, Foucault and Derrida perform the same operation on the texts of Bataille and Blanchot: in either case the various consequences of political, social, and textual automutilation are avoided. Those consequences, however, and that automutilation, always return to haunt Foucault's and Derrida's readings. Derrida and Foucault thus cannot be said to have been simply "influenced" by Bataille or Blanchot, nor do they simply continue in a dialectical history or "tradition." Instead, they repeat and double Blanchot and Bataille, while at the same time they violently forget a part of the earlier writers' texts. That cursed part here returns—in this text: it is the remainder that cannot remain unread. This may still be a dialectical relation, with its temporality and extension; but it is a dialectic with the difference of a mutilation.

As we have seen, Blanchot is not willing to recognize this problem of textual and political conflict to the same extent as Bataille. We noted that the tendency on Derrida's part to privilege "writing" is something that is probably traceable to Blanchot.

What is needed, then, is a theory of reading that recognizes and analyzes this automutilation and its refusal. Our theory will not see itself as *above* automutilation, turning out a master plan that writes the truth of "écriture" or Nietzschean power or language. On the contrary: not only will it be impossibly cognizant of its own fissured political status, but it will read in other texts the spaces and silences in which the fissure of textual/political conflict that it repeats is silenced. That silencing is for us *ideology*, whether we are analyzing it in "primary" "literary" texts (as in the works of Bataille, Blanchot, Roussel, Leiris, and Ponge), or in "secondary" texts that strip from the "primary" ones the mutilation that can be read through them (as in Derrida and Foucault).

The method of reading that we are proposing, and whose outlines we will sketch in the following chapter, will owe much to Althusserian critics (Macherey, Marin, Eagleton, Jameson), because they attempt to read in the unknowable or unwriteable "utopian" spaces of works a political unconscious. But we will differ from their approach in that we will never lose "sight" of the doubleness of our own repulsive commentary, of the extent to which, as ideology or utopia, it incessantly infects and invalidates itself. In other words, we cannot forget the heterogeneity of Bataille's Nietzsche.

Chapter Eight
Reading Avant-Garde Utopias

Avant-garde utopias—as we have seen in our readings of Bataille, Blanchot, Roussel, Leiris, and Ponge—are concerned less with the formulation of specific guidelines and elaborate plans for a society in which all misfortune will be banished (the kind of utopia Marx excoriated) than they are with attempting in some way to envisage the implementation of a radical negativity (or evil) in society, and the role of a transformed *writing* in that implementation. This is not to say that on some level all the texts we are concerned with do not work to repress or refuse the political consequences of this implementation. Even if only negatively, they allow us to read the problem of a future society or social experience built around negativity, and the role of writing in the consitution and obfuscation of that future. Needless to say, these concerns are quite different from what we would expect to find in the more "classical" utopias of More, Campanella, or Fourier.

It is perhaps significant that the most rigorous analysis of utopias, Louis Marin's *Utopiques: jeux d'espaces* [*Utopias: Plays of Spaces*],[1] analyzes primarily Renaissance utopias: More's *Utopia*, as well as various seventeenth-century maps. When he comes to contemporary utopias—Disneyland, the vertical cities of Xenakis—Marin labels them "degenerate" (*Utopiques*, 256). Because Marin is writing as a Marxist, and Marxists necessarily criticize utopias as unscientific,[2] he sees these contemporary utopias as simple products of ideology, whereas the earlier ones, in Marin's view, are battlegrounds of conflicting ideologies and are,

124

at the same time, latent critiques of the reigning social and class configurations. Marxism has established the fundamental laws of economic and social change; therefore, utopias formulated today are simply *wrong*.

Yet if we consider Marin's basic argument—and his revisions of that argument—we will see that the repressed aspect of his own text is precisely an avant-garde utopia that is not "degenerate" (in Marin's sense of the term, at least): when investiaged, it will allow us better to understand the forces at play in the utopias analyzed in the preceding chapters.

We cannot hope to examine the complexities of Marin's analysis of More's *Utopia* here. Instead, we will only try to reflect on the theoretical grounding of the notions of "utopia" or the "neutral space" in Marin, how those notions are seen as ideological, how they are critical, and finally, the subject of their critique.

The utopian or neutral space as first outlined by Marin is an alogical and adialectical space—"ni être ni néant, ni négation ni affirmation" (*Utopiques*, 45) ["neither being nor nothingness, neither negation nor affirmation"]; it is a "self-reflexive" space to the extent that it calls attention to the impossibility of its own representation—("C'est . . . la 'réflexion' de la figure sur elle-même . . . une référence sans référent" (145) ["It is . . . the reflection of the figure upon itself . . . a reference without referent"].

As it is elaborated at the beginning of *Utopiques*, through a reading of Husserl's commentary on an engraving by Dürer (42–3), this reflexive utopian space seems to be a challenge not only to the law of contradiction, but to the very possibility of a philosophy grounded on utility: "La modification de la croyance que cherche à isoler Husserl ne biffe pas, n'agit pas, 'elle est pour la conscience tout le contraire d'une action: elle en est la neutralisation.' Sa puissance consiste à *enlever* la force propre de n'importe quelle position" (46) ["The modification of belief that Husserl tries to isolate does not cross out, does not act: 'for consciousness, it is the opposite of action; it is the neutralization of it.' Its strength consists of *taking away* the force of any given position"].

The backbone of Marin's reading of More, however, is a political and ideological critique: the "neutral space" is now read through a methodology (Marxism) that is very far indeed from a "neutralization" incapable of logically consistent acts. In a sense Marin puts this "neutrality" to work by harnessing it to a Marxist analysis. In More (according to Marin) the "neither/nor" of the utopian/neutral space is a refusal both of the declining feudal configurations of More's time, and of the ascending capitalist structures of the period. The utopian space here is not simply a reflection of the ideology of the day, or even of the ideological contradictions of the day; rather it is an attempt at working out a solution to those contradictions.[3] The neutral space becomes a blind spot of the text, an irreducible gap, to the extent that it is where the contradictions within and between ideologies would be resolved—but where this resolution cannot take place, precisely because More lacks a scientific method (Marxism).

Thus Marin is uninterested in seeing More's utopia, or any utopia, as a possible configuration that in some way could be "implemented" in "reality." Instead, his interest lies in reading the utopia as a critical tool that reveals the interaction of reigning ideologies through their incoherencies. Hence the "neither/nor" aspect of the utopia, and its "self-reflexive" status: it is neither one ideology nor another, and it is more than a simple ideology because it can be used as a critical tool that, when read from a position that is aware of the utopia's historical and political position (i.e., Marin's own metatext), can indicate "les instruments conceptuels théoriques permettant de penser [les] contradictions" (255) ["the conceptual theoretical instruments permitting one to think (the) contradictions"] between self-canceling ideological constructs.

This is not to argue, however, that the utopia is not at the same time an effort at constructing a pure, timeless ideology, a locus of ideal and impossible solutions to real problems. In Marin's analysis of More, the utopia brings about the impossible resolution of three distinct problems. First, the text obscures—by presenting its reversed image—the inscription of money and capitalist economic power within the borders of Utopia. Thus in Utopia, gold and silver are made into chamber pots and chains for prisoners rather than used as exchangeable money. Similarly, the workers of Utopia are seen to participate in a kind of reversed model of the feudal system, an "honest industry of wool" in which

Les valets d'escorte des seigneurs seront remplacés par les moutons . . . il s'agit de . . . retrouver un manoir d'un nouveau type d'où seront exclus les vices de chômage et du sous-emploi, comme ceux de la richesse et du loisir aritsocratiques. (193)

The armed valets of the lords will be replaced by sheep . . . it is a question of . . . finding a new kind of manor, from which the vices of unemployment and underemployment will be excluded, as will those of wealth and aristocratic leisure.

Thus in a period of the decline of feudalism (and the rise of capitalism) in England, when peasants were being driven off the land by aristocrats who would raise sheep for wool rather than farm, More proposes a utopia bearing the traces of occulted feudalism and capitalism.

A third conflict obscured in a utopia is the necessary split between writing and the fiction of the society it would describe, and the concomitant split between modes of representation. If a utopia can only be conceived as written product—it is a society that precisely cannot be carried out in the real—it will necessarily have to forget the traces of its writing as well (that is, until the utopian text critically calls attention to those traces through the metatext that reads it). At this point, Marin would have it that his project intersects Derrida's (30): the neutral space is a function of modes of representation that are not compatible with one another, of modes of writing that in spite of themselves refer back to their own fictionality, to their status as figures or writing—instead of simply effacing themselves before a signified that they can somehow transmit without mediation. Marin, then, can write of "la trace de la production utopique dans le produit textuel où l'utopie s'expose et se décrit" (201) ["the trace of utopian production in the textual product, where the utopia reveals itself and describes itself"]. One of these traces, these junctures, is between different and irreconcilable modes of representation: Marin devotes an important chapter of his book to the conflict between typography and illustration in the layout of seventeenth-century maps (chapter 10, "Le Portrait de la ville dans ses utopiques" ["The Portrait of the City in Its Utopias"]).

Utopias, then, are critical tools to the extent that their spaces of non-congruence call attention to their own workings as ideology. But only from a stable position can these spaces be read critically; it is the scientific basis of Marxism that allows this reading:

La force critique de la figure utopique qu'au début des temps modernes More avait dressée *dans un livre* restait efficace, même si nous disposions d'une théorie scientifique . . . qui permett[ait] . . . d'accomplir dans le concept ce qu'elle [l'utopie] retraçait pluriellement et à vide dans la figure. (48)

The critical force of the utopian figure which, at the beginning of modern times, More had worked out *in a book* remained efficacious, even if we have at our disposal a scientific theory . . . which permitted . . . us to accomplish in a concept what [utopia] retraced plurally and in a void in the figure.

But what of the very stability of the Marxist position? Marxism reflects in a "concept" what the utopia can only "laisse . . . apparaître comme manque interne . . . à sa propre cohérence" (351) ["allow . . . to appear as an internal lack . . . in its own coherence"]. To what extent, however, is the stability of the Marxist concept simply a repetition, on a dialectically higher level, of the *stability* of utopia as ideological obfuscation? We recall here the earlier reading of the neutral space in Husserl. There the "neither/nor" aspect of negation was precisely a "reference without referent," a doing away with all coherent positions (46). Now, in order to see the neutral space in action, undermining opposing positions, it is necessary for Marin to posit an ultimate coherent position, or concept.

A few years after completing *Utopiques*, Marin did a sort of autocritique in the pages of *Glyph*.[4] He could now recognize that the Marxist scientific "concept" itself was utopian to the extent that it refuses to see its own "internal gaps":

To be effective . . . a critical discourse on utopia has to lean back against the wall [against the thesis] of a final truth of history, a place from which it is formulated. But what would happen to its authority if the wall cracks and splits? . . . My critical discourse (in *Utopiques*) was formulated in terms of a topic and its fabricated utopian figure consisted in making coherent those spatial inconsistencies which the utopian image structured as a whole. . . . This production was possible only *après coup*, in a site supposed to be the true knowledge of the end of history that is the end of utopia as well. (*Glyph 1*, 52)

Perhaps I was not aware five years ago that my own discourse in the past and, in a sense, the paper I publish today are also degenerate utopias, critical myths, theoretical fantasies. (66)

Ironically, this autocritique is published along with a recapitulation of Marin's reading of the "degenerate utopia," Disneyland (chapter 12 of *Utopiques*). That critique still depends, as it did in *Utopiques*, on a position whose parameters include a Lukácsian critique of the reification of commodities and consumers ("The individual is shown to be progressively mastered, dominated by utensility" [63]). But if utopian, scientific Marxism has as a base been "shattered," how can Marin still perform the same Lukácsian-Marxist critique?

At this point, of course, we must start considering the neutral or utopian space of Marin's own discourse on utopias. Both *Utopiques* and the *Glyph* autocritique are structured around a blind spot, which in each case is situated between the same two contrary positions. In *Utopiques*, the neutral space associated with Husserl's reading of Dürer, which would seem to corrode all coherent positions, enters into conflict with the neutral space associated with Marxist analysis, which depends on the stable vantage point of a Marxist "concept." Conversely, the *Glyph* article criticizes and refuses the stability of the Marxist critical framework (and thus valorizes an all-corrosive space) but is still dependent on what is essentially a Marxist analysis.

Just as Marin recognizes the space of conflict and silence in More's text, so we recognize a similar space in Marin's. Marin, however, could move to a dialectically higher position and survey *Utopia* (to see the true significance of its silences and spaces), because he had the stability of the Marxist theoretical edifice. Similarly, if we would survey Marin's *Utopiques*, we too must move dialectically "beyond" his utopian space and survey it from a more advanced theoretical position. But this is the rub: it is the very possibility of such a stable position that we criticize in *Utopiques*, by seeing it (the stable position) as an oppositional term that is criticized (unawares) in the spaces or gaps of Marin's own work.

The position from which we analyze the utopian space of Marin's own utopia will thus necessarily be split, and it will be aware of this split: we will have a way of analyzing history, but instead of positing truth or equalization or stability as an endpoint, we will see the end of history as a moment of destructive division. Moreover, the excessive negativity of this division will be revealed as the "driving force" of history. Such an end of history is, as we have already seen in chapter 6, the utopian State that somehow recognizes "excess," posited at the end of Bataille's *La Part maudite*. This state is a self-rending negativity because it recognizes itself and constitutes itself, at the same time sundering and betraying itself, through an (impossible) awareness of a negativity that can never work to constructively elaborate history or its end, the State.

Bataille certainly saw his conception of history going beyond, but retaining the undeniably valid progress made by Marxism. Thus there is a dialectical continuity between the two approaches (Marx's and Bataille's). If, in rewriting Marin, we replace the Marxist end of history with Bataille's end of history, the neutral space in the texts we read will necessarily change as well. According to Marin, the critical neutral space in More is elaborated in the gap of conflict between capitalist and feudal ideologies: once Marxism has definitely explained the repressed aspects of these neutral spaces, any utopia subsequently written will be "degenerate," a mere symptom:

Ce discours cesse alors d'avoir la valeur anticipatrice critique . . . pour ne garder . . . qu'une valeur symptomale affinée que la théorie sociale peut exploiter pour critiquer et dénoncer l'idéologie dont il est alors le simple produit. (256)

This discourse then ceases to have any critical anticipatory value . . . only to retain . . . a refined symptomatic value that social theory can use to criticize and denounce the ideology of which it is then the simple product.

But if Marxism itself has been (dialectically) negated but maintained, contemporary utopias will be more than simple "degenerate" symptoms or products of ideology. And if Marin's analysis, from the point of view of Marxism, can see the utopian conflict as one between capitalism and feudalism, our analysis, moving one dialectical stage beyond Marin's (to Bataille's State at the end of history that "recognizes" excess), can see the conflict in contemporary utopias as one between Marxism and capitalism (or its various irrational avatars, such as fascism), between use value and mindless, destructive expenditure.

We have examined texts of this sort in this book, and our method of reading owes much to (and perverts much of) Marin's method in *Utopiques*. It is degenerate avant-garde writing that attempts to explode the pure rationalism of a future society with all that escapes it: the result may often be sinister (as in the case of Céline's pamphlets).[5] But the position or vantage point from which we write cannot offer any political or moral superiority. It is not more "human" than another position. The State that recognizes and would inevitably rationalize excess is sundered, and must (in spite of itself) face its own self-betrayal. It cannot establish itself in a region of pristine omniscience, and in this way it is different from a simple knowledge at the end of history. At the end of history, as foreseen by Bataille, dialectically nonrecuperable negativity is "recognized"— but that recognition itself is liable to be betrayed by what it impossibly recognizes.[6] In the same way, the intellectual who would "utilize" this sundered absolute knowledge will be unable to definitively lose his or her guilt. To that extent the gap between our Bataillean metatext and the avant-garde texts we read is less than the gap between Marin's Marxism and the utopianism of More. Strictly speaking our double bind rigorously repeats the one faced by these avant-garde utopias, these urtexts of deconstruction. The "ideology" we read, however, in these works comes from their refusal to recognize their own doubled positions, the betrayal and guilt of inherent negativity, and the repetitious necessity of analysis. This utopian ideology is the unwriteable space in the text that embraces types of silence (Blanchot, Ponge), or loquacity (Leiris), or various repressive fictional alternatives—the mechanization of corpses and language, for example (Roussel). These are the alternatives to self-mutilation that in the end are even more guilty than that mutilation itself, because they would suture over the mutilation and substitute a position that is violently innocent. Fascism is always the most extreme example of this tendency: there the most aggressive destruction and self-destruction (on the part of the executioner or writer) is covered over or repressed by an utterly banal and finally irrational justification. (The most extreme example of this is, again, the pamphleteering of Céline, which conceals an irresolvable struggle between Marxism and an orgiastic violence behind an insipid but hallucinatory harangue.) Yet to think that we could ever simply leave behind any guilty ideology is as utopian as the espousal of that ideology, because Marxism (or a rationalized model of any type, including Bataille's utopia, at the end of *La Part maudite*, where negativity is somehow, in the future, recognized) will always see what defies it as an irrational, fascistic betrayal—and there is no higher vantage point from which we could prove Marxism wrong and argue for our own "human" perspective. Even though our viewpoint might be "dialectically" an "advance" over Marxism, it ultimately lacks the recuperative stability of the "Aufhebung." It is a dialectical advance that recognizes, by rewriting the dialectic, a radically defiant or unrecuperable negativity. To that extent, it is both a dialectical advance over Marxism, and therefore a continuation of the rationalizing tendency of Marxism (in theory and practice), *and* a defiant betrayal of Marxism (as well as of itself) in a repetitious dyadic struggle whose negativity cannot be simply integrated or put to work. In the same instant, at a crucial point, our viewpoint is both a dialectical move and a subversion of all dialectic. At that moment, as critical doubles of Bataille, we incessantly betray our own methodology (and thus we betray Bataille). In and out of the text.

Notes

Notes

Introduction: Utopias of Conflict, Urtexts of Deconstruction

1. See Georg Lukács's *Writer and Critic*, trans. Arthur D. Kahn (New York: Grosset and Dunlap, 1971:

> In the profound pessimism of their art and ideologies, leading writers reflect capitalism's hostility to art and the general ugliness of life under capitalism. Artists and thinkers become increasingly overwhelmed by the bleakness of life in the age of imperialism. Though they represent the inhumanity of capitalism with ever-greater intensity, they no longer manifest a rebellious fury but exhibit a conscious or unconscious respect for its "monumentality." The Greek ideal of beauty disappears and is replaced by a modern orientalism or a modernized glorification of the Gothic or the baroque. Nietzsche completes the ideological transformation by pronouncing the harmonious man of Greece a myth and by transfiguring Greece and the Renaissance "realistically" into civilizations of "monumental inhumanity and bestiality." Fascism inherits these decadent tendencies of bourgeois development and adapts them to its own demagogic purposes, using them to provide an ideological rationale for its prisons and torture chambers. (101-2)

The citation is from the essay "The Ideal of the Harmonious Man in Bourgeois Aesthetics," in *Writer and Critic*. See also the essay "Healthy or Sick Art?" in the same volume:

> Any sterile, impotent opposition to the dominant social system or, rather, to certain cultural symptoms of this system must inflate and distort the concrete problem of capitalist inhumanity into a hazy, universal, "cosmic" inhumanity. And since, as we have seen, there are strong elements of capitulation in every sterile opposition, this falsely universalized, desocialized inhumanity is itself transformed into a principle of art. (108)

2. See Julia Kristeva's *La Révolution du langage poétique* [*The Revolution of Poetic Language*] (Paris: Seuil, 1974) and, for the remarks on Céline, the chapter "D'une identité l'autre" ["From One Identity to the Other"] in *Polylogue* (Paris: Seuil, 1977), especially pp. 170-71.

135

3. For Jean-Paul Sartre's remarks on Bataille, Blanchot, and Ponge, see his *Situations I* (Paris: Gallimard, 1947), pp. 113–22, 133–74, and 226–70.

4. See Jacques Derrida's article on Bataille and Hegel, "De l'économie restreinte à l'économie générale" in *L'Ecriture et la différence* (Paris: Seuil, 1967), pp. 369–407. (English translation: *Writing and Difference*, trans. A. Bass [Chicago: University of Chicago Press, 1978], pp. 251–77.) We will return to this essay in chapter 7.

5. Derrida's reading of Husserl is *La Voix et le phénomène* (Paris: P.U.F., 1967); his reading of Plato, "La Pharmacie de Platon" in *La Dissémination* (Paris: Seuil, 1972). pp. 69–197. (English translation: "Plato's Pharmacy," in *Dissemination*, trans. B. Johnson [Chicago: University of Chicago Press, 1981], pp. 61–171.)

6. See Georges Bataille's "La Pratique de la joie devant la mort" ["The Practice of Joy before Death"] in his *Oeuvres Complètes*, vol. I (Paris: Gallimard, 1970), p. 557.

7. See Michael Ryan's *Marxism and Deconstruction* (Baltimore: Johns Hopkins University Press, 1982).

Chapter 1. Politics, Mutilation, Writing

1. All references are to Georges Bataille's *Oeuvres Compètes*, 9 vol. (Paris: Gallimard, 1970–). The three essays mentioned here are in volume I, pp. 302–20, 339–71, and 277–90, respectively. The first number refers to the volume; the second to the page.

2. See Jean Wahl's *Etudes Kierkegaardiennes* [*Kierkegaardian Studies*] (Paris: Aubier, 1938). The 1930s French readings of Kierkegaard (by Jean Wahl) as well as of Heidegger and of Hegel (by Kojève) greatly influenced not only Bataille, Blanchot, and Queneau, but also Sartre.

3. All page references to Kierkegaard refer to *Either/Or*, vol. I (Princeton: Princeton University Press, 1943).

4. Citations from *Le Bleu du ciel* in English are taken from the translation by Harry Mathews, *Blue of Noon* (New York: Urizen, 1978). The page numbers of *Le Bleu du ciel* refer first to the French original in the *Oeuvres Complètes* (in vol. III), then to the Urizen Press version. I have modified Mathews's translation slightly when fidelity to the original syntax was necessitated by my argument.

5. In essays like "La Vieille taupe et le préfixe *sur* dans les mots *surhomme* et *surréaliste*" (II, 93–109) ["The Old Mole and the Prefix *sur* in the Words *surhomme* (Superman) and *Surrealist*"] (written around 1930), Bataille presents two alternative versions of explosive revolt: one is the glorious heavenward ascension of the superman and surrealist, which Bataille associates with fascism, and the other is the "low" subversive "grubbing" movement of Marx's (and Hegel's) famous mole. By the time *Le Bleu du ciel* was written, however (in 1935), the embrace of "blood and soil" had taken on distinctly unsavory overtones. *Both* alternatives, then—sky and earth—may be tainted.

Chapter 2. Blanchot and the Silence of Specificity

1. See Jeffrey Mehlman's "Blanchot at *Combat*: Of Literature and Terror," *MLN* 95, no. 4 (1980): 808–29.

2. Maurice Blanchot, *Faux pas* (Paris: Gallimard, 1943). Quotes from "De l'angoisse au langage" are taken from "From Dread to Language" in *The Gaze of Orpheus*, trans. L. Davis (New York: Station Hill, 1981), pp. 3–20. The page numbers refer first to the French original, then to the Davis translation. The translation has been modified slightly. All other translations from the works of Blanchot used in this chapter (and from all other French authors used in this book, when not attributed to a specific published translation) are by Allan Stoekl.

3. Maurice Blanchot, *Le Très-Haut* (Paris: Gallimard, 1948).

4. Michel Foucault, "La Pensée du dehors" ["The Thought of the Outside"], *Critique* 229 (1966): 523–46.

5. This convergence of nihilistic destruction and absolute knowledge in Blanchot's entropic future State is very reminiscent of Camus's vision of the identity of pointless individual violence and the systematized utilitarian violence of the State in *L'Homme révolté*; for Bataille's comments on this problem in Camus, see chapter 6. It should also be noted that *Le Très-Haut* can be read as a critique of Camus's *La Peste* (1947), another novel using the plague as a metaphor of social crisis.

6. This position is held by Foucault in "La Pensée du dehors"; see also the sections on *Le Très-Haut* in Evelyne Londyn's *Maurice Blanchot: Romancier* [*Maurice Blanchot: Novelist*] (Paris: Nizet, 1976), pp. 181–200.

7. For an exposition of the problem of "utopias" and the neutral space, see Louis Marin's *Utopiques: jeux d'espaces* (Paris: Minuit, 1973). *Utopiques* will be discussed in chapter 8.

Chapter 3. Roussel's Revivifications of History

1. Michel Foucault, *Raymond Roussel* (Paris: Gallimard, 1963). Raymond Roussel, *Comment j'ai écrit certains de mes livres* (Paris: J-J Pauvert, 1963).

2. Laurent Jenny raises a similar problem in his essay "Structure et fonctions du cliché" ["Structure and Functions of the Cliché"] (in *Poétique* 12 [1972]: 495–517). He argues that Roussel's "procedure" could not function if it did not borrow from larger cultural (and, we would add, political) codes: Roussel's presentation of the "procedure" does not, however, by itself explain why certain expressions and narratives are generated, and others are not.

3. Raymond Roussel, *Locus Solus* (Paris: Gallimard, 1963). The English versions of passages from *Locus Solus* used in this chapter are from the translation by Rupert C. Cuningham: *Locus Solus* (Berkeley and Los Angeles: University of California Press, 1970). Page numbers of the French (Gallimard) edition precede those of the English translation.

4. Popular histories of the Revolution and the Terror emphasize the contrasting *personae* of Danton and Robespierre; see Stanley Loomis's *Paris in the Terror* (Philadelphia: Lippincott, 1964) and Hilaire Belloc's *Danton* (New York: AMS Press, 1969; reprint of the 1928 edition). Both of these histories recount Danton's last words on the scaffold and the insult to Robespierre during his last attempt at making a speech (see Loomis, pp. 320 and 393). The glorification of Danton during the Third Republic can be seen (in solid form) in the statue erected in his honor on the Boulevard Saint-Germain in Paris.

5. We do not mean to imply here that the historical Roussel was himself a fascist, that he would have had any truck with fascists, or on the other hand, that fascists would ever have tolerated his literary experimentation. All we mean to say is that, as an ideological construct, Roussel's text misreads what is at stake in the dualities it reinscribes and reenacts, and consequently it performs a function comparable to that of fascist literature. Roussel's text, rather than overtly revealing this ideological overdetermination, this complicity, precisely obscures it in a unique way through the fantasy of physical revivification and the practice of textual revivification. When read critically, however, it permits, through this very obfuscation, a more thoroughgoing analysis of the ideological elements at play in avant-garde utopias. For more on the analysis of these utopias, see chapter 8.

Chapter 4. Leiris's Unwritten Autobiography

1. Michel Leiris in fact was personally acquainted with Roussel, through his father. Leiris's review of Raymond Roussel's *Comment j'ai écrit certains de mes livres* [*How I Wrote Several of My Books*] can be found in *Brisées* [*Markers*] (Paris: Mercure de France, 1966), pp. 58–61.

2. Page numbers refer to the four-volume *La Règle du jeu* (Paris: Gallimard, 1948—): I. *Biffures* (1948), II. *Fourbis* (1955), III. *Fibrilles* (1966), IV. *Frêle Bruit* (1976).

3. At least for Leiris, in his own project, the figural aspect of language is primarily written: the project of linking words through the interrelations of their meanings cannot be seen outside of Leiris's project of writing his autobiography, of collecting and collating notecards on which experiences and endless bifurcations of meaning are inscribed. Hence he can write:

Et j'ai choisi, pour le signe sous lequel les placer [les expériences] le nom tout à la fois floral et souterrain de Perséphone, arraché ainsi à ses noiceurs terrestres et haussé jusqu'au ciel d'une tête de chapitre. (I, 85)

And I chose, as the sign under which to place [these experiences] the both floral and subterranean name Persephone, torn out of its terrestrial darkness and raised up to the sky of a chapter heading.

Persephone rises out of the earth, out of Hades, and reaches not the clear blue sky, but the head of a chapter.

4. *Le Petit Robert* (Paris: Societe du nouveau Littré, 1977). p. 68.

5. Jeffrey Mehlman's chapter, "Reading with Leiris," to which I am indebted, can be found in his *Structural Study of Autobiography* (Ithaca: Cornell University Press, 1974), pp. 65-150. Jacques Derrida cites the part of the "Perséphone" section that describes the "Graphophone" in his introductory "Tympan" chapter of *Marges de la philosophie* (Paris: Minuit, 1972).

6. See above all Derrida's *De la grammatologie* (Paris: Minuit, 1967); English translation: *Of Grammatology*, trans. Gayatri Spivak (Baltimore: Johns Hopkins University Press, 1976).

7. Georges Bataille's *Acéphale* writings can be found in his *Oeuvres Complètes* (Paris: Gallimard, 1970—), vol. I, pp. 442-90 and 552-58.

8. This letter can be found in volume II of Bataille's *Oeuvres Complètes*, pp. 454-55. All the lectures given at the *Collège de Sociologie*—by Bataille, Leiris, and Caillois, along with many others—can be found in *Le Collège de Sociologie*, ed. Denis Hollier (Paris: Gallimard, Collection "Idées," 1979).

9. See the *Nouvelle Revue Française* 298 (July 1938): 26-38. This text can also be found in Hollier's edition of the *Collège de Sociologie.*

10. This text appears as an introduction to Leiris's *L'Age d'homme* (Paris: Gallimard, Collection "Folio," 1973). A later citation from *L'Age d'homme* itself is from this same edition.

11. Maurice Blanchot raises this very question with regard to Leiris's "De la litterature considérée comme une tauromachie." See Blanchot's "Regards d'outre-tombe" ["Glances from Beyond the Tomb"] in *La Part du feu* [*The Fire's Share*] (Paris: Gallimard, 1949), pp. 238-48, and especially p. 240.

12. Jean-Paul Sartre makes a similar point in his 1945 article "Paris sous l'occupation" ["Paris under the Occupation"], in *Situations III* (Paris: Gallimard, 1949), pp. 15-42 (see especially pp. 35-38). For Sartre, there is a considerable paradox in the fact that, simply by living and doing one's job, one inevitably collaborated, even if at the same time one actively supported the Resistance. Any farmer producing food not only fed French people, but Nazis. Any railroad worker, keeping his nation alive by keeping its trains running, also aided the German war effort. Sartre concludes:

Le mal était partout, tout choix était mauvais et pourtant il fallait choisir et nous étions responsables; chaque battement de notre coeur nous enfonçait dans une culpabilité dont nous avions horreur. (37-38)

Evil was everywhere, all choices were bad and nevertheless it was necessary to choose, and we were responsible; each heartbeat drove us further into a horrifying guilt.

13. D. A. Miller, "The Novel and the Police," in *Glyph 8* (Baltimore: Johns Hopkins University Press, 1980), pp. 127-47.

14. *Nuits sans nuit et quelques jours sans jour* (Paris: Gallimard, 1961).

15. A text by Anatole Lewitzky presented before the Collège de Sociologie can be found in Hollier's edition of the Collège lectures (see note 8).

16. In other words, the sacrificial rites of mutilation, death, and rebirth , seen politically (as in Acéphale).

17. The epigraph to *Nuits sans nuit et quelques jours sans jour.*

Chapter 5. Ponge's Photographic Rhetoric

1. Page references are to Francis Ponge's three-volume *Le Grand recueil* [*The Large Collection*] (Paris: Gallimard, 1961): I. *Lyres*, II. *Méthodes*, III. *Pièces*, and to Ponge's *Le Parti pris des choses* (Paris: Gallimard, Collection "Poésie," 1972). The English translation of "Le Soleil placé en abîme" ["The Sun Placed in the Abyss"], is found in Serge Gavronsky's collection of Ponge writings, *The Sun Placed in the Abyss and Other Texts* (New York: Sun, 1977), pp. 43–63. "Text on Electricity," also translated by Gavronsky, is in his Ponge anthology, *The Power of Language* (Berkeley: University of California Press, 1979), pp. 157–213. "Notes toward a Shell" and "Flora and Fauna" are in Beth Archer's Ponge anthology, *The Voice of Things* (New York: McGraw-Hill, 1972), pp. 58–61. In each case in the text, the page number of the French original precedes that of the English translation. All translations are modified.

2. Daniel Breazeale, *Philosophy and Truth: Selections from Nietzsche's Notebooks of the Early 1870's* (New Jersey: Humanities Press, 1979), pp. 79–97.

3. Jacques Derrida, "La Mythologie blanche," in *Marges de la philosophie* (Paris: Minuit, 1972), pp. 247–324. See English translation: "White Mythology: Metaphor in the Text of Philosophy," in *Margins of Philosophy*, trans. A. Bass (Chicago: University of Chicago Press, 1982), pp. 207–71. (The page numbers of the French original precede those of the English translation.)

4. The reader is referred to the chapter on Ponge, "Surdétermination dans le poème en prose (II): Francis Ponge" ["Overdetermination in the Prose Poem (II): Francis Ponge"], in Michael Riffaterre's *La Production du texte* [*The Production of the Text*] (Paris: Seuil, 1979), pp. 267–85.

5. Bernard Groethuysen, *Origines de l'esprit bourgeois en France* [*Origins of the Bourgeois Mind in France*] (Paris: Gallimard, 1927), *Anthropologie philosophique* (Paris: Gallimard, 1952), etc.

6. *Le Petit Robert* (Paris: Société du nouveau Littré, 1977), p. 1114.

Chapter 6. Betrayal in the Later Bataille

1. All quotes from Bataille in this chapter refer to the *Oeuvres Complètes* (Paris: Gallimard, 1970—). The volume number (in roman numerals) precedes the page number. (Page numbers of *L'Abbé C.* refer first to the original [in vol. III of the *Oeuvres*], then to the English translation by Philip A. Facey [London and New York: Marion Boyars, 1983]. All translations have been modified.) The only exceptions to this are several articles that have not yet been collected in the *Oeuvres Complètes*: they can be found in the issues of the review *Critique* indicated in this chapter.

2. Camus's most forceful statements on violence can be found in the section of *L'Homme révolté* entitled "Le Meurtre historique." See the *Essais d'Albert Camus* (Paris: Gallimard, Bibliothèque de la Pléiade, 1965), pp. 689–96. The English translation is *The Rebel*, trans. A. Bower (New York: Knopf,1956), pp. 286–93.

3. The citations from Sartre are taken from the chapter "Situation de l'écrivain en 1947" of *Qu'est-ce que la littérature?* in *Situations II* (Paris: Gallimard, 1948), pp. 202–317. The English translation, from which our quotes are taken, is: *What Is Literature?* trans. B. Frechtman (New York: Philosophical Library, 1949), pp. 161–297. The page numbers refer first to the French original, then to the English translation.

4. The "State" that Bataille valorizes is directly related to the (American) State power assoc-

iated with the Marshall Plan (VII, 174–75). Bataille's point is that when a State sets itself the task of *giving* (rather than expecting profits or producing war matériel) it inevitably leaves capitalism behind and becomes "socialist" and centralized. Bataille thus implies that only a socialist State (and not a Stalinist or capitalist one) can hope to monitor "spending without return" and guarantee it. This management of "pure expenditure" will lead to a kind of "apotheosis" or "self-awareness" at the end of history (VII, 178–79)—an "apotheosis" related in fundamental ways to a secular mystical experience, which can only be impossibly conveyed (or betrayed) by *silence*. Absurd and utopian as all this may seem, it must be pointed out that any other projection into the future of a society that in any way *recognizes* discontinuity or expenditure will not be different in kind. And whatever the regime—socialist, anarchist, or what have you—a future society that recognizes expenditure will itself be liable to be betrayed, or expended by silence or violence. (This certainly applies to any alternatives to the present power structure that Michel Foucault can propose; see chapter 7.)

Chapter 7. Derrida, Foucault, and Their "Precursors"

1. For a general history of French philosophy since 1933, see Vincent Descombes's *Le Même et l'autre* (Paris: Minuit, 1979); English translation: *Modern French Philosophy*, trans. L. Scott-Fox and J. M. Harding (New York: Cambridge University Press, 1980). Descombes argues that "contemporary" French philosophy begins in the year 1933, with Kojève's first lectures on Hegel.

2. See the section on Nietzsche in *L'Homme révolté* (Paris: Gallimard, Pléiade edition, 1965), pp. 475–89; English translation: *The Rebel*, trans. A. Bower (New York: Knopf, 1956), pp. 65–80. Camus's short story "Le Renégat" ["The Renegade"] in *L'Exil et le royaume* (Paris: Gallimard, 1957), pp. 45–72—English translation: *Exile and the Kingdom* (New York: Knopf, 1958), pp. 34–61—is also a good example of his condemnation of a nihilistic, brutal, and "Nietzschean" social order.

3. *Huis clos* (Paris: Gallimard, 1943); English translation: *No Exit*, trans. S. Gilbert (New York: Knopf, 1946).

4. Sartre's espousal of the notion of scarcity, and his condemnation of repetition (or recurrence), is most clearly worked out in *La Critique de la raison dialectique* (Paris: Gallimard, 1960); English translation: *The Critique of Dialectical Reason* (London: NLB, 1976). On scarcity, see "Rareté et mode de production," pp. 200–224 (English translation, pp. 122–52). On recurrence as a phenomenon of seriality, see the section "Les Collectifs," pp. 306–77 (English translation, pp. 256–341).

5. Georges Bataille's most extended meditation on Nietzsche is *Sur Nietzsche* [*On Nietzsche*], published in 1945 (collected in vol. VI of Bataille's *Oeuvres Complètes* [Paris: Gallimard, 1970—]). See also my article "Nietzsche in the Text of Bataille," in *Glyph 6* (Baltimore: Johns Hopkins University Press, 1979), pp. 42–67.

6. All quotes from Bataille in this chapter are from his *Oeuvres Complètes*.

7. Alexandre Kojève, *Introduction à la lecture de Hegel*, ed. Raymond Queneau (Paris: Gallimard, 1947); English translation: *Lectures on the Phenomenology of Spirit*, ed. A. Bloom, trans. J. H. Nichols, Jr. (Ithaca: Cornell University Press, 1980). See also Jean Hyppolite's *Genèse et structure de la Phénoménologie de l'esprit de Hegel* (Paris: Aubier, 1946); English translation: *Genesis and Structure of Hegel's Phenomenology of Spirit*, trans. S. Cherniak and J. Heckman (Evanston: Northwestern University Press, 1974).

8. The status of the impossible knowledge of nonknowledge in Bataille is explored in Denis Hollier's book on Bataille, *La Prise de la concorde* [*The Taking of the Concorde*] (Paris: Gallimard, 1974).

9. The "vicious circle" of Nietzsche's philosophy has been extensively studied by Pierre Klossowski in *Nietzsche et le cercle vicieux* [*Nietzsche and the Vicious Circle*] (Paris: Mercure de France, 1969). (Klossowski's earliest writings on Nietzsche date from the 1930s: see "Création du monde,"

in *Acéphale* 2–3 [January 1937]: 25–27. Klossowski, of course, was a collaborator with Bataille in the Acéphale group.) Gilles Deleuze's Nietzschean philosophy owes much to Klossowski: see Deleuze's *Nietzsche et la philosophie* (Paris: PUF, 1962).

10. For Michel Leiris, the mythic Nietzschean sacrificial or acephalic figure was transmuted into the experience of language in everyday life; see chapter 4. For Klossowski, a Catholic, there was an intimate connection between "transgression" and "transsubstantiation": see his essay on Bataille's *L'Abbé C.*, "La Messe de Georges Bataille" ["Georges Bataille's Mass"] in the collection *Un si funeste désir* [*So Deadly a Desire*] (Paris: Gallimard, 1963), pp. 123–32. (Klossowski also collaborated with Leiris and Bataille in their "Collège de sociologie" group; his lecture presented there can be found in Denis Hollier's *Collège de sociologie* anthology.)

11. On the scandalous "friendship" between Bataille, Blanchot, and Klossowski, see Jane Gallop's *Intersections* (Lincoln: University of Nebraska Press, 1981).

12. For example, Bataille quotes from *Aminadab* in *Le Coupable* (V, 323–24). Bataille also discusses the relation between his own project and those of Levinas, Heidegger, and Blanchot in the second part of his essay "De l'existentialisme au primat de l'économie" ["From Existentialism to the Primacy of Economics"] (*Critique* 20 [February 1948]: 127–41).

13. This quote is taken from the chapter "Du coté de chez Nietzsche" ["Nietzsche's Way"], in Maurice Blanchot's *La Part du feu* [*The Fire's Share*] (Paris: Gallimard, 1949). Another important essay by Blanchot on Nietzsche can be found in *L'Entretien infini* [*The Infinite Interview*] (Paris: Gallimard, 1969), pp. 201–55.

14. In *La Part du feu*, pp. 293–331; English translation: "Literature and the Right to Death," in *The Gaze of Orpheus*, trans. Lydia Davis (New York: Station Hill, 1981), pp. 3–20. The page number of the French precedes that of the English text.

15. Despite the fact that both Blanchot and Bataille ground their notions of negativity in a Heideggerian "es gibt" or the seemingly contrary Levinasian "il y a." See Blanchot's footnote on p. 320 (p. 51 of the English translation) of "La Littérature et le droit à la mort" ("quand il n'y a rien, *il y a* de l'être") ["when there is nothing, *there is* being"]. On the connections between Blanchot and Heidegger, see Levinas's "Le Regard du poète" ["The Gaze of the Poet"] in his collection of essays *Sur Maurice Blanchot* [*On Maurice Blanchot*] (Montpellier: Fata Morgana, 1973). The problem of the limits of Blanchot's rewriting of Heidegger is unfortunately beyond the scope of this chapter.

16. A philosophy often seen as Heideggerian.

17. Marx is almost totally lost in the process, but not completely. In one of his later collections of essays, *L'Amitié* [*Friendship*], Blanchot finally subordinates Marx to "writing" ("L'écriture")—and thus makes him minor—by pointing out that (Marxist) science itself inevitably falls under the sway of literature, and literature itself is "le jeu insensé d'écrire" (*L'Amitié* [Paris: Gallimard, 1971], p. 117).

18. See Sartre's *Qu'est-ce que la littérature?* (Paris: Gallimard, 1948), p. 326, in which he condemns Bataille as a good example of the prewar author of the "littérature de consommation"—rather than the "littérature de construction," as represented by Malraux, Saint-Exupéry, and himself. (English translation: *What Is Literature?* trans. B. Frechtman [New York: Philosophical Library, 1949], p. 205). Sartre's reading of Blanchot can be found in *Situations I* (Paris: Gallimard, 1947), pp. 113–32.

19. In *L'Ecriture et la différence* (Paris: Seuil, 1967); English translation: *Writing and Difference*, trans. A. Bass (Chicago: University of Chicago Press, 1978). The page number of the French precedes that of the English text.

20. Such an element is "writing" ("l'écriture") in the context of Husserl's phenomenology. See Derrida's *La Voix et le phénomène* (Paris: PUF, 1967). English translation: *Speech and Phenomena*, trans. D. Allison (Evanston: Northwestern University Press, 1973).

21. In *L'Ecriture et la différence*.

22. For another view of Sartre and Derrida on Bataille, see Michele Richman's *Reading Georges Bataille* (Baltimore: Johns Hopkins University Press, 1982), pp. 112–20 and 141–50.

23. See Bataille's *Oeuvres Complètes*, I, 379–412.

24. Especially of interest here is a little-known, never-republished postwar essay by Bataille entitled "Mensonge politique" ["Political Lie"] (*Critique* 25, June 1948), as well as the chapter on Soviet industrialization in *La Part maudite* (VII, 139–58).

25. *La Folie du jour* (Montpellier: Fata Morgana, 1973); English translation: *La Folie du jour/Madness of the Day*, trans. L. Davis (New York: Station Hill, 1981).

26. In *Glyph 7* (Baltimore: Johns Hopkins University Press, 1980), pp. 176–201. The English translation, "The Law of Genre," trans. A. Ronnell, immediately follows the French version in the same issue of *Glyph* (pp. 202–32).

27. See *L'Ecriture et la différence*, p. 397, note 1 (*Writing and Difference*, p. 337, note 33).

28. In Levinas's article on Blanchot, "Le Regard du poète," in *Sur Maurice Blanchot* (Montpellier: Fata Morgana, 1975), we see a remarkable coming together of themes associated with Blanchot, Bataille, Heidegger, and even Derrida (the article dates from 1956):

Blanchot détermine ansi l'écriture comme une structure quasi folle, dans l'économie générale de l'être et par laquelle l'être n'est plus une économie, car il ne porte plus, abordé à travers l'écriture—aucune habitation, ne comporte aucune intériorité. Il est espace littéraire, c'est à dire extériorité absolue—exteriorité de l'absolue exil.(17)

Blanchot thus determines writing as an almost mad structure, in the general economy of being, and by which being is no longer an economy, for it no longer carries, brought forth across writing—any shelter, no longer carries with itself any interiority. It is literary space, in other words absolute exteriority—exteriority of absolute exile.

Bataille, however, and Derrida along with him, would never argue that anything simply is "no longer" an economy, or that at any point the general economy (of "being"?) ceases to be an economy.

29. See Foucault's *Surveiller et punir* (Paris: Gallimard, 1975); English translation: *Discipline and Punish*, trans. A. Sheridan (New York: Pantheon, 1977). See also *La Volonté de savoir, Histoire de la sexualité*, I (Paris: Gallimard, 1976); English translation: *The History of Sexuality*, trans. R. Hurley (New York: Pantheon, 1978).

30. In *Critique*, 195–96 (August-September, 1963): 751–69. The English translation is in Donald F. Bouchard's collection of Foucault essays, *Language, Counter-Memory, Practice* (Ithaca: Cornell University Press, 1977), pp.29–52. The page number of the French precedes that of the English text.

31. *L'Ordre du discours* (Paris: Gallimard, 1971); English translation: *The Discourse on Language*, in *The Archaeology of Knowledge*, trans. A. M. Sheridan Smith (New York: Pantheon, 1972), pp. 215–37. The page number of the French precedes that of the English text.

32. See note 9. See also, in this context, Foucault's essay on Nietzsche, "Nietzsche, la généalogie, l'histoire," in *Hommage à Jean Hyppolite* (Paris: PUF, 1971), pp. 145–72. This essay appears in translation in *Language, Counter-Memory, Practice*, on pp. 139–64.

33. "Revolutionary Action: Until Now." translated in *Language, Counter-Memory, Practice*, pp. 218–33. I have not been able to locate the original of this article, which appeared in French in *Actuel* 14 (1971).

34. Foucault would probably argue that, if anything, his plans for the future should be identified with "heterotopias" rather than with "utopias." He associates utopias with elaborate and precise social plans, carried out for the pacification of individuals; heterotopias, on the other hand, such as those in Borges, "dessèchent le propos, arrêtent les mots sur eux-mêmes, contestent, dans sa racine, toute possibilité de grammaire" ["dessicate speech, stop words in their tracks, contest the very

possibility of grammar at its source"] (*Les Mots et les choses* [Paris: Gallimard, 1966], pp. 9–10; English translation: *The Order of Things* [London: Tavistock, 1970], p. xviii). No doubt Foucault would also identify the visions of Bataille, Blanchot, Roussel, Leiris, and Ponge as heterotopias, to the extent that they too "ruinent . . . d'avance la 'syntaxe' . . . qui fait 'tenir ensemble' . . . les mots et les choses" ["destroy . . . (the) 'syntax' that causes words and things . . . to 'hold together' "]. And yet if our readings of these authors have accomplished anything, they have shown that this easy distinction does not hold and that heterotopias are precisely avant-garde utopias, with their own unconventional but perfectly comprehensible ideal realms in which the implementation of negativity in language and society is foreseen, and with their own textual and ideological blind spots.

35. With the difference, of course, that the official 1960s hippy discovers his "true self" through sex and drugs, whereas Foucault's hippy continuously reinvents or creates pleasure through sex and drugs. These two alternatives might not be so different, however, since what Foucault's hippy ultimately discovers—through a reading of Foucault—is the truth in the form of his pleasure, a pleasure that is (or rather should be) constant, even though it is continuously reinvented or created.

36. See, for example, Foucault's interview with Bob Gallagher and Alexander Wilson in *The Advocate*, August 7, 1984, p. 26.

37. See *Les Mots et les choses*, p. 395; English translation: *The Order of Things*, p. 384.

38. Indeed John Rajchman has argued, in "Foucault, or the Ends of Modernism" (in *October* 24 [Spring 1983]: 37–62) that a profound change takes place in Foucault's work of the 1970s: turning away from a vision of an all-inclusive "transgressive" language and turning away as well from the valorization of a literary avant-garde, Foucault, according to Rajchman, comes to focus on a "complex political reality no linguistic play can dispel" (p. 59).

It seems that one cannot analyze the history of Foucault's antidialectical project without finding in it (as Rajchman does) a thoroughly dialectical moment of negation, leading to a higher, perfected stage of development. Hubert L. Dreyfus and Paul Rabinow, in their book *Michel Foucault: Beyond Structuralism and Hermeneutics* (Chicago: The University of Chicago Press, 1982), find a similar definitive turning point (again taking place around 1970), this time marking the transition from "Archaeology" to "Genealogy" (see pp. 79–125).

39. In this light, it is clear that Derrida's reading of Bataille—situating Bataille as he does *in* Hegel—is a critique of Foucault (who sees in Bataille a rejection of the dialectic), as well as of Sartre. In *L'Ecriture et la différence*, Derrida moreover devotes a chapter to a critique of Foucault ("Cogito et histoire de la folie" ["Cogito and the History of Madness"]).

40. Peggy Kamuf, in her article "Peneolope at Work: *A Room of One's Own*," *Novel* 16, no. 1 (Fall 1982): 5–8, points out that Foucault's discourse is still moored in the "privileged domain of patriarchal thought" to the extent that it has been trained "to think without interruption" (p. 13). Foucault's first-person "I," in fact, is never questioned: a strange security for the proponent of the "death of man."

Chapter 8. Reading Avant-Garde Utopias

1. *Utopiques: jeux d'espaces* (Paris: Minuit, 1973).

2. In this context, see Marin's chapter of *Utopiques* treating Marx's critique of a utopia (chapter 14, "L'Utopie n'est pas un projet politique ou 'Le Projet du citoyen Cabet' " ["Utopia Is Not a Political Project, or the 'Project of Citizen Cabet' "]).

3. Marin's approach here is very similar to that of Pierre Macherey in *Pour une théorie de la production littéraire* [Toward a Theory of Literary Production] (Paris: Maspero, 1966). See especially chapter 19, "Lénine, critique de Tolstoy" [Lenin, Critic of Tolstoy"] and "L'Image dans le

miroir'' [''The Image in the Mirror'']. For similar projects in English, see Terry Eagleton's *Criticism and Ideology* (London: NLB, 1977) and Fredric Jameson's *The Political Unconscious* (Ithaca: Cornell University Press, 1981).

4. *Glyph 1* (Baltimore: Johns Hopkins University Press, 1977): 50–66.

5. See, for example, Céline's *Bagatelles pour un massacre* [*Trifles for a Massacre*] (Paris: Denoel, 1937), *Les Beaux draps* [*A Fine Mess!*] (Paris: Nouvelles éditions françaises, 1941), etc.

6. In this context, see the ''Hegel'' section of Bataille's *L'Expérience intérieure* [*The Inner Experience*] (V, 127–30), as well as the concluding pages of *La Part maudite* (VII, 177–79).

Selected Bibliography

Selected Bibliography

Georges Bataille

Primary Works

Oeuvres Complètes, vol. I-IX. Paris: Gallimard, 1970—.
Le Bleu du ciel (1935). In *Oeuvres Complètes*, vol. III.
L'Expérience intérieure (1943). In *Oeuvres Complètes*, vol. V.
Le Coupable (1944). In *Oeuvres Complètes*, vol. V.
Sur Nietzsche (1945). In *Oeuvres Complètes*, vol. VI.
La Part maudite (1949). In *Oeuvres Complètes*, vol. VII.
L'Abbé C. (1950). In *Oeuvres Complètes*, vol. III.
L'Histoire de l'érotisme (ca. 1950). In *Oeuvres Complètes*, vol. VIII.
La Souveraineté (ca. 1953). In *Oeuvres Complètes*, vol. VIII.
L'Erotisme. Paris: Minuit, 1957.
    Translated by Mary Dalwood. London: John Calder, 1962. *Death and Sensuality.*
Blue of Noon. Translated by Harry Mathews. New York: Urizen, 1978.
L'Abbé C. Translated by Philip A. Facey. London and New York: Marion Boyars, 1983.
Visions of Excess (Selected Writings, 1927-1939). Translated and edited by Allan Stoekl. Minneapolis: University of Minnesota Press, 1985.

"La Mutilation sacrificielle et l'oreille coupée de Van Gogh" (1930). In *Oeuvres Complètes*, vol. I, pp. 258-70.
"La Vieille taupe et le préfixe *sur* dans les mots *surhomme* et *surrealiste* (1930?). In *Oeuvres Complètes*, vol. II, pp. 93-109.
"La Notion de dépense" (1933). In *Oeuvres Complètes*, vol. I, pp. 302-20.
"La Structure psychologique du fascisme" (1933). In *Oeuvres Complètes*, vol. I, pp. 339-71.
"La Pratique de la joie devant la mort (1939). In *Oeuvres Complètes*, vol. I, pp. 552-58.
(The above five articles, translated as "Sacrificial Mutilation and the Severed Ear of Vincent Van

Gogh," "The Old Mole and the Prefix *sur* in the Words *surhomme* (*Superman*) and *Surrealist*," "The Notion of Expenditure," "The Psychological Structure of Fascism," and "The Practice of Joy before Death" can be found in the anthology *Visions of Excess.*
"La Morale de la malheur: La Peste." In *Critique* 13/14 (1947): 3–15.
"S. S. et déportés." In *Critique* 17 (1947): 337–42.
"De l'existentialisme au primat de l'économie (I)." In *Critique* 19 (1947): 515–26.
"De l'existentialisme au primat de l'économie (II)." In *Critique* 20 (1948): 127–41.
"Mensonge politique." In *Critique* 25 (1948): 561–65.

Secondary Works

Cérisy Colloquium. Edited by P. Sollers, *Bataille*. Paris: 10/18, 1973.
Gallop, Jane. *Intersections: A Reading of Sade with Bataille, Blanchot, and Klossowski*. Lincoln: University of Nebraska Press, 1981.
Gasché, Rodolphe. "L'Echange héliocentrique." In *L'Arc* 48 (1971): 11–26.
Hollier, Denis. *La Prise de la Concorde*. Paris: Gallimard, 1974.
———, ed. *Le Collège de Sociologie*. Paris: Gallimard, Collection "Idées," 1979.
Richman, Michele. *Reading Georges Bataille: Beyond the Gift*. Baltimore: Johns Hopkins University Press, 1982.
Sasso, Robert. *Georges Bataille*. Paris: Minuit, 1979.
Stoekl, Allan. "Nietzsche in the Text of Bataille." In *Glyph* 6: 42–67. Baltimore: Johns Hopkins University Press, 1979.

More complete bibliographies may be found in:

Critique 195/196 (1963). Issue devoted to Bataille.
L'Arc 32 (1967). Issue devoted to Bataille.
Semiotexte 2, no. 2 (1976). Issue devoted to Bataille.
Hawley, Daniel. *Bibliographie annotée de la critique sur Georges Bataille de 1929 à 1975*. Paris: Honoré Champion, 1976.

Maurice Blanchot

Primary Works

Thomas l'obscur. Paris: Gallimard, 1941.
Faux pas. Paris: Gallimard, 1943.
L'Arrêt de Mort. Paris: Gallimard, 1948.
Le Très-Haut. Paris: Gallimard, 1948.
La Part du feu. Paris: Gallimard, 1949.
Au moment voulu. Paris: Gallimard, 1951.
L'Espace littéraire. Paris: Gallimard, 1955.
L'Entretien infini. Paris: Gallimard, 1969.
L'Amitié. Paris: Gallimard, 1971.
La Folie du jour. Montpellier: Fata Morgana, 1973.
Death Sentence. Translated by Lydia Davis. New York: Station Hill, 1979.
The Gaze of Orpheus. Translated by Lydia Davis. New York: Station Hill, 1981.
The Madness of the Day/La Folie du jour. Translated by Lydia Davis. New York: Station Hill, 1981.
The Space of Literature. Translated by Ann Smock. Lincoln: University of Nebraska Press, 1982.

Secondary Works

Collin, Françoise. *Maurice Blanchot et la question de l'écriture*. Paris: Gallimard, 1971.

De Man, Paul. "Impersonality in the Criticism of Maurice Blanchot." In *Blindness and Insight*, pp. 60–78. New York: Oxford University Press, 1971.

Laporte, Roger. *Deux lectures de Maurice Blanchot*. Montpellier: Fata Morgana, 1973.

Levinas, Emmanuel. *Sur Maurice Blanchot*. Montpellier: Fata Morgana, 1975.

Londyn, Evelyne. "L'Allégorie dans *Le Très-Haut*" and "Le Fantastique et le merveilleux dans *Le Très-Haut*." In *Maurice Blanchot: Romancier*, pp. 181–200. Paris: Nizet, 1976.

Mehlman, Jeffrey. "Blanchot at *Combat*: Of Literature and Terror." In *MLN* 95, no. 4 (1980): 808–29.

Ungar, Steven. "Night Moves: Spatial Perception and the Place of Blanchot's Early Fiction." In *Yale French Studies* 57 (1979): 124–35.

Todorov, Tzvetan. "Reflections on Literature in Contemporary France." In *New Literary History*, Spring 1979, 511–31.

More complete bibliographies may be found in:

Critique 229 (1966). Issue devoted to Blanchot.

Sub-Stance 14 (1977). Issue devoted to Blanchot.

Raymond Roussel

Primary Works

La Doublure (1897). Paris: Pauvert, 1963.

Impressions d'Afrique (1910). Paris: Pauvert, 1963.

Locus Solus (1914). Paris: Gallimard, 1963.

Comment j'ai écrit certains de mes livres (1933). Paris: Pauvert, 1963.

Impressions of Africa. Translated by L. Foord and R. Heppenstall. Berkeley: University of California Press, 1967.

Locus Solus. Translated by R. C. Cuningham. Berkeley: University of California Press, 1970.

Secondary Works

Amiot, Anne-Marie. *Un Mythe moderne*. Paris: Lettres Modernes, 1977.

Heppenstall, Rayner. *Raymond Roussel*. Berkeley: University of California Press, 1967.

Jenny, Laurent. "Structure et fonctions du cliché." In *Poétique* 12 (1972): 495–517.

Leiris, Michel. "Conception et réalité chez Raymond Roussel." In *Critique* 89 (1954): 821–35.

———. "Comment j'ai écrit certains de mes livres." In *Brisées*, pp. 58–61. Paris: Mercure de France, 1966.

Lovitt, Carl. "*Locus Solus*: Literary Solitaire." In *Sub-Stance* 10 (1974): 95–109.

Veschambre, Christiane. "Sur *Les Impressions d'Afrique*." In *Poétique* I (1970): 64–78.

Michel Leiris

Primary Works

Miroir de la tauromachie. Paris: GLM, 1938.

L'Age d'homme. Paris: Gallimard, 1939.

———, preceded by "De la littérature considérée comme une tauromachie." Paris: Gallimard, folio ed., 1973.

La Règle du jeu. Vol. I: *Biffures*. Paris: Gallimard, 1948.

———. Vol. II: *Fourbis*. Paris: Gallimard, 1955.

———. Vol. III: *Fibrilles*. Paris: Gallimard, 1966.

———. Vol. IV: *Frêle Bruit*. Paris: Gallimard, 1976.

Nuits sans nuit et quelques jours sans jour. Paris: Gallimard, 1961.
Brisées. Paris: Mercure de France, 1966.
Mots sans mémoire. Paris: Gallimard, 1969.
"Le Sacré dans la vie quotidienne." In *La Nouvelle Revue Française* 298 (July 1938): 26–38.

Secondary Works

Blanchot, Maurice. "Regards d'outre-tombe." In *La Part du feu*, pp. 238–48. Paris: Gallimard, 1949.
Boyer, Alain-Michel. *Leiris*. Paris: Editions Universitaires, 1974.
Chappuis, Pierre. *Leiris*. Paris: Seghers, 1974.
Hewitt, Leah D. "Historical Intervention in Leiris' Bif(f)ur(e)s." In *French Forum* 7, no. 2 (1982): 132–45.
Hollier, Denis. "La Poésie jusqu'à Z." In *L'Ire des vents* 3–4 (1981): 141–54.
Leigh, James. "Figure of Autobiography." In *MLN* 93, no. 4 (1978): 33–49.
Lejeune, Philippe. *Lire Leiris*. Paris: Klincksieck, 1975.
Mehlman, Jeffrey. "Reading (with) Leiris." In *A Structural Study of Autobiography*, pp. 65–150. Ithaca: Cornell University Press, 1974.
Sturrock, J. "New Model Autobiographer." In *New Literary History*, Autumn 1977, 51–63.
Sub-Stance 11/12 (1976). Issue devoted to Leiris; includes bibliography.

Francis Ponge

Primary Works

Le Parti pris des choses. Paris: Gallimard, 1942. Reprint. Paris: Gallimard, Collection Poesie, 1972.
Le Grand receuil. Vol. I: *Lyres*. Paris: Gallimard, 1961.
——. Vol. II: *Méthodes*. Paris: Gallimard, 1961.
——. Vol. III: *Pièces*. Paris: Gallimard, 1961.
Pour l'araignée. Paris: Gallimard, 1965.
Pour un Malherbe. Paris: Gallimard, 1965.
Le Savon. Paris: Gallimard, 1967.
La Fabrique du pré. Paris: Gallimard, 1971.
The Voice of Things. Translated and edited by B. Archer. New York: McGraw-Hill, 1972.
"The Sun Placed in the Abyss." In *The Sun Place in the Abyss and Other Texts*, pp. 43–68. Translated and edited by Serge Gavronsky. New York: Sun, 1977.
The Power of Language. Translated by Serge Gavronsky. (Contains "Text on Electricity," pp. 157–213.) Berkeley: University of California Press, 1979.

Secondary Works

Genette Gérard. "Le Parti pris de mots." *Romanic Review*, November 1975, 283–87.
Mowitt, John. "Towards a Non-Euclidean Rhetoric." In *Sub-Stance* 30 (1981): 63–84.
Cérisy Colloquium. *Ponge, inventeur et classique*. Paris: 10/18, 1975.
Riffaterre, Michael. "Surdétermination dans le poème en Prose (II): Francis Ponge." In *La Production du texte*, pp. 267–85. Paris: Seuil, 1979.
Spada, Marcel. Francis Ponge. Paris: Seghers, 1974. Contains bibliography.
Digraphe 8 (1976). Issue devoted to Ponge.

Jacques Derrida

Primary Works

De la grammatologie. Paris: Minuit, 1967.
L'Ecriture et la différence. Paris: Seuil, 1967.
La Voix et le phénomène. Paris: PUF, 1967.
La Dissémination. Paris: Seuil, 1972.
Marges de la philosophie. Paris: Minuit, 1972.
Speech and Phenomena. Translated by D. Allison. Evanston: Northwestern University Press, 1973.
Of Grammatology. Translated by G. Spivak. Baltimore: Johns Hopkins University Press, 1976.
Writing and Difference. Translated by A. Bass. Chicago: University of Chicago Press, 1978.
"De l'économie restreinte à l'économie générale." In *L'Ecriture et la différence* (1967): 369–407. (On Bataille.)
"La Mythologie blanche." In *Poetique* 5 (1971): 1–52. Reprint in *Marges de la philosophie*, pp. 247–324. Paris: Minuit, 1972.
"Tympan." In *Marges de la philosophie* (1972), pp. i–xxv. (With a long citation from Leiris.)
Signéponge/Signsponge. (Essay on Ponge written in 1975, published with a translation by Richard Rand.) New York: Columbia University Press, 1984.
"From Restricted to General Economy: A Hegelianism without Reserve." In *Writing and Difference*, pp. 251–77. Translated by A. Bass. Chicago: University of Chicago Press, 1978.
"La Loi du genre." In *Glyph* 7: 176–20. Baltimore: Johns Hopkins University Press, 1980. (On Blanchot.)
"The Law of Genre." Translated by A. Ronnell. In *Glyph 7* (1980).
"White Mythology." In *Margins of Philosophy*, pp. 207–71. Translated by A. Bass. Chicago: University of Chicago Press, 1982.
"Tympan." In *Margins of Philosophy*, pp. x–xxix.

Michel Foucault

Primary Works

Raymond Roussel. Paris: Gallimard, 1963.
Les Mots et les choses. Paris: Gallimard, 1966.
L'Archéologie du savoir. Paris: Gallimard, 1969.
L'Ordre du discours. Paris: Gallimard, 1971.
Surveiller et punir. Paris: Gallimard, 1975.
La Volonté de savoir: vol. I, *Histoire de la sexualité*. Paris: Gallimard, 1976.
The Order of Things. London: Tavistock, 1970.
The Archaeology of Knowledge and *The Discourse on Language*. Translated by A. M. Sheridan-Smith. New York: Pantheon, 1972.
Discipline and Punish. Translated by A. Sheridan. New York: Pantheon, 1977.
Language, Counter-Memory, Practice. Translated by D. F. Bouchard and S. Simon. Ithaca: Cornell University Press, 1977.
"Préface à la transgression." In *Critique* 195–96 (1963): 751–69. Translation in *Language, Counter-Memory, Practice* (1977), pp. 29–52. (On Bataille.)
"La Pensée du dehors." In *Critique* 229 (1966): 523–46. (On Blanchot.)
"Nietzsche, la généalogie, l'histoire." In *Hommage À Jean Hyppolite*. Paris: PUF, 1971. Translation in *Language, Counter-Memory, Practice* (1977), pp. 145–72.

"Revolutionary Action: 'Until Now.' " In *Language, Countery-Memory, Practice* (1977), pp. 218–33.

"An Interview: Sex, Power, and the Politics of Identity." With Bob Gallagher and Alexander Wilson. In *The Advocate*, 7 August 1984, 26.

Secondary Works

Dreyfus, Hubert L., and Paul Rabinow. *Michel Foucault: Beyond Structuralism and Hermeneutics.* Chicago: University of Chicago Press, 1982.

Kamuf, Peggy. "Penelope at Work: *A Room of One's Own.*" In *Novel* 16, no. 1 (Fall 1982): 5–18.

Rajchman, John. "Foucault, or the Ends of Modernism." In *October* 24 (Spring 1983): 37–62.

Other Works Cited

Belloc, Hilaire. *Danton.* New York: AMS Press, 1969; reprint of 1929 edition.

Benda, Julien. *La Trahison des clercs.* Paris: Grasset, 1927.

Camus, Albert. *L'Exil et le royaume.* Paris: Gallimard, 1957.

———. *Exile and the Kingdom.* New York: Knopf, 1958.

———. *L'Homme révolté.* Paris: Gallimard (Pléiade edition), 1965.

———. *The Rebel.* Translated by A. Bower. New York: Knopf, 1956.

———. *La Peste.* Paris: Gallimard, 1948.

Céline, Louis-Ferdinand. *Bagatelles pour un massacre.* Paris: Denoel, 1937.

———. *Les Beaux draps.* Paris: Nouvelles éditions françaises, 1941.

Deleuze, Gilles. *Nietzsche et la philosophie.* Paris: PUF, 1962.

Descombes, Vincent. *Le Même et l'autre. Quarante-cinq ans de philosophie française* (1933–1978). Paris: Minuit, 1979.

———. *Modern French Philosophy.* Translated by L. Scott-Fox and J. M. Harding. New York: Cambridge University Press, 1980.

Eagleton, Terry. *Criticism and Ideology.* London: NLB, 1977.

Groethuysen, Bernard. *Anthropologie philosophique.* Paris: Gallimard, 1952.

———. *Origines de l'esprit bourgeois en France.* Paris: Gallimard, 1927.

Hegel, G. W. F. *The Phenomenology of Spirit.* Translated by A. V. Miller. Oxford: Clarendon Press, 1977.

Hyppolite, Jean. *Genèse et structure de la Phénoménologie de l'esprit.* Paris: Aubier, 1946.

———. *Genesis and Structure of Hegel's Phenomenology of Spirit.* Translated by S. Cherniak and J. Heckman. Evanston: Northwestern University Press, 1974.

Jameson, Fredric. *The Political Unconscious.* Ithaca: Cornell University Press, 1981.

Janet, Pierre. *De l'angoisse à l'extase.* Paris: Alcan, 1926–28.

Jünger, Ernst. *On the Marble Cliffs.* Translated by Stuart Hood. New York: Penguin, 1983 (originally published in 1939).

Kierkegaard, Søren. *Either/Or.* Vol. I. Translated by D. F. and L. M. Swenson. Princeton: Princeton University Press, 1943.

Klossowski, Pierre. "Creation du monde." In *Acéphale* 2–3 (January 1937): 25–27.

———. "La Messe de Georges Bataille." In *Un si funeste desir*, pp. 123–32. Paris: Gallimard, 1963.

———. *Nietzsche et le cercle vicieux.* Paris: Mercure de France, 1969.

Kojève, Alexandre. *Introduction à la lecture de Hegel.* Edited by Raymond Queneau. Paris: Gallimard, 1947.

———. *Lectures on the Phenomenology of Spirit.* Translated by J. H. Nichols Jr. Edited by A. Bloom. Ithaca: Cornell University Press, 1980.

Kristeva, Julia. *Polylogue.* Paris: Seuil, 1977.

——. *La Révolution du langage poétique*. Paris: Seuil, 1974.

Loomis, Stanley. *Paris in the Terror*. Philadelphia: Lippincott, 1964.

Lukács, Georg. *Writer and Critic*. Translated by A. D. Kahn. New York: Grosset and Dunlap, 1971.

Macherey, Pierre. *Pour une théorie de la production littéraire*. Paris: Maspéro, 1966.

Marin, Louis. *Utopiques: jeux d'espaces. Paris: Minuit, 1973*.

——. *"Disneyland, A Degenerate Utopia."* In *Glyph 1*: 50–66. Baltimore: Johns Hopkins University Press, 1977.

Milosz, Czeslaw. *The Captive Mind*. Translated by J. Zielonko. New York: Knopf, 1953.

——. *The Seizure of Power*. Translated by C. Wieniewska. New York: Criterion, 1955.

Nietzsche, Friedrich. *Beyond Good and Evil*. Translated by W. Kaufman. New York: Vantage Books, 1966.

——. *"On Truth and Lie in a Nonmoral Sense."* In *Philosophy and Truth: Selections from Nietzsche's Notebooks of the Early 1870's*, pp. 79–97. Edited and translated by Daniel Breazeale. New Jersey: Humanities Press, 1979.

——. *The Will to Power*. Translated by W. Kaufman. New York: Random House, 1967.

Rousset, David. *Les Jours de notre mort*. Paris: Editions du Pavois, 1947.

Rousset, Jean. *Forme et signification*. Paris: Corti, 1963.

Ryan, Michael. *Marxism and Deconstruction*. Baltimore: Johns Hopkins University Press, 1982.

Sartre, Jean-Paul. *Critique de la raison dialectique*. Paris: Gallimard, 1960.

——. *Critique of Dialectical Reason*. Translated by A. Sheridan-Smith. London: NLB, 1976.

——. *Huis clos*. Paris: Gallimard, 1943.

——. *No Exit*. Translated by Stuart Gilbert. New York: Knopf, 1946.

——. *Situations I*. Paris: Gallimard, 1947.

——. *"Aminadab* ou du fantastique considéré comme un langage." In *Situations I*. (On Blanchot.)

——. *"L'Homme et les choses."* In *Situations I*, pp. 226–70. (On Ponge.)

——. *"Un Nouveau mystique."* In *Situations I*, pp. 133–74. (On Bataille.)

——. *"Qu'est-ce que la littérature?"* In *Situations II*. Paris: Gallimard, 1948.

——. *"Paris sous l'occupation."* In *Situations III*, pp. 15–42. Paris: Gallimard, 1949.

——. *What is Literature?* Translated by B. Frechtman. New York: Philosophical Library, 1949.

Wahl, Jean. *Etudes Kierkegaardiennes*. Paris: Aubier, 1938.

Index

Index

Allan Stoekl is assistant professor of comparative literature and French at Yale University. He edited and translated Georges Bataille's *Visions of Excess: Selected Writings, 1927–1939*, a volume in Minnesota's Theory and History of Literature series.